Chaucer

GOLDENTREE BIBLIOGRAPHIES
In Language and Literature
under the series editorship of
O. B. Hardison, Jr.

Chaucer

SECOND EDITION

compiled by

Albert C. Baugh

University of Pennsylvania

AHM Publishing Corporation
Arlington Heights, Illinois 60004

ISBN: 0-88295-557-8, paper
ISBN: 0-88295-563-2, cloth

Library of Congress Card Number: 75-42975

PR
1905
B33
1977

PRINTED IN THE UNITED STATES OF AMERICA
737

Contents

v

CONTENTS

CONTENTS

CONTENTS

Preface

THE SECOND EDITION of this bibliography is brought up-to-date by more than 800 new items selected according to the principles of the original edition. It is intended for graduate and advanced students who desire a convenient guide to scholarship on Chaucer and related subjects. The listing is necessarily selective, but every effort has been made to provide ample coverage of the major works and topics, with emphasis on work published in the twentieth century.

In order to keep this bibliography to a practical size a great number of pertinent references had to be left out. With a bare handful of exceptions in two or three categories, the classes of excluded references are as follows:

School editions

Short articles on minor points

Popular and semipopular books and articles

Doctoral dissertations abstracted in *Microfilm Abstracts* or *Dissertation Abstracts* but not otherwise available in printed form.

In general, the compiler has attempted to steer a middle course between the brief lists of references included in the average textbook and the long professional bibliography in which significant items are often lost in the sheer number of references given. This bibliography should materially assist the student in his effort to survey a topic, write reports and term papers, prepare for examinations, and do independent reading. Attention is called to four features intended to enhance its utility.

1. Extra margin on each page permits listing of library call numbers of often-used items.

2. Space at the bottom of every page permits inclusion of additional entries, and blank pages for notes follow the index.

3. An index by author follows the bibliography proper.

4. All entries are numbered consecutively throughout the book. Thus, the index uses individual numbers for each entry, rather than page numbers. Cross references appear both in standard forms ("see also," "reprinted in") and as follows for cross reference 264:

392 ELLIOTT, R. W. V. "Chaucer's Reading." 264, pp. 46–68.

An asterisk following an entry indicates a work of "special importance" in the field. Other annotations which may conclude an entry are: (1) abbreviations, given in brackets, of paperback publishers and series numbers, all based on the list of abbreviations given in *Paperbound Books in Print*; (2) a phrase describing the subject of an allusive title.

In a small number of places the elimination of an item inadvertently entered twice has resulted in the elimination of a number. There are no items numbered 598, 854, 880, 1055, 1754, 1963, 2287, 2536, 2771, 2888.

Abbreviations

Symbols for journals and series cited herein generally follow the standard forms given at the beginning of recent *PMLA* Bibliographies. The symbols and their meanings are as follows:

AJP	American Journal of Philology
AN&Q	American Notes and Queries
AnM	Annuale Mediaevale
Archiv	Archiv für das Studium der neueren Sprachen und Literaturen
AS	American Speech
AWR	Anglo-Welsh Review
BJRL	Bulletin of the John Rylands Library
BUSE	Boston Univ. Studies in English
BYUS	Brigham Young Univ. Studies
C&M	Classica et Mediaevalia
CE	College English
CFMA	Classiques français du moyen âge
ChauR	Chaucer Review
CJ	Classical Journal
CJL	Canadian Journal of Linguistics
CL	Comparative Literature
CLAJ	College Language Association Journal
CR	Critical Review
CRAS	Centennial Review of Arts and Sciences (Michigan)
CritQ	Critical Quarterly
EA	Études anglaises
E&S	Essays and Studies by Members of the English Association
EHR	English Historical Review
EIC	Essays in Criticism
EJ	English Journal
ELH	Journal of English Literary History
ELN	English Language Notes
EM	English Miscellany
ES	English Studies
ESA	English Studies in Africa
ESt	Englische Studien
FMod	Filología Moderna
GRM	Germanisch-romanische Monatsschrift

ABBREVIATIONS

HAB	Humanities Association Bulletin
HLQ	Huntington Library Quarterly
HSELL	Hiroshima Studies in English Language and Literature
IJES	Indian Journal of English Studies
JEGP	Journal of English and Germanic Philology
JHI	Journal of the History of Ideas
JMRS	Journal of Medieval and Renaissance Studies
L&P	Literature and Psychology
LangQ	Language Quarterly
LeedsSE	Leeds Studies in English
MÆ	Medium Ævum
M&H	Medievalia et Humanistica
MLN	Modern Language Notes
MLQ	Modern Language Quarterly
MLR	Modern Language Review
MP	Modern Philology
MS	Mediaeval Studies
N&Q	Notes and Queries
NDQ	North Dakota Quarterly
Neophil	Neophilologus
NM	Neuphilologische Mitteilungen
NS	Die Neueren Sprachen
PBSUV	Papers of the Bibliographical Society of the Univ. of Virginia
PLL	Papers on Language & Literature
PMASAL	Papers of the Michigan Academy of Science, Arts, and Letters
PMLA	Publication of the Modern Language Association of America
PQ	Philological Quarterly
PTRSC	Proceedings and Transactions of the Royal Society of Canada
QJS	Quarterly Journal of Speech
QR	Quarterly Review
REL	Review of English Literature
RES	Review of English Studies
RLC	Revue de littérature comparée
RPh	Romance Philology
RR	Romanic Review
RUO	Revue de l'Université de Ottawa
SAQ	South Atlantic Quarterly
SATF	Société des anciens textes français
SB	Studies in Bibliography: Papers of the Bibliographical Society of the Univ. of Virginia
SELit	Studies of English Literature (Univ. of Tokyo)
SFQ	Southern Folklore Quarterly
SMed	Studi Medievali
SN	Studia Neophilologica
SP	Studies in Philology
SR	Sewanee Review
SSF	Studies in Short Fiction
TLS	Times Literary Supplement (London)

ABBREVIATIONS

TSE	Tulane Studies in English
TSL	Tennessee Studies in Literature
TSLL	Texas Studies in Literature and Language
TWA	Trans. of the Wisconsin Academy of Science, Arts, and Letters
UCSLL	Univ. of Colorado Studies in Language and Literature
UMSE	Univ. of Mississippi Studies in English
UTQ	Univ. of Toronto Quarterly
WVUPP	West Virginia Univ. Philological Papers
YCGL	Yearbook of Comparative and General Literature
YES	Yearbook of English Studies

Note: *The publisher and compiler invite suggestions for additions to future editions of the bibliography.*

Bibliographies and Surveys of Scholarship

1 *Abstracts of English Studies,* published by the National Council of Teachers of English. Boulder, Colo., 1958–.

2 ACKERMAN, Robert W. "Middle English Literature to 1400" (bibliographical survey). 179, pp. 75–123.

3 "American Bibliography," Comp. Albert C. Baugh, et al. (Surveys for previous years in *The American Year Book;* became international as "Annual Bibliography" in 1957; superseded in 1964 by 20.)

4 *Annual Bibliography of English Language & Literature,* published by the Modern Humanities Research Association, 1920–.

5 BATESON, F. W., ed. *The Cambridge Bibliography of English Literature.* 4 vols. Cambridge: Cambridge Univ. Press, 1941. Suppl., 1957.

6 BAUGH, Albert C. "Fifty Years of Chaucer Scholarship." *Speculum,* 26 (1951), 659–672.

7 BENSON, L. D. "A Reader's Guide to Writings on Chaucer." 260, pp. 321–372.

8 CRAWFORD, William R. *Bibliography of Chaucer 1954–63.* Seattle and London: Univ. of Washington Press, 1967.

9 CRAWFORD, William R. "The House of Chaucer's Fame." *ChauR,* 3 (1969), 191–203.

10 *Dissertation Abstracts* (formerly *Microfilm Abstracts*). Ann Arbor: University Microfilms, 1952–.

11 *Dissertations in English and American Literature: Theses Accepted by American, British, and German Universities, 1865–1964,* ed. Lawrence F. McNamee. New York: Bowker, 1968.

12 GRIFFITH, Dudley D. *Bibliography of Chaucer 1908–1953.* Seattle: Univ. of Washington Press, 1955.

13 HAMMOND, Eleanor P. *Chaucer: A Bibliographical Manual.* New York: Macmillan, 1908. Reprinted, New York: Peter Smith, 1933.

14 *International Guide to Medieval Studies:* A Quarterly Index to Periodical Literature. Darien, Conn.: American Bibliographic Service, 1961–.

15 *International Medieval Bibliography.* Leeds: Univ. of Leeds, 1967–.

16 KIRBY, Thomas A. "Chaucer Research, 1966." *ChauR,* 1 (1967), 186–199. Continued annually.

17 KIRBY, Thomas A. "Chaucer Research in Progress." *NM,* 70 (1969), 545–555. Continued annually.

18 KOCH, John. "Die Chaucerforschung seit 1900." *GRM,* 1 (1909), 490–507. Cf. other surveys by Koch in *Anglia Beiblatt,* 22 (1911), 265–282; 25 (1914), 327–342; 28 (1917), 152–160; *ESt,* 46 (1912), 98–114; 48 (1914), 251–281; *Anglia,* 49 (1926), 193–243.

1

19 MARTIN, Willard E., Jr. *A Chaucer Bibliography 1925–1933.* Durham, N.C.: Duke Univ. Press, 1935.

20 *MLA International Bibliography of. . . Modern Languages and Literature. PMLA,* 79 (1964), May issue. Also separately; continued annually.

21 NEWSTEAD, Helaine. "Chaucer's Canterbury Tales." In *Recent Middle English Scholarship and Criticism: Survey and Desiderata,* ed. J. Burke Severs. Pittsburgh: Duquesne Univ. Press, 1971.

22 PURDY, Rob Roy. "Chaucer Scholarship in England and America: A Review of Recent Trends." *Anglia,* 70 (1951), 345–381.

23 *Quarterly Check-list of Medievalia:* An International Index of Current Books, Monographs, Brochures and Separates. Darien, Conn.: American Bibliographic Service, 1958–.

24 SEVERS, J. Burke, and Albert E. HARTUNG, eds. *A Manual of the Writings in Middle English, 1050–1500.* 4 vols. New Haven: Connecticut Acad., 1967–, in progress.

25 WELLS, John Edwin. *A Manual of the Writings in Middle English 1050–1400.* New Haven: Yale Univ. Press, 1916. [Nine supplements, 1919–51. For new edition, see 24.]

26 *The Year's Work in English Studies,* published by the English Association. London, 1921–.

27 *The Year's Work in Modern Language Studies,* published by the Modern Humanities Research Association, 1931–.

Societies and Journals

28 *The Chaucer Review: A Journal of Medieval Studies and Literary Criticism.* Pennsylvania State Univ. Press, 1968–.

29 CHAUCER SOCIETY: Publications. First Ser. [mainly texts], 99 vols, London, 1868–1912; Second Ser., 56 vols., 1869–1925. Reprinted (First Ser.) New York: Johnson, 1965.

30 EARLY ENGLISH TEXT SOCIETY. Original Ser., 1864–; Extra Ser., 1867–1920.

31 SOCIÉTÉ DES ANCIENS TEXTES FRANÇAIS. Paris, 1875–.

Reference Works

(Acquaintance with the pertinent general dictionaries is assumed: *New English Dictionary, Middle English Dictionary,* and the Old French dictionaries of Godefroy and Tobler-Lommatzsch.)

2

REFERENCE WORKS

32 CARTER, Henry H. *A Dictionary of Middle English Musical Terms*, ed. George B. Gerhard *et al.* Bloomington, Ind.: Indiana Univ. Press, 1961.

33 CORSON, Hiram. *Index of Proper Names and Subjects to Chaucer's Canterbury Tales*, together with Comparisons and Similes, Metaphors and Proverbs, Maxims, etc., in the Same. London, 1911 (Chaucer Soc., 72).

34 CROMIE, Henry. *Ryme-Index to the Ellesmere Manuscript of Chaucer's Canterbury Tales.* London, 1875 (Chaucer Soc., First Ser., 45); reprinted, 1875 (First Ser., 46). Notes and Corrections, 1875 (First ser., 47).

34a DILLON, Bert. *A Chaucer Dictionary: Proper Names and Allusions Excluding Place Names.* Boston: G. K. Hall, 1974.

35 FLÜGEL, Ewald. "Prolegomena and Side-Notes of the Chaucer Dictionary." *Anglia,* 34 (1911), 354–422.

36 FURNIVALL, F. J., ed. *Autotype Specimens of the Chief Chaucer MSS.* London, 1877–86 (Chaucer Soc., 48, 56, 62, 74).

37 HAECKEL, Willi. *Das Sprichwort bei Chaucer.* Erlangen, 1890 (*Erlanger Beiträge,* 8).

38 HEIDRICH, Käte. *Das geographische Weltbild des späteren englischen Mittelalters mit besonderer Berücksichtigung der Vorstellungen Chaucer's und seinen Zeitgenossen.* Freiburg, 1915 (diss.).

39 MAGOUN, Francis P., Jr. *A Chaucer Gazetteer.* Chicago: Univ. of Chicago Press; Uppsala: Almqvist & Wiksell, 1961. [Embodies material previously published in *MS,* 15–17.]

40 MARSHALL, Isabel, and Lela PORTER. *Ryme-Index to the Manuscript Texts of Chaucer's Minor Poems.* London, 1887 (Chaucer Soc., 78); reprinted 1889 (Chaucer Soc., 80).

41 MORAWSKI, J. *Proverbes français antérieurs au XV* siècle.* Paris, 1925 (*CFMA*).

42 SINGER, Samuel. *Sprichwörter des Mittelalters. 3 vols.* Bern: Lang, 1944–47.

43 SKEAT, W. W. *A Ryme-Index to Chaucer's Troilus and Criseyde.* London, 1892 (Chaucer Soc., 84).

44 TATLOCK, John S. P., and A. G. KENNEDY. *Concordance to the Complete Works of Geoffrey Chaucer and to the Romaunt of the Rose.* Washington, D.C.: Carnegie Institution, 1927. Reprinted, Gloucester, Mass.: Peter Smith, 1963.*

45 WALTHER, Hans. *Proverbia Sententiaeque Latinitatis Medii Aevi: Lateinische Sprichwörter und Sentenzen des Mittelalters.* 6 vols. Göttingen: Vandenhoeck & Ruprecht, 1963–67 (*Carmina Medii Aevi Posterioris Latina,* 2/1–6). [In progress.]

46 WHITING, B. J. *Chaucer's Use of Proverbs.* Cambridge, Mass.: Harvard Univ. Press, 1934 (*Harvard Stud. in Compar. Lit.,* 11). Reprinted, New York: AMS Press, 1973.

47 WHITING, Bartlett J. and Helen W. *Proverbs, Sentences, and Proverbial Phrases from English Writings Mainly before 1500.* Cambridge, Mass.: Harvard Univ. Press, 1968.*

Testimonial Volumes — Festschriften

(containing four or more articles on Chaucer)

48 [BAUGH] *Studies in Medieval Literature in Honor of . . . Albert Croll Baugh,* ed. MacEdward Leach. Philadelphia: Univ. of Pennsylvania Press, 1961.

49 [BROWN] *Essays and Studies in Honor of Carleton Brown.* New York: New York Univ. Press, 1940.

50 [FURNIVALL] *An English Miscellany Presented to Dr. Furnivall . . .* Oxford: Clarendon Press, 1901.

51 [KITTREDGE] *Anniversary Papers by Colleagues and Pupils of George Lyman Kittredge.* Boston: Ginn, 1913; reprinted, New York: Russell & Russell, n.d.

52 [MUSTANOJA] *Studies Presented to Tauno F. Mustanoja on . . . His Sixtieth Birthday.* Helsinki, 1972 (*NM,* 73, No. 1–2).

53 [ROBBINS] *Chaucer and Middle English Studies in Honour of Rossell Hope Robbins,* ed. Beryl Rowland. London: Allen & Unwin; Kent, Ohio: Kent State Univ. Press, 1974.

54 [SCHIRMER] *Chaucer und seine Zeit: Symposion für Walter F. Schirmer,* ed. Arno Esch. Tübingen: Niemeyer, 1968.

55 [SCHLAUCH] *Studies in Language and Literature in Honor of Margaret Schlauch.* Warszawa, 1966.

56 [UTLEY] *Medieval Literature and Folklore Studies: Essays in Honor of Francis Lee Utley,* ed. Jerome Mandel and Bruce A. Rosenberg. New Brunswick: Rutgers Univ. Press, 1970.

57 [WHITING] *The Learned and the Lewd: Studies in Chaucer and Medieval Literature,* ed. Larry D. Benson. Cambridge, Mass.: Harvard Univ. Press, 1974.

Life

Collections of Documents

58 CROW, Martin M., and Clair C. OLSON, eds. *Chaucer Life-Records,* from materials compiled by John M. Manly and Edith Rickert, with the assistance of Lilian J. Redstone and others. Oxford: Clarendon Press, 1966.*

59 KUHL, E. P. "Index to *The Life-Records of Chaucer*" [61]. *MP,* 10 (1913), 527–552.

60 NICOLAS, N. Harris, ed. *The Controversy between Sir Richard Scrope and Sir Robert Grosvenor in the Court of Chivalry.* 2 vols., London, 1832.

61 SELBY, W. D., F. J. FURNIVALL, E. A. BOND, and R. E. G. KIRK. *Life Records of Chaucer.* London, 1875–1900 (Chaucer Soc., 2nd Ser., 12, 14, 21, 32).

62 STEWART-BROWN, R. "The Scrope-Grosvenor Controversy." *TLS,* June 12, 1937, p. 447. Cf. *N&Q,* 146 (1924), 225–227.

Special Topics

63 ARDENNE, S. R. T. O. d'. "Chaucer the Englishman." 54, pp. 47–54.

64 BAUGH, Albert C. "The Background of Chaucer's Mission to Spain." 54, pp. 55–69.

65 BAUGH, Albert C. "Chaucer the Man." 296, pp. 1–19.

66 BLAND, D. S. "Chaucer and the Inns of Court: A Reexamination." *ES,* 33 (1952), 145–155.

67 BLAND, D. S. "When Was Chaucer Born?" *TLS,* April 26, 1957, p. 264. Cf. *ibid.,* May 10, p. 289 (M. Galway), May 17, p. 305 (O. Warner, C. E. Welch), June 28, p. 397 (G. D. G. Hall), July 12, p. 427 (M. Galway).

68 BOLTON, W. F. "Chaucer's Life." 161, pp. 159–161.

69 BRADDY, Haldeen. "Chaucer and Dame Alice Perrers." *Speculum,* 21 (1946), 222–228. Reprinted in 258.

70 BRADDY, Haldeen. "Chaucer's Philippa, Daughter of Panneto." *MLN,* 64 (1949), 342–343. Reprinted in 258.

71 BRADDY, Haldeen. "Froissart's Account of Chaucer's Embassy in 1377." *RES,* 14 (1938), 63–67. Reprinted in 258.

72 BRADDY, Haldeen. "New Documentary Evidence Concerning Chaucer's Mission to Lombardy." *MLN,* 48 (1933), 507–511. Cf. *ibid.,* 49 (1934), 209–216 (J. M. Manly).

73 BRESSIE, Ramona. "Was Chaucer at the Siege of Paris?" *JEGP,* 39 (1940), 209–221.

74 BROOKS, Eric S. "Chaucer's Mother." *New England Hist. and Geneal. Register,* 83 (1929), 391–393.

75 CALL, Reginald. "The Plimpton Chaucer and Other Problems of Chaucerian Portraiture." *Speculum,* 22 (1947), 135–144.

76 CARPENTER, Nan C. "A Note on Chaucer's Mother." *MLN,* 60 (1945), 382–383.

77 [CHAUCER'S LEASE OF 1399] Reproduced in fascimile, Palaeographical Soc.: Facsimiles, Vol. II, plate 224.

78 CHUTE, Marchette. *Geoffrey Chaucer of England.* New York: Dutton, 1946.

79 COOK, Albert S. "The Last Months of Chaucer's Earliest Patron [Lionel, Duke of Clarence]." *Trans. Connecticut Acad.,* 21 (1916–17), 1–144.

80 COOK, Albert S. See 365.

81 COULTON, George G. "Chaucer's Captivity." *MLR,* 4 (1909), 234–235.

82 DU BOULAY, F. R. H. "The Historical Chaucer." 260, pp. 33–57.

83 EMERSON, Oliver F. "Chaucer's First Military Service—A Study of Edward Third's Invasion of France in 1359–60." *RR,* 3 (1912), 321–361. Reprinted in 395.

84 EMERSON, Oliver F. "Chaucer's Testimony as to His Age." *MP,* 11 (1913–14), 117–125. Reprinted in 395.

85 "F. U." "Did Chaucer Meet Petrarch and Boccaccio?" *Anglo-Italian Rev.,* 1 (1918), 121–135.

86 FERRIS, Sumner. "Chaucer, Richard II, Henry IV, and 13 October." 53, pp. 210–217.

87 FURNIVALL, Frederick J. [Communication identifying Chaucer's father for the first time.] *Athenaeum,* Nov. 29, 1873, p. 698.

88 GALWAY, Margaret. "Chaucer's Journeys in 1368." *TLS,* April 4, 1958, p. 183.

89 GALWAY, Margaret. "Geoffrey Chaucer, J. P. and M. P." *MLR,* 36 (1941), 1–36.

90 GALWAY, Margaret. "Philippa Pan, Philippa Chaucer." *MLR,* 55 (1960), 481–487.

91 GALWAY, Margaret. " 'Pullesdon' in the *Life-Records of Chaucer.*" *N&Q,* 202 (1957), 371–374.

92 GALWAY, Margaret. "Walter Roet and Philippa Chaucer." *N&Q,* 199 (1954), 48–49.

93 GARBÁTY, Thomas J. "Chaucer in Spain, 1366: Soldier of Fortune or Agent of the Crown?" *ELN,* 5 (1967), 81–87.

94 HONORÉ-DUVERGÉ, Suzanne. "Chaucer en Espagne? (1366)." *Recueil de Travaux offert à M. Clovis Brunel.* 2 vols., Paris, 1955, II, 9–13.

95 HULBERT, James R. "Chaucer and the Earl of Oxford." *MP,* 10 (1912–13), 433–437.

96 HULBERT, James R. *Chaucer's Official Life.* Menasha, Wis., 1912.*

97 JAMES, Margery K. "Gilbert Maghfeld, a London Merchant of the Fourteenth Century." *Economic Hist. Rev.,* 2nd ser. 8 (1956), 364–376.

98 JENKINS, T. A. "Deschamps' Ballade to Chaucer." *MLN,* 33 (1918), 268–278.

99 JUSSERAND, J. J. "Did Chaucer Meet Petrarch?" *Nineteenth Century,* 39 (1896), 993–1005.

100 JUSSERAND, J. J. "On the Possible Meeting of Chaucer and Petrarch." *The School for Ambassadors and Other Essays,* pp. 325–341. (New York: Putnam, 1925).

101 KERN, Alfred A. *The Ancestry of Chaucer.* Baltimore, 1906.*

102 KRAUSS, Russell. "Chaucerian Problems: Especially the Petherton Forestership and the Question of Thomas Chaucer." In *Three Chaucer Studies,* ed. Carleton Brown. New York, 1932. (621)

103 KRAUSS, Russell. "Notes on Thomas, Geoffrey and Philippa Chaucer." *MLN,* 47 (1932), 351–360.

104 KUHL, Ernest P. "Chaucer and Aldgate." *PMLA,* 39 (1924), 101–122.

105 KUHL, Ernest P. "Chaucer and the 'Fowle Ok.' " *MLN,* 36 (1921), 157–159. Reprinted in 475.

106 KUHL, Ernest P. "Chaucer and Westminster Abbey." *JEGP,* 45 (1946), 340–343. Reprinted in 475.

107 KUHL, Ernest P. "Some Friends of Chaucer." *PMLA,* 29 (1914), 270–276. Reprinted in 475.

108 KUHL, Ernest P. "Why Was Chaucer Sent to Milan in 1378?" *MLN,* 62 (1947), 42–44. Reprinted in 475.

109 LAM, George L., and Warren H. SMITH. "George Vertue's Contributions to Chaucerian Iconography." *MLQ,* 5 (1944), 303–322.

110 LANGHANS, V. "Chaucers Heirat." *Anglia,* 54 (1930), 297–306.

111 MANLY, John M. "Chaucer as Controller." *MP,* 25 (1927–28), 123. Cf. *TLS,* June 9, 1937, p. 408.

112 MANLY, John M., and Edith RICKERT. "Chaucer in a New Setting." *TLS,* Aug. 19, 1926, p. 549. Cf. *ibid.,* Sept. 2, p. 580 (Angus McBain).

113 MANLY, John M. "Mary Chaucer's First Husband." *Speculum,* 9 (1934), 86–88. [John Heyroun.]

114 MANLY, John M. "A Portrait of Chaucer." *TLS,* March 29, 1934, p. 229. Cf. *ibid.,* April 5, p. 244 (M. H. Spielmann).

115 MATHER, F. J. "On the Asserted Meeting of Chaucer and Petrarch." *MLN,* 12 (1897), 1–21.

116 MITCHELL, Jerome. "Hoccleve's Supposed Friendship with Chaucer." *ELN,* 4 (1966), 9–12.

117 MOORE, Samuel. "Studies in the Life-Records of Chaucer." *Anglia,* 37 (1913), 1–26.*

118 OLSON, Clair C. *The Emerging Biography of a Poet* (The Third Annual College of the Pacific Research Lecture), 1953.

119 PARKS, George B. "The Route of Chaucer's First Journey to Italy." *ELH,* 16 (1949), 174–187.

120 PLUCKNET, T. F. T. "Chaucer's Escapade." *Law Quar. Rev.,* 64 (1948), 33–36.

121 PRATT, Robert A. "Geoffrey Chaucer, Esq., and Sir John Hawkwood." *ELH,* 16 (1949), 188–193.

122 REDSTONE, Vincent B. "Chaucer A Norfolk Man." *Academy,* 75 (1908), 425.

123 REDSTONE, Vincent B. "The Chaucer Seals." *Athenaeum,* 1908, 1, 670.

124 REDSTONE, Vincent B., and Lilian J. REDSTONE. "The Heyrons of London: A Study in the Social Origins of Geoffrey Chaucer." *Speculum,* 12 (1937), 182–195.

125 RICKERT, Edith. "Chaucer Abroad in 1369." *MP,* 25 (1927–28), 511–512.

126 RICKERT, Edith. "Chaucer and the Treasurer of Calais." *TLS,* Nov. 17, 1932, p. 859.

127 RICKERT, Edith. "Chaucer at School." *MP,* 29 (1931–32), 257–274. See also *TLS,* Feb. 4, 1932, p. 76.

128 RICKERT, Edith. "Chaucer Called to Account." *TLS,* Dec. 8, 1932, p. 943.

129 RICKERT, Edith. "Chaucer's Debt to Walter Bukholt." *MP,* 24 (1926–27), 503–505.

130 RICKERT, Edith. "Extracts from a Fourteenth-Century Account Book." *MP,* 24 (1926–27), 111–119, 249–256. See 97.

131 RICKERT, Edith. "New Life Records of Chaucer." *TLS,* Sept. 27, 1928, p. 684; Oct. 4, p. 707. Cf. *ibid.,* Oct. 11, p. 736 (H. W. Garrod).

132 RICKERT, Edith. "Was Chaucer a Student at the Inner Temple?" *Manly Anniversary Studies* (Chicago, 1923), pp. 20–31.

133 Rye, Walter. *Chaucer: A Norfolk Man.* Norwich: Privately printed, 1915; *Chaucer, A Norfolk Man: Appendix III* [paged 105–124, to follow the preceding]. Norwich, 1916.

134 Scott, Florence R. "Chaucer and the Parliament of 1386." *Speculum,* 18 (1943), 80–86.

135 Shugrue, Michael. "The Urry *Chaucer* (1721) and the London Uprising of 1384: A Phase in Chaucerian Biography." *JEGP,* 65 (1966), 229–237.

136 Spielmann, M. H. "The Portraits of Chaucer." 360, pp. 111–141. Also separately, Chaucer Soc., 2nd Ser., No. 31 (1900).

137 Stanley-Wrench, M. *Teller of Tales: The Life of Goeffrey Chaucer.* Surrey: Tadsworth, 1967. (World's Work).

138 Tatlock, John S. P. "The Duration of Chaucer's Visits to Italy." *JEGP,* 12 (1913), 118–121.

139 Vibert, Lionel. "Chaucer and Henry Yevele." *Ars Quatuor Coronatorum,* 44 (1931), 239–241.

140 Watts, P. R. "The Strange Case of Geoffrey Chaucer and Cecilia Chaumpaigne." *Law Quar. Rev.,* 63 (1947), 491–515.

Children and Descendants

141 Anderson, Marjorie. "Alice Chaucer and Her Husbands." *PMLA,* 60 (1945), 24–47.

142 Baugh, Albert C. "Kirk's Life Records of Thomas Chaucer." *PMLA,* 47 (1932), 461–515.

143 Baugh, Albert C. "Thomas Chaucer, One Man or Two?" *PMLA,* 48 (1933), 328–339.

144 Kittredge, George L. "Lewis Chaucer or Lewis Clifford." *MP,* 14 (1916–17), 513–518.

145 Lamborn, E. A. G. "The Arms on the Chaucer Tomb at Ewelme." *Oxoniensia,* 5 (1940), 78–93.*

146 Lamborn, E. A. G. "A Chaucer Seal." *N&Q,* 184 (1943), 287.

147 Manly, John M. "Litel Lowis My Sone." *TLS,* June 7, 1928, p. 430.

148 Manly, John M. "Thomas Chaucer, Son of Geoffrey." *TLS,* Aug. 3, 1933, p. 525. See *ibid.,* Aug. 10, p. 537 (Oswald Barron and E. S. Brooks); Aug. 17, p. 549 (Barron).

149 Rickert, Edith. "Elizabeth Chausir a Nun at Barking." *TLS,* May 18, 1933, p. 348. Cf. *ibid.,* June 8, p. 396 (A. H. Fowler).

150 Ruud, Martin B. *Thomas Chaucer.* Minneapolis, 1926 (*Research Pub. of the Univ. of Minnesota: Stud. in Lang. and Lit.,* No. 9).*

Literary, Political, and Social Environment

151 ACKERMAN, Robert W. *Backgrounds to Medieval English Literature.* New York: Random House, 1966. [SLL 7]

152 ALLEN, Judson B. *The Friar as Critic: Literary Attitudes in the Later Middle Ages.* Nashville: Vanderbilt Univ. Press, 1971.

153 ANDERSON, George K. "Old and Middle English Literature ... to 1485." *A History of English Literature,* ed. Hardin Craig, pp. 1–172. New York: Oxford Univ. Press; 1950.

154 BAUGH, Albert C. "The Middle English Period (1100–1500)." *A Literary History of England,* ed. Albert C. Baugh, pp. 107–312. New York: Appleton-Century-Crofts, 1948; 2nd ed., 1967; since 1974 Prentice-Hall.

155 BEICHNER, Paul E. "The Allegorical Interpretation of Medieval Literature." *PMLA,* 82 (1967), 33–38. Reprinted in 211.

156 BENNETT, H. S. *Chaucer and the Fifteenth Century.* Oxford: Oxford Univ. Press, 1947.

156a BENNETT, J. A. W. *Chaucer at Oxford and at Cambridge.* Oxford: Clarendon Press; Toronto: Toronto Univ. Press, [1974].

157 BERGNER, Heinz. "Das Fabliau in der mittelenglischen Literatur." *Sprachkunst: Beiträge zur Literaturwissenschaft,* 3 (1972), 298–312. (Österreichische Akad.)

158 BIRD, Ruth. *The Turbulent London of Richard II.* London: Longmans, 1949.

159 BLAKE, N. F. "Chaucer in His Time." 282, pp. 1–7.

160 BLOOMFIELD, Morton W. *Essays and Explorations: Studies in Ideas, Language, and Literature.* Cambridge, Mass.: Harvard Univ. Press, 1970. (Collected essays; pertinent items are separately listed.)

161 BOLTON, W. F., ed. *History of Literature in the English Language.* Vol. I: *The Middle Ages.* London: Barrie and Jenkins, 1970.

162 BOYD, Beverly. *Chaucer and the Medieval Book.* [San Marino, Calif.:] Huntington Library, 1973.

163 BREWER, Derek S. *Chaucer in His Time.* London: Nelson, 1963.

164 BREWER, Derek S. "The Relationship of Chaucer to the English and European Traditions." In 339, pp. 1–38.

165 BRODY, Saul N. *The Disease of the Soul: Leprosy in Medieval Literature.* Ithaca: Cornell Univ. Press, 1974.

166 BURROW, J. A. *Ricardian Poetry: Chaucer, Gower, Langland, and the Gawain Poet.* New Haven: Yale Univ. Press; London: Routledge & Kegan Paul, 1971.

167 COTTLE, Basil. *The Triumph of English, 1350–1400.* New York: Barnes and Noble, 1969.

168 COULTON, G. G. *Chaucer and His England.* With a New Bibliography by T. W. Craik. London: Methuen; New York: Barnes and Noble, 1963. [UP 46-B&N]

169 COULTON, G. G. *Medieval Panorama: The English Scene from Conquest to Reformation.* Cambridge: Cambridge Univ. Press, 1938.

170 CURRY, Walter C. *Chaucer and the Medieval Sciences.* New York: Oxford Univ. Press, 1926; 2nd ed., New York: Barnes and Noble, 1960; paperback, 1962.

171 CURTIUS, Ernst R. *Europäische Literatur und lateinisches Mittelalter.* Bern: Francke, 1948; 2nd ed., 1954. English trans. by Willard R. Trask, *European Literature and the Latin Middle Ages.* New York: Pantheon Books, 1953.

172 DENOMY, Alexander J. "Courtly Love and Courtliness." *Speculum,* 28 (1953), 44–63.

173 DENOMY, Alexander J. *The Heresy of Courtly Love.* New York: D. X. McMullen, 1947.

174 DENOMY, Alexander J. "An Inquiry into the Origins of Courtly Love." *MS,* 6 (1944), 175–187.

175 DONALDSON, E. T. "The Myth of Courtly Love." *Ventures,* 5 (1965), 16–23. Reprinted in 273.

176 ECONOMOU, George D. *The Goddess Natura in Medieval Literature.* Cambridge, Mass.: Harvard Univ. Press, 1972.

177 EVANS, W. O. " 'Cortaysye' in Middle English." *MS,* 29 (1967), 143–157.

178 EVERETT, Dorothy. *Essays on Middle English Literature.* Ed. Patricia Kean. Oxford: Clarendon Press, 1955.

179 FISHER, John H., ed. *The Medieval Literature of Western Europe: A Review of Research, Mainly 1930–1960.* New York: MLA, 1966 (Revolving Fund Ser., No. 22).

180 FLEMING, John V. *The Roman de la Rose: A Study in Allegory and Iconography.* Princeton: Princeton Univ. Press, 1969.

181 FORD, Boris, ed. *The Pelican Guide to English Literature:* I. *The Age of Chaucer.* London and Baltimore: Penguin Books, 1954. [A 290-Pen]

182 FRANK, Don K. "The Corporeal, the Derogatory and the Stress on Equality in Andreas' *De Amore.*" *M&H,* 16 (1964), 30–38.

183 FRIEDMAN, John B. *Orpheus in the Middle Ages.* Cambridge, Mass.: Harvard Univ. Press, 1970.

184 GLUNZ, H. H. *Die Literarästhetik des europäischen Mittelalters: Wolfram-Rosenroman-Chaucer-Dante.* Bochum-Langendreer: Poppinghaus, 1937.

185 GROSS, Charles. *The Sources and Literature of English History from the Earliest Times to about 1485.* 2nd ed. London: Longmans, 1915.

186 GUNN, Alan M. F. *The Mirror of Love: A Reinterpretation of 'The Romance of the Rose.'* Lubbock, Tex., 1952 (*Texas Tech. Coll. Research Pub.*).

187 HILL, Betty. "Systematic Bibliography of Middle English Literature, c. 1150–1500: A Select Guide." *NM,* 74 (1973), 473–479.

188 HILL, Mary C. *The King's Messengers, 1199–1377: A Contribution to the History of the Royal Household.* London: Arnold, 1961.

189 HUSSEY, Maurice. *Chaucer's World: A Pictorial Companion.* Cambridge: Cambridge Univ. Press, 1967.

190 JACKSON, W. T. H. "The *De Amore* of Andreas Capellanus and the Practice of Love at Court." *RR,* 49 (1958), 243–251.

191 KLEINSTÜCK, J. W. *Chaucers Stellung in der Mittelalterlichen Literatur.* Hamburg: Cram, de Gruyter, 1956 (*Britannica et Americana,* I).

192 KNOWLTON, Edgar C. "The Goddess Nature in Early Periods." *JEGP,* 19 (1920), 224–253.

193 KNOWLTON, Edgar C. "Nature in Middle English." *JEGP,* 20 (1921), 186–207.

194 LOOMIS, Laura H. *Adventures in the Middle Ages: A Memorial Collection of Essays and Studies.* New York: Franklin, 1962.

195 LOOMIS, Roger S. *A Mirror of Chaucer's World.* Princeton: Princeton Univ. Press, 1965.

196 LOOMIS, Roger S. *Studies in Medieval Lieterature: A Memorial Collection of Essays.* New York: Burt Franklin, [1970].

197 McFARLANE, K. B. "The Education of the Nobility in Later Medieval England." *The Nobility of Later Medieval England: The Ford Lectures for 1953 and Related Studies.* London: Oxford Univ. Press, 1973.

198 McKEON, Richard. "Rhetoric in the Middle Ages." *Speculum,* 17 (1942), 1–32.

199 McKISACK, May. *The Fourteenth Century, 1307–1399.* Oxford: Clarendon Press, 1959 (*Oxford Hist. of England,* V).

200 MAHONEY, John J. "Ovid and Medieval Courtly Love Poetry." *Classical Folia,* 15 (1961), 14–27.

201 MATHEW, Gervase. "Marriage and *Amour Courtois* in Late Fourteenth-Century England." In *Essays Presented to Charles Williams.* Oxford: Oxford Univ. Press, 1947. Reprinted in 211.

202 MATHEW, Gervase. *The Court of Richard II.* London: Murray, 1968.

203 MEANS, Michael H. *The Consolatio Genre in Medieval English Literature.* Gainesville: Univ. of Florida Press, 1972 (*Univ. of Florida Humanities Monograph,* No. 36).

204 MEIER, Hans H. "Middle English Styles in Action." *ES,* 55 (1974), 193–204.

205 MILLER, Joseph M., *et al.,* eds. *Readings in Medieval Rhetoric.* Bloomington: Indiana Univ. Press, 1973.

206 MILLS, Mabel H. "The London Customs House during the Middle Ages." *Archaeologia,* 83 (1933), 307–325.

207 MURPHY, James J. "Literary Implications of Instruction in the Verbal Arts in Fourteenth-Century England." *LeedsSE,* 1 (1967), 119–135.

208 MURPHY, James J., ed. *Three Medieval Rhetorical Arts.* Berkeley: Univ. of California Press, 1971.

209 MUSCATINE, Charles. *Poetry and Crisis in the Age of Chaucer.* Notre Dame: Univ. of Notre Dame Press, 1972.

210 NEWMAN, F. X., ed. *The Meaning of Courtly Love.* Albany: State Univ. of New York Press, [1969].

211 NEWSTEAD, Helaine, ed. *Chaucer and His Contemporaries: Essays on Medieval Literature and Thought.* Greenwich, Conn.: Fawcett, [1968].

212 OLSON, Clair C. "Chaucer and Fourteenth-Century Society." 296, pp. 20–37.

213 OLSON, Glending. "Deschamps' *Art de dictier* and Chaucer's Literary Environment." *Speculum,* 48 (1973), 714–723.

11

214 PAETOW, Louis J. *A Guide to the Study of Medieval History.* Rev. ed., New York: Crofts, 1931.

215 PANTIN, W. A. *The English Church in the Fourteenth Century.* Cambridge: Cambridge Univ. Press, 1955. [NDP-23]

216 PARRY, John J., trans. *The Art of Courtly Love.* New York: Columbia Univ. Press, 1941 (*Records of Civilization,* No. 33). Abridged by Frederick W. Lock. New York: Ungar, n.d. [M 104-Ungar]

217 PATCH, Howard R. *The Goddess Fortuna in Medieval Lieterature.* Cambridge, Mass.: Harvard Univ. Press, 1927.

218 PATCH, Howard R. "The Individual and the Type in Medieval Literature." *The McAuley Lectures, 1954: Christian Humanism in Letters,* pp. 25–41. West Hartford, Conn.: St. Joseph College, 1954.

219 PATCH, Howard R. *The Tradition of Boethius: A Study of His Importance in Medieval Culture.* New York: Oxford Univ. Press, 1935.

220 POOLE, Austin L., ed. *Medieval England,* 2 vols. Oxford: Clarendon Press, 1958.

221 QUILLER-COUCH, Sir Arthur T. *The Age of Chaucer.* London: Dent, [1926].

222 RICKERT, Edith. *Chaucer's World,* ed. C. C. Olson and M. M. Crow. New York: Columbia Univ. Press, 1948. [30–Col].

223 ROBBINS, Rossell H. "The English Fabliau: Before and after Chaucer." *Moderna Språk* (Stockholm), 64 (1970), 231–244.

224 ROBERTSON, D. W. *Chaucer's London.* New York: Wiley, [1968].

225 ROBERTSON, D. W. "The Subject of the *De Amore* of Andreas Capellanus." *MP,* 50 (1952–53), 145–161.

226 RODAX, Yvonne. *The Real and the Ideal in the Novella of Italy, France and England: Four Centuries of Change in the Boccaccian Tale.* Chapel Hill: Univ. of No. Carolina Press, 1968.

227 ROWLAND, Beryl. *Animals with Human Faces: A Guide to Animal Symbolism.* [Knoxville]: Univ. of Tennessee Press, [1973].

228 ROWLAND, Beryl. *Blind Beasts: Chaucer's Animal World.* [Kent, Ohio]: Kent State Univ. Press, [1971].

229 SCHLAUGH, Margaret. *English Medieval Literature and Its Social Foundations.* Warszawa: Panstwowe Wydawn.naukowe, 1956.

230 SCHLÖSSER, Felix. *Andreas Capellanus, Seine Minnelehre und das christliche Weltbild um 1200.* Bonn, 1960 (*Abhandlungen zur Kunst-, Musik- und Literaturwissenschaft,* XV).

231 SPEARING, A. C. *Criticism and Medieval Poetry.* London: Arnold, 1964; 2nd ed., 1972.

232 STEADMAN, John M. " 'Courtly Love' as a Problem of Style." 54, pp. 1–33.

233 SUTHERLAND, D. R. "The Love Meditation in Courtly Literature." *Studies in Medieval French Presented to Alfred Ewert,* pp. 165–193. Oxford: Oxford Univ. Press, 1961.

234 TALBOT, C. H. *Medicine in Medieval England.* London: Oldbourne, [1967].

235 TALBOT, C. H. "Dame Trot and Her Progeny." *Essays and Studies, 1972: In Honor of Beatrice White*, ed. T. S. Dorsch, pp. 1–14. New York: Humanities, 1972. (*Essays and Stud. Collected for the English Assoc.*, n.s. 25). [On medieval women doctors]

236 THOMPSON, A. Hamilton. *The English Clergy and Their Organization in the Later Middle Ages.* Oxford: Clarendon Press, 1947.

237 THRUPP, Sylvia L., *The Merchant Class of Medieval London (1300–1500).* Chicago: Univ. of Chicago Press, 1948. [AA 72]

238 TOUT, T. F. "Literature and Learning in the English Civil Service in the Fourteenth Century." *Speculum,* 4 (1929), 365–389.

239 TREVELYAN, G. M. *England in the Age of Wycliffe.* 4th ed., London: Longmans, 1909. [TB 1112]

240 VARTY, Kenneth. *Reynard the Fox: A Study of the Fox in Medieval English Art.* Leicester: Leicester Univ. Press, 1967.

241 VASTA, Edward, ed. *Middle English Survey: Critical Essays.* Notre Dame, Ind.: Univ. of Notre Dame Press, 1965.

242 WEDEL, T. O. *The Mediaeval Attitude Toward Astrology, Particularly in England.* New Haven, 1920 (*Yale Stud. In Eng.,* 60).

243 WEIGAND, Hermann J. *Three Chapters on Courtly Love in Arthurian France and Germany.* Chapel Hill, 1956 (*Univ. of No. Carolina Stud. in the Germanic Lang. and Lit.,* 17).

244 WHITMORE, Sister M. Ernestine. *Medieval English Domestic Life and Amusements in the Works of Chaucer.* Washington, D.C., 1937 (Cath. Univ. of Amer. diss.). Reprinted New York: Cooper Square, 1972.

245 WILHELM, James J. *The Cruelest Month: Spring, Nature, and Love in Classical and Medieval Lyrics.* New Haven: Yale Univ. Press, 1965.

246 WIMSATT, James I. *Allegory and Mirror: Tradition and Structure in Middle English Literature.* New York: Pegasus, 1970.

247 ZESMER, David M., and Stanley B. GREENFIELD. *Guide to English Literature from Beowulf through Chaucer and Medieval Drama.* New York: Barnes & Noble, 1961.

Collective Editions

Critical Texts

248 BAUGH, Albert C., ed. *Chaucer's Major Poetry.* New York: Appleton-Century-Crofts, 1963; since 1974 Prentice-Hall.

249 BREWER, D. S., ed. *Geoffrey Chaucer: The Works* [Thynne], *1532.* London: Scholar Press Facsimiles, 1969, 1974.

250 DONALDSON, E. T., ed. *Chaucer's Poetry: An Anthology for the Modern Reader.* New York: Ronald Press, 1958.

251 POLLARD, A. W., M. H. LIDDELL, H. F. HEATH, W. S. McCORMICK, eds. *The Works of Geoffrey Chaucer.* London: Macmillan, 1908. [The Globe Chaucer.]

252 ROBINSON, F. N., ed. *The Works of Geoffrey Chaucer.* Boston: Houghton Mifflin, 1933; 2nd ed., 1957.*

253 SKEAT, W. W., ed. *The Complete Works of Geoffrey Chaucer.* 7 vols., Oxford: Clarendon Press, 1894–7. [The Oxford Chaucer.]*

Modernizations

254 MORRISON, Theodore. *The Portable Chaucer.* Selected and translated. New York: Viking, 1949 (verse). [P 47-Vik]

255 TATLOCK, John S. P., and Percy MACKAYE. *The Complete Poetical Works of Geoffrey Chaucer.* New York: Macmillan, 1912. *The Modern Reader's Chaucer.* New York, 1914 (prose). [93241-FreeP]

Criticism

Comprehensive and General

256 BAUM, Paull F. *Chaucer: A Critical Appreciation.* Durham, N.C.: Duke Univ. Press, 1958.

257 BOWDEN, Muriel. *A Reader's Guide to Geoffrey Chaucer.* New York: Farrar, Straus, 1964.

258 BRADDY, Haldeen. *Geoffrey Chaucer: Literary and Historical Studies.* Port Washington: Kennikat Press, [1971]. (Studies previously published, listed separately.)

259 BREWER, D. S. *Chaucer.* London and New York: Longmans, 1953; 3rd ed., 1973.

260 BREWER, Derek, ed. *Geoffrey Chaucer.* London: Bell, 1974. (Writers and their Background)

261 BRONSON, Bertrand H. *In Search of Chaucer.* Toronto: Univ. of Toronto Press, 1960 (The Alexander Lectures, 1958–59). [UTP]*

262 BRUSENDORFF, Aage. *The Chaucer Tradition.* London: Oxford Univ. Press; Copenhagen: Branner, 1925.*

263 BURROW, John A., ed. *Geoffrey Chaucer: A Critical Anthology.* Harmondsworth: Penguin, 1969.

264 CAWLEY, A. C., ed. *Chaucer's Mind and Art.* Edinburgh: Oliver & Boyd, 1969. (Items, some reprinted, listed separately.)

265 CHESTERTON, G. K. *Chaucer.* New York: Farrar & Rinehart; London: Faber, 1932.

266 CLEMEN, Wolfgang. *Chaucers frühe Dichtung.* Göttingen: Vandenhoeck and Ruprecht, 1963. [A revision of 268]

267 CLEMEN, Wolfgang. *Chaucer's Early Poetry,* trans. C. A. M. Sym. London: Methuen, 1963. [A trans. of 266]*

CRITICISM

268 CLEMEN, Wolfgang. *Der junge Chaucer: Grundlagen und Entwicklung seiner Dichtung.* Bochum-Langendreer, 1938 (*Kölner Anglistische Arbeiten,* 33).

269 COGHILL, Nevill. *The Poet Chaucer.* London: Oxford Univ. Press, 1949; 2nd ed., 1968.

270 COGHILL, Nevill. *Geoffrey Chaucer.* London: Longmans, 1956. (Writers and Their Work, No. 79).

271 COWLING, G. H. *Chaucer.* London: Methuen, 1927.

272 DE SELINCOURT, Aubrey. "Geoffrey Chaucer, 1340–1400." In *Six Great Poets,* pp. 9–39. London: Hamilton, 1956.

273 DONALDSON, E. Talbot. *Speaking of Chaucer.* New York: Norton, [1970].

274 FRENCH, Robert D. *A Chaucer Handbook.* New York: Crofts, 1927; 2nd ed., 1947.

275 GROSE, Michael. *Chaucer.* London: Evans, 1967.

276 HADOW, Grace E. *Chaucer and His Times.* New York: Holt, 1914; 2nd ed., 1926.

277 HALLIDAY, F. E. *Chaucer and His World.* London: Thames and Hudson; New York: Viking, 1968.

278 HOWARD, Edwin J. *Geoffrey Chaucer.* New York: Twayne, 1964.

279 HUSSEY, S. S. *Chaucer: An Introduction.* London: Methuen, 1971. [B&N 224]

280 HUSSEY, Maurice, A. C. SPEARING, and James WINNY. *An Introduction to Chaucer.* Cambridge: Cambridge Univ. Press, 1965.

281 HUXLEY, Aldous. "Chaucer." *London Mercury,* 2 (1920), 170–189; reprinted in *On the Margin* (London: Chatto & Windus, 1923) and *EIC,* 15 (1965), 6–21.

282 JOHNSON, William C., Jr. and Loren C. GRUBER, eds. *New Views on Chaucer: Essays in Generative Criticism.* Denver: Soc. for New Lang. Study, 1973.

283 KITTREDGE, George L. *Chaucer and His Poetry.* Cambridge, Mass.: Harvard Univ. Press, 1915.*

284 LANGHANS, Viktor. *Untersuchungen zu Chaucer.* Halle: Niemeyer, 1918.

285 LAWLOR, John. *Chaucer.* London: Hutchinson; New York: Harper, 1968.

286 LEGOUIS, Emile. *Geoffrey Chaucer.* Trans. L. Lailavoix. London: Dent, 1913. [French original, Paris, 1910.]

287 LOWES, John L. *Geoffrey Chaucer and the Development of His Genius.* Boston: Houghton Mifflin, 1934. Reprinted as *Geoffrey Chaucer.* Bloomington, Ind.: Indiana Univ. Press, 1958. [MB-8]*

288 MALONE, Kemp. *Chapters on Chaucer.* Baltimore: Johns Hopkins Univ. Press, 1951.

289 MASEFIELD, John. *Chaucer.* Cambridge: Cambridge Univ. Press, 1931.

290 McNABB, Fr. Vincent. *Geoffrey Chaucer: A Study in Genius & Ethics.* London: Pepler and Sewell, 1934.

291 NORTON-SMITH, John. *Geoffrey Chaucer.* London: Routledge & Kegan Paul, 1974.

292 PATCH, Howard R. *On Rereading Chaucer.* Cambridge, Mass.: Harvard Univ. Press, 1939.

293 POLLARD, A. W. *Chaucer.* London: Macmillan, 1893; 2nd ed., 1931.

294 PRESTON, Raymond. *Chaucer.* London and New York: Sheed and Ward, 1952.

295 ROOT, Robert K. *The Poetry of Chaucer.* 2nd ed., Boston: Houghton Mifflin, 1922. Reprinted Gloucester, Mass.: Peter Smith, 1957.*

296 ROWLAND, Beryl, ed. *Companion to Chaucer Studies.* Toronto: Oxford Univ. Press, 1968; also paperback. (The items are separately listed.)

297 SEDGWICK, Henry D. *Dan Chaucer: An Introduction to the Poet, His Poetry and His Times.* Indianapolis: Bobbs-Merrill, 1934.

298 SHELLY, Percy V. D. *The Living Chaucer.* Philadelphia: Univ. of Pennsylvania Press, 1940.*

299 SKEAT, W. W. *The Chaucer Canon.* Oxford: Clarendon Press, 1900.*

300 SPEIRS, John. *Chaucer the Maker.* London: Faber, 1951; 2nd ed., 1960. [Embodies articles in *Scrutiny,* 11 (1942–43), 84–108, 189–211; 12 (1943–44), 35–57.]

301 STROUD, Theodore A. "Genres and Themes: A Reaction to Two Views of Chaucer." *MP,* 72 (1974), 60–70. [Review article on 390 and 1383]

302 TATLOCK, John S. P. *The Development and Chronology of Chaucer's Works.* London, 1907 (Chaucer Soc., 2nd Ser., No. 37). Reprinted Gloucester, Mass.: Peter Smith, 1964.*

303 TATLOCK, John S. P. *The Mind and Art of Chaucer.* Syracuse, N.Y.: Syracuse Univ. Press, 1950. Reprinted New York: Stechert, 1966.*

304 TEN BRINK, Bernard. *Chaucer: Studien zur Geschichte seiner Entwicklung und zur Chronologie seiner Schriften.* Munster: Russell, 1870.

305 WAGENKNECHT, Edward. *The Personality of Chaucer.* Norman, Okla.: Univ. of Oklahoma Press, 1968.

306 WARD, A. W. *Chaucer.* London: Macmillan, 1880 (English Men of Letters Ser.).

307 WILLIAMS, George. *A New View of Chaucer.* Durham, N.C.: Duke Univ. Press, 1965.

308 ZANCO, Aurelio. *Chaucer e il suo mondo.* Torino: Petrini, 1955.

Special Topics

309 ADAMS, George R., and Bernard S. LEVY. "Good and Bad Fridays and May 3 in Chaucer." *ELN,* 3 (1966), 245–248. [*KnT, NPT, TC*]

310 ADOLPHUS, A. E. "Chauceriana." *N&Q,* 10 Ser. 8 (1907), 202–203. [*NPT, CIT, PF*]

311 ALDERSON, William L., and Arnold C. HENDERSON. *Chaucer and Augustan Scholarship.* Berkeley: Univ. of Calif. Press, 1970. (*Univ. of Calif. Pubns, English Stud.,* 35)

312 ANDERSON, William L. "A Check-List of Supplements to Spurgeon's Chaucer Allusions." *PQ,* 32 (1953), 418–427.

313 BADENDYCK, J. Lawrence. "Chaucer's Portrait Technique and the Dream Vision Tradition." *English Record,* 21, i (1970), 113–125.

314 BALDWIN, Charles S. "Cicero on Parnassus." *PMLA,* 42 (1927), 106–112.

315 BAUER, Gero. "Historisches Präsens und Vergegenwärtigung des epischen Geschehens: Ein erzähltechnischer Kunstgriff Chaucers." *Anglia,* 85 (1967), 138–160.

CRITICISM

316 BAUM, Paull F. "Chaucer's Nautical Metaphors." *SAQ*, 49 (1950), 67–73.

317 BAUM, Paull F. "Chaucer's Puns." *PMLA*, 71 (1956), 225–246.

318 BAUM, Paull F. "Chaucer's Puns: A Supplementary List." *PMLA*, 73 (1958), 167–170.

319 BAWCUTT, Priscilla. "The Lark in Chaucer and Some Later Poets." *YES*, 2 (1972), 5–12.

320 BENHAM, Allen R. "Three Chaucer Studies." *SAQ*, 20 (1921), 330–348. [Chaucer and the Renaissance, Chaucer and Ovid, Chaucer and Molière.]

321 BENNETT, Josephine W. "The Mediaeval Loveday." *Speculum*, 33 (1958), 351–370.

322 BENSON, Larry D., and Theodore M. ANDERSON, eds. *The Literary Context of Chaucer's Fabliaux*. Indianapolis: Bobbs-Merrill, [1971]. [LL 28]

323 BESSINGER, J. B. "Chaucer: A Parliament of Critics." *UTQ*, 29 (1959), 91–96.

324 BETHURUM, Dorothy. "Chaucer's Point of View as Narrator in the Love Poems." *PMLA*, 74 (1959), 511–520. Reprinted in 593.

325 BIRNEY, Earle. "The Beginnings of Chaucer's Irony." *PMLA*, 54 (1939), 637–655.

326 BIRNEY, Earle. "Is Chaucer's Irony a Modern Discovery?" *JEGP*, 41 (1942), 303–319.

327 BIRNEY, Earle. "The Two Worlds of Geoffrey Chaucer." *Manitoba Arts Rev.*, 4, No. 4 (1941), 3–16.

328 BLAKE, N.F. "Chaucer and the Alliterative Romances." *ChauR*, 3 (1969), 163–169.

329 BLOOMFIELD, Morton W. "Authenticating Realism and the Realism of Chaucer." *Thought*, 39 (1964), 335–358. Reprinted in 160.

330 BLOOMFIELD, Morton W. "Chaucer's Sense of History." *JEGP*, 51 (1952), 301–313. Reprinted in 546.

331 BLOOMFIELD, Morton W. "The Gloomy Chaucer." In *Eliot in His Time*, ed. A. Walton Litz, pp. 57–68. Princeton: Princeton Univ. Press, 1973.

332 "BOMBARDIER." "Chaucer: Ornithologist." *Blackwood's Mag.*, 256 (1944), 120–125.

333 BOOTHMAN, Janet. " 'Who Hath No Wyf, He is No Cokewold': A Study of John and January in Chaucer's Miller's and Merchant's Tales." *Thoth*, 4 (1963), 3–14.

334 BOYD, Beverly. *Chaucer and the Liturgy*. Philadelphia: Dorrance, 1967.

335 BRADDY, Haldeen. "Chaucer's Bawdy Tongue." *SFQ*, 30 (1966), 214–222.

336 BRADDY, Haldeen. "Three Chaucer Notes." *Essays and Studies in Honor of Carleton Brown* (New York, 1940), pp. 91–99. [Symbolic colors, Ceys and Alcione, Sir Guichard d'Angle.] Reprinted in 258.

337 BRADDY, Haldeen. "Chaucer—Realism or Obscenity?" *Arlington Quar.*, 2 (1969), 121–138. Reprinted in 258.

338 BRADLEY, Ruth J. "The Use of Cockney Dialect by Chaucer." *QJS*, 29 (1943), 74–76.

339 BREWER, D. S., ed. *Chaucer and Chaucerians: Critical Studies in Middle English Literature*. London: Nelson; University, Ala.: Univ. of Alabama Press, 1966. [Pertinent contents entered separately.]

CRITICISM

340 BREWER, D. S. "Children in Chaucer." *REL,* 5, iii (1964), 52–60.

341 BREWER, D. S. "The Humour of Chaucer: The Artist as Insider." In *Proteus: Studies in English Literature,* pp. 69–132. Tokyo: Kenkyusha, 1958.

342 BREWER, D. S. "Images of Chaucer 1386–1900." 339, pp. 240–270.

343 BREWER, D. S. "Love and Marriage in Chaucer's Poetry." *MLR,* 49 (1954), 461–464.

344 BREWER, D. S. "Chaucer and Chrétien and Arthurian Romance." 53, pp. 255–259.

345 BREWER, D. S. "Class Distinction in Chaucer." *Speculum,* 43 (1968), 290–305.

346 BREWER, D. S. "The Criticism of Chaucer in the Twentieth Century." 264, pp. 3–28.

347 BREWER, D. S. "The Fabliaux." 296, pp. 247–267.

348 BREWER, Derek. "Gothic Chaucer." 260, pp. 1–32.

349 BREWER, D. S. "Honour in Chaucer." *Essays and Stud. of the English Assoc.,* ed. J. Lawlor, pp. 1–19. London: Murray, 1973.

350 BREWER, D. S. "Some Metonymic Relationships in Chaucer's Poetry." *Poetica,* 1 (1974), 1–20.

351 BRONSON, Bertrand H. "Chaucer's Art in Relation to His Audience." *Five Studies in Literature,* pp. 1–53. Berkeley, 1940. (*Univ. of Calif. Pub. in English,* VII, No. 1).

352 BROOKHOUSE, Christopher. "Chaucer's *Impossibilia.*" *MÆ,* 34 (1965), 40–42.

353 BROOKHOUSE, Christopher. "In Search of Chaucer: The Needed Narrative." 57, pp. 67–80.

354 BROWNE, William H. "Notes on Chaucer's Astrology." *MLN,* 23 (1908), 53–54.

355 BÜHLER, Curt A. "Wirk alle thyng by conseil." *Speculum,* 24 (1949), 410–412.

356 CALDWELL, Robert A. "The Scribe of the Chaucer MS, Cambridge University Library Gg 4.27." *MLQ,* 5 (1944), 33–44.

357 CAMPBELL, J. M. "Patristic Studies and the Literature of Medieval England." *Speculum,* 8 (1933), 465–478.

358 CAPONE, Gino. *I poemi minori di Chaucer: saggio critico.* Modica: Papa, 1900.

359 CAWLEY, A. C. "A Note on Chaucer's Prioress and Criseyde." *MLR,* 43 (1948), 74–77.

360 *Chaucer Memorial Lectures, 1900,* ed. Percy W. Ames. London: Asher, 1900. [Contents listed separately.]

361 CHIAPPELLI, Carolyn. "Chaucer's Use of *Solas.*" *Comitatus,* 2 (1971), 91–92.

362 COFFMAN, George R. "Old Age from Horace to Chaucer." *Speculum,* 9 (1934), 249–277.

363 COFFMAN, George R. "Old Age in Chaucer's Day." *MLN,* 52 (1937), 25–26. Cf. *ibid.,* 53 (1938), 181–182 (C. Philip).

364 COGHILL, Nevill. *Chaucer's Idea of What Is Noble.* London: English Assoc., 1971. (Presidential address)

365 COOK, Albert S. "Chaucerian Papers—I." *Trans. Conn. Acad.,* 23 (1919), 1–63.

CRITICISM

366 Corsa, Helen S. *Chaucer, Poet of Mirth and Morality.* Notre Dame, Ind.: Univ. of Notre Dame Press, 1964.

367 Cox, S. H. "Chaucer's Cheerful Cynicism." *MLN,* 36 (1921), 475–481.

368 Crosby, Ruth. "Chaucer and the Custom of Oral Delivery." *Speculum,* 13 (1938), 413–432.

369 Curry, Walter C. "Chaucer's Science and Art." *Texas Rev.,* 8 (1923), 307–322.

370 Dean, Nancy. "Chaucer's *Complaint,* a Genre Descended from the *Heroides.*" *CL,* 19 (1967), 1–27.

371 Delasanta, Rodney. "Chaucer and the Exegetes." *Stud. in the Literary Imagination,* 4, ii (1971), 1–10.

372 Deligiorgis, S. "Structuralism and the Study of Poetry: A Parametric Analysis of Chaucer's *Shipman's Tale* and *Parlement of Foules.*" *NM,* 70 (1969), 297–306.

373 Dempster, Germaine. *Dramatic Irony in Chaucer.* Stanford University, 1932 (*Stanford Univ. Pub. in Lang. and Lit.,* 4, No. 3); New York: Humanities Press, 1959.

374 DeNeef, A. Leigh. "Robertson and the Critics." *ChauR,* 2 (1968), 205–234.

375 Dent, A. A. "Chaucer and the Horse." *Proc. Leeds Philos. and Lit. Soc.,* 9, Part 1 (Dec. 1959).

376 de Selincourt. E. *Oxford Lectures on Poetry.* Oxford: Clarendon Press, 1934. ["Chaucer" (pp. 24–49), *TC* (pp. 50–77).]

377 Diekstra, F. N. M. *Chaucer's Quizzical Mode of Exemplification.* Nijmegen, 1974.

378 Dodd, William G. *Courtly Love in Chaucer and Gower.* Boston: Ginn, 1913.

379 Donahue, Charles. See 380.

380 Donaldson, E. Talbot. "Patristic Exegesis in the Criticism of Medieval Literature: The Opposition." *Critical approaches to Medieval Literature: Selected Papers from the English Institute, 1958–1959,* ed. Dorothy Bethurum, pp. 1–26, 155–157. New York: Columbia Univ. Press, 1960. Cf. *ibid.,* "The Defense," pp. 27–60, 158–159 (R. E. Kaske); "Summation," pp. 61–82, 160–162 (Charles Donahue). Donaldson reprinted in 273.

381 Donaldson, E. Talbot. "The Manuscripts of Chaucer's Works and Their Use." 260, 85–108.

382 Donaldson, E. Talbot. "The Psychology of Editors of Middle English Texts." 273, pp. 102–118.

383 Donaldson, E. Talbot. "The Masculine Narrator and Four Women of Style." 273, pp. 46–64.

384 Donaldson, E. Talbot. "Chaucer and the Elusion of Clarity." In *Essays and Studies, 1972: In Honor of Beatrice White,* ed. T. S. Dorsch, pp. 23–44. New York: Humanities, 1972. (*Essays and Studies Collected for the English Assoc.,* n.s. 25)

385 Donner, Morton. "Chaucer and His Narrators: The Poet's Place in His Poems." *Western Humanities Rev.* 27 (1973), 189–195.

386 Dronke, Peter, and Jill Mann. "Chaucer and the Medieval Latin Poets." 260, pp. 154–183.

387 Dunleavy, Gareth W. "Natural Law as Chaucer's Ethical Absolute." *TWA,* 52 (1963), 177–187.

CRITICISM

388 DUNNING, T. P. "Chaucer's Icarus-Complex: Some Notes on His Adventures in Theology." *English Studies Today,* ed. G. I. Duthie, 3rd Ser. (1964), pp. 89–106.

389 EDWARDS, A. S. G. "The Case of the Stolen Chaucer Manuscript." *Book Collector,* 21 (1972), 380–385. [Cardigan MS]

390 ELIASON, Norman E. *The Language of Chaucer's Poetry: An Appraisal of the Verse, Style, and Structure.* Copenhagen: Rosenkilde and Bagger, 1972. (*Anglistica,* 17)

391 ELIASON, Norman E. "Chaucer the Love Poet." 528, pp. 9–26.

392 ELLIOTT, R. W. V. "Chaucer's Reading." 264, pp. 46–68.

393 ELLIOTT, R. W. V. "When Chaucer Swears." *Australasian Universities Lang. and Lit. Assoc.: Proc. . . . The Twelfth Congress,* pp. 417–434. (Sydney: AAULA, 1970).

394 EMERSON, O. F. "Chaucer and Medieval Hunting." *RR,* 13 (1922), 115–150. Reprinted in 395.

395 EMERSON, O. F. *Chaucer Essays and Studies: A Selection from the Writings of . . . (1860–1927).* Cleveland: Western Reserve Univ. Press, 1929.

396 EMERSON, O. F. "Some Notes on Chaucer and Some Conjectures." *PQ,* 2 (1923), 81–96. Reprinted in 395 [*BD, PF, TC, Mars,* A 164, *KnT*]

397 ENKVIST, Nils E. *Geoffrey Chaucer.* Stockholm: Natur och Kultur, 1964.

398 *Essays on Chaucer, His Words and Works.* 6 parts, London, 1868–92 (Chaucer Soc., 2nd Ser., Nos. 2, 9, 16, 18, 19, 29).

399 EVANS, Joan. "Chaucer and Decorative Art." *RES,* 6 (1930), 408–412.

400 EVERETT, Dorothy. "Some Reflections on Chaucer's 'Art Poetical.' " *Proc. Brit. Acad., 1950,* pp. 131–154. Reprinted in 178.

401 FARRELL, William J. "Chaucer's Use of the Catalogue." *TSLL,* 5 (1963), 64–78.

402 FIFIELD, Merle. "Chaucer the Theater-goer." *PLL,* 3, Summer Suppl. (1967), 63–70.

403 FISHER, John H. "Chaucer's Horses." *SAQ,* 60 (1961), 71–79.

404 FOX, Denton. "Chaucer's Influence on Fifteenth-Century Poetry." 294, pp. 385–402.

405 FRANCIS, W. Nelson. "Chaucer Shortens a Tale." *PMLA,* 68 (1953), 1126–1141.

406 FURNIVALL, F. J. *Trial-Forewords to my Parallel-Text Edition of Chaucer's Minor Poems.* London, 1871 (Chaucer Soc., 2nd Ser., No. 6).

407 GALWAY, Margaret. "Chaucer, Graunson, and Isabel of France." *RES,* 24 (1948), 273–280.

408 GALWAY, Margaret. "Court Poets' I.O.U's." *TLS,* Oct. 16, 1953, p. 668.

409 GARBÁTY, Thomas J. "The Degradation of Chaucer's 'Geffrey.' " *PMLA,* 79 (1974), 97–104.

410 GEROULD, Gordon H. *Chaucerian Essays.* Princeton: Princeton Univ. Press, 1952.

411 GETTY, Agnes K. "Chaucer's Changing Conception of the Humble Lover." *PMLA,* 44 (1929), 202–216.

412 GETTY, Agnes K. "The Mediæval-Modern Conflict in Chaucer's Poetry." *PMLA,* 47 (1932), 385–402.

413 GIFFIN, Mary. *Studies on Chaucer and His Audience.* Quebec, 1956 (for private distribution).

CRITICISM

414 GILLIE, Christopher. "Women by Chaucer: The Wife of Bath, Criseyde." In *Character in English Literature,* pp. 41–55. (New York: Barnes & Noble, 1965).

415 GILLMEISTER, Heiner. *Discrecioun: Chaucer und die Via Regia.* Bonn: Grundmann, 1972.

416 GOFFIN, R. C. "Chaucer and Elocution," *MÆ,* 4 (1935), 127–142.

417 GOFFIN, R. C. "Chaucer and 'Reason.' " *MLR,* 21 (1926), 13–18.

418 GOLDEN, Samuel A. "Chaucer in Minsheu's *Guide into the Tongues.*" *ChauR,* 4 (1970), 49–54.

419 GREEN, A. Wigfall. "Chaucer's Clerks and the Mediæval Scholarly Tradition as Represented by Richard de Bury's *Philobiblon,*" *ELH,* 18 (1951), 1–6.

420 GREEN, Richard H. "Classical Fable and English Poetry in the Fourteenth Century." 380, pp. 110–133.

421 GRIMM, Florence M. *Astronomical Lore in Chaucer,* Lincoln, Neb., 1919 (*Univ. of Nebraska Stud. in Lang., Lit., and Crit.,* No. 2).

• 422 HAKETHAL, Marietta. *Aufbau und Erzählstruktur der Erzählungen Chaucers.* München, 1966 (Munich diss.)

423 HAMILTON, Marie P. "Notes on Chaucer and the Rhetoricians." *PMLA,* 47 (1932), 403–409.

424 HAMMOND, Eleanor P. "A Scribe of Chaucer." *MP,* 27 (1929–30), 27–33 (with facs.).

425 HAMMOND, Eleanor P. "Two Chaucer Cruces." *MLN,* 22 (1907), 51–52. [Lollius, St. Loy.]

426 HARBERT, Bruce. "Chaucer and the Latin Classics." 259, 137–153.

427 HARRISON, Thomas P. *They Tell of Birds: Chaucer, Spenser, Milton, Drayton.* Austin: Univ. of Texas Press, 1956. [Chaucer, pp. 32–52.]

428 HAYMES, Edward R. "Chaucer and the English Romance Tradition." *South Atlantic Bull.,* 37, iv (1972), 35–43.

429 HEATHER, P. J. "Seven Planets." *Folklore,* 54 (1943), 338–361.

430 HÉRAUCOURT, Will. "Chaucers Vorstellung von den geistig-seelischen Kräften des Menschen." *Anglia,* 65 (1941), 255–302.

431 HÉRAUCOURT, Will. "Das Hendiadyoin als Mittel zur Hervorhebung des Werthaften bei Chaucer." *ESt,* 73 (1938–39), 190–201.

432 HÉRAUCOURT, Will. *Die Wertwelt Chaucers, die Wertwelt einer Zeitwende.* Heidelberg: Winter, 1939 (Kulturgeschichtliche Bibliothek, n.f., Dritte Reihe, I).

433 HERBEN, Stephen J., Jr. "Arms and Armor in Chaucer." *Speculum,* 12 (1937), 475–487.

434 HEYDON, Peter N. "Chaucer and the *Sir Orfeo* Prologue of The Auchinleck MS." *PMASAL,* 51 (1966), 529–545.

435 HIBBARD, Laura A. "Chaucer's 'Shapen was my Sherte.' " *PQ,* 1 (1922), 222–225.

436 HIEATT, Constance B. *The Realism of Dream Visions: The Poetic Exploitation of the Dream-Experience in Chaucer and His Contemporaries.* The Hague: Mouton, 1967.

437 HILL, Betty. "On Reading Chaucer." *Proc. Leeds Philos. Soc., Lit. & Hist. Sect.,* 14 (1971), 207–220.

CRITICISM

438 HILL, Mary A. "Rhetorical Balance in Chaucer's Poetry." *PMLA*, 42 (1927), 845–861.

439 HINCKLEY, Henry B. "Chauceriana." *PQ*, 6 (1927), 313–314.

440 HINTON, Norman D. "More Puns in Chaucer." *AN&Q*, 2 (1964), 115–116.

441 HIRA, Toshinori. "Chaucer's Gentry in the Historical Background." *Essays in English and American Literature: In Commemoration of Professor Takejiro Nakayama's Sixty-first Birthday.* Tokyo: Shohakusha, 1961, pp. 31–44.

442 HIRA, Toshinori. "Two Phases of Chaucer, Moral and Mortal." *Maekawa Shunichi Kyoju Kanreki Kinenronbunshu* [Maekawa Festschrift], pp. 91–114. Tokyo: Eihosha, 1968.

443 HOWARD, Donald R. "Chaucer the Man." *PMLA*, 80 (1965), 337–343. Reprinted in 264.

444 HUPPÉ, Bernard F., and D. W. ROBERTSON, Jr. *Fruyt and Chaf: Studies in Chaucer's Allegories.* Princeton: Princeton Univ. Press, 1963. [*BD, PF*]

445 HUSSEY, S. S. "The Minor Poems and the Prose." 161, 229–262.

446 JOHNSON, William C., Jr. "Chaucer's Language of Inevitability." 282, pp. 17–27.

447 JORDAN, Robert M. "The Limits of Illusion: Faulkner, Fielding, and Chaucer." *Criticism*, 2 (1960), 278–305.

448 JORDAN, Robert M. *Chaucer and the Shape of Creation: The Aesthetic Possibilities of Inorganic Structure.* Cambridge, Mass.: Harvard Univ. Press, 1967.

448a JORDAN, Robert M. "Chaucerian Narrative." 296, 85–102.

449 KANE, G. *The Autobiographical Fallacy in Chaucer and Langland Studies.* London: Lewis, 1966.

450 KASKE, Robert E. See 380.

451 KASKE, Robert E. "Chaucer and Medieval Allegory." *ELH*, 30 (1963), 175–192.

452 KEAN, P. M. *Chaucer and the Making of English Poetry.* Vol. I: *Love Vision and Debate;* Vol. II: *The Art of Narrative.* 2 vols. London: Routledge & Kegan Paul, 1972.

453 KEE, Kenneth. "Two Chaucerian Gardens." *MS*, 23 (1961), 154–162.

454 KELLETT, E. E. "Chaucer as a Critic of Dante." *London Mercury*, 4 (1921), 282–291.

455 KELLOGG, Alfred L. "Chaucer's Self-Portrait and Dante's." *MÆ*, 29 (1960), 119–120. Reprinted in 456.

456 KELLOGG, Alfred L. *Chaucer, Langland, Arthur: Essays in Middle English Literature.* New Brunswick: Rutgers Univ. Press, [1972]. (Pertinent items are listed separately.)

457 KELLOGG, Alfred L., and Robert C. Cox. "Chaucer's St. Valentine: A Conjecture." 456, pp. 108–145.

458 KELLOGG, Alfred L., and Robert C. Cox. "Chaucer's May 3 and Its Contexts." 456, pp. 155–198.

459 KIRALIS, Karl. "William Blake as an Intellectual and Spiritual Guide to Chaucer's *Canterbury Pilgrims.*" *Blake Studies*, 1 (1969), 139–190.

460 KIRBY, Thomas A. "Arnold and Chaucer." 52, pp. 127–133.

461 KITTREDGE, George L. "Chauceriana." *MP*, 7 (1910), 465–483.

CRITICISM

462 KNIGHT, Stephen. "Chaucer—a Modern Writer?" *Balcony,* No. 2 (1966), 37–43.

463 KOCH,John. "Alte Chaucerprobleme und neue Lösungsversuche." *ESt,* 55 (1921), 161–225.

464 KOCH, John. "Ein Beitrag zur Kritik Chaucers." *ESt,* 1 (1877), 249–293. [Contains his interpretation of *PF.*]

465 KOCH, John. *The Chronology of Chaucer's Writings.* London, 1890 (Chaucer Soc., 2nd Ser., No. 27).

466 KOCH, John. "On 1. An Original Version of the *Knight's Tale;* 2. The Date and Personages of the *Parlement of Foules;* 3. *Quene Anelida and the False Arcyte;* 4. a. Lollius; b. Chaucer and Boccaccio's Decamerone." *Essays on Chaucer,* Part IV, pp. 357–415 (Chaucer Soc., 2nd Ser., No. 18).

467 KÖKERITZ, Helge. "Rhetorical Word-Play in Chaucer." *PMLA,* 69 (1954), 937–952.

468 KOLVE, F. A. "Chaucer and the Visual Arts." 260, pp. 290–320.

469 KORSCH, Hedwig. *Chaucer als Kritiker.* Berlin: Mayer and Müller, 1916 (Berlin diss.).

470 KREISLER, Nicolai von. "A Recurrent Expression of Devotion in Chaucer's *Book of the Duchess, Parliament of Fowls,* and *Knight's Tale.*" *MP,* 68 (1970), 62–64.

471 KROG, Fritz. *Studien zu Chaucer und Langland.* Heidelberg: Winter, 1928 (*Anglistische Forsch.,* 65).

472 KUHL, Ernest P. "Chaucer and the Church." *MLN,* 40 (1925), 321–338. Reprinted in 475.

473 KUHL, Ernest P. "Chaucer and the Red Rose." *PQ,* 24 (1945), 33–38. Reprinted in 475.

474 KUHL, Ernest P. "Chaucer the Patriot." *PQ,* 25 (1946), 227–280. Reprinted in 475.

475 KUHL, Ernest P. *Studies in Chaucer and Shakespeare.* Beloit: Belting Pubs, [1971]. (Pertinent articles reprinted here are listed separately.)

476 LANAGHAN, R. T. "The Clerk of Venus: Chaucer and Medieval Romance." 57, pp. 31–43.

477 LANGE, Hugo. "Chaucer und Mandeville's Travels." *Archiv,* 174 (1938), 79–81.

478 LANGE, Hugo. "Geoffrey Chaucer als Hof- und Gelegenheitsdichter." *Archiv,* 158 (1930), 36–54.

479 LANGE, Hugo. "Hat Chaucer den Kompass gekannt und benutzt?" *Anglia,* 58 (1934), 333–344.

480 LANGHANS, Viktor. "Die Datierung der Prosastücke Chaucers." *Anglia,* 53 (1929), 235–268.

481 LANGHANS, Viktor. "Zu Chaucers Traumgedichten und deren Auffassung durch A. Brusendorff." *Anglia,* 51 (1927), 323–353.

482 LANGHANS, Viktor. "Zu J. Kochs Artikel in *Anglia* 37, 193." *Anglia,* 49 (1926), 356–360.

483 LANHAM, Richard A. "Game, Play, and High Seriousness in Chaucer's Poetry." *ES,* 48 (1967), 1–24.

484 LAWLOR, John. "The Earlier Poems." In 339, pp. 39–64.

CRITICISM

485 LAWRENCE, C. E. "The Personality of Geoffrey Chaucer." *QR*, 242 (1924), 315–333.

486 LEVER, Katherine. "The Christian Classicist's Dilemma." *CJ*, 58 (1963), 356–361.

487 LEVY, H. L. " 'As myn auctour seyth.' " *MÆ*, 12 (1943), 25–39.

488 LEYERLE, John. "The Heart and the Chain." 57, pp. 113–145.

489 LONG, E. Hudson. "Chaucer as a Master of the Short Story." *Delaware Notes*, Sixteenth Ser. (1943), 11–29.

490 LOOMIS, Dorothy B. "The Venus of Alanus de Insulis and the Venus of Chaucer." *Philological Essays in Honor of Herbert Dean Meritt*, pp. 182–195. The Hague: Mouton, 1970.

491 LOOMIS, Dorothy B. "Chaucer and Shakespeare." 264, 166–190.

492 LOOMIS, Laura H. "Chaucer and the Breton Lays of the Auchinleck MS." *SP*, 38 (1941), 14–33. Reprinted in 194.

493 LOOMIS, Roger S. "Was Chaucer a Free Thinker?" 48, pp. 21–44.

494 LOOMIS, Roger S. "Was Chaucer a Laodicean?" 49, pp. 129–148. Reprinted in 195, 1686.

495 LOOTEN, [Camille]. *Chaucer, ses modèles, ses sources, sa religion.* Lille, 1931 (*Mémoires et Travaux des Facultés catholiques de Lille*, 38).

496 LOOTEN, [Camille]. "Chaucer et la dialectique." *Revue Anglo-Americaine*, 7 (1929), 193–214.

497 LOOTEN, [Camille]. "Les portraits dans Chaucer: leurs origines." *RLC*, (1927), 397–437.

498 LOUNSBURY, Thomas R. *Studies in Chaucer.* 3 vols., New York: Harper, 1892. Reprinted New York: Russell, 1962.

499 LOWES, John L. *The Art of Geoffrey Chaucer.* Sir Israel Gollancz Memorial Lecture, British Acad., 1930. London: Milford, 1931. Reprinted in *Essays in Appreciation*, pp. 75–118. Boston: Houghton Mifflin, 1936.

500 LOWES, John L. "Illustrations of Chaucer, drawn Chiefly from Deschamps." *RR*, 2 (1911), 113–128.

501 LÜDEKE, H. *Die Funktionen des Erzählers in Chaucers Epischer Dichtung.* Halle, 1928 (*Studien zur engl. Phil.*, 72).

502 MACAULAY, G. C. "Notes on Chaucer." *MLR*, 4 (1908), 14–19.

503 MACCRACKEN, Henry N. "Notes Suggested by a Chaucer Codex." *MLN*, 23 (1908), 212–214. [*Truth, Stedfastnesse.*]

504 MACKAIL, J. W. "Chaucer." *The Springs of Helicon*, pp. 1–69. (London: Longmans, 1909).

505 MADELEVA, Sister Mary. *Chaucer's Nuns and Other Essays.* New York: Appleton, 1925.

506 MADELEVA, Sister Mary. *A Lost Language and Other Essays on Chaucer.* New York: Sheed and Ward, 1951.

507 MAHONEY, John F. "Chaucerian Tragedy and the Christian Tradition." *AnM*, 3 (1962), 81–99.

508 MANLY, John M. *Chaucer and the Rhetoricians.* London, [1926] (Warton Lecture on English Poetry, 17: Proc. Brit. Acad.). Reprinted in 1700.

24

CRITICISM

509 MANLY, John M. *Some New Light on Chaucer: Lectures Delivered at the Lowell Institute.* New York: Holt, 1926.*

510 MANLY, John M. "Three Recent Chaucer Studies." *RES,* 10 (1934), 257–272.

511 MANZALAOUI, M. "Chaucer and Science." 260, pp. 224–261.

512 MARCUS, Hans. "Chaucer, der Freund des einfachen Mannes." *Archiv,* 171 (1937), 174–182; 172 (1937), 28–41.

513 MARKMAN, Alan. "The Concern of Chaucer's Poetry." *AnM,* 7 (1966), 90–103.

514 MASUI, Michio. "The Language of Love in Chaucer." *SELit,* English Number (1960), 1–36.

515 MASUI, Michio. *A Study of Chaucer.* Tokyo: Kenkyusha, 1962.

516 MASUI, Michio. "Chaucer's Tenderness and the Theme of Consolation." 52, pp. 214–221.

517 MASUI, Michio. "Some Thoughts on the Continuity of Themes in Chaucer." *Poetica,* 1 (1974), 114–121.

518 MAXFIELD, Ezra K. "Chaucer and Religious Reform." *PMLA,* 39 (1924), 64–74.

519 McCALL, John P. "Chaucer's May 3." *MLN,* 76 (1961), 201–205.

520 McNALLY, John J. "Chaucer's Topsy-Turvy Dante." *Stud. in Medieval Culture,* 2 (1966), 104–110.

521 McPEEK, James A. S. "Chaucer and the Goliards." *Speculum,* 26 (1951), 332–336.

522 McPEEK, James A. S. "Did Chaucer Know Catullus?" *MLN,* 46 (1931), 293–301.

523 MEAD, Douglas S. "Verse Tags." *Essays in Honor of A. Howry Espenshade,* pp. 119–145. New York: Nelson, 1937.

524 MEHL, D. *Geoffrey Chaucer: Eine Einführung in seine erzählenden Dichtungen.* Berlin: E. Schmidt, [1973]. (*Grundlagen der Anglistik und Amerikanistik,* 7)

525 MEYER, Emil. *Die Charakterzeichnung bei Chaucer.* Halle: Niemeyer, 1913 (*Studien zur engl. Phil.,* 48).

526 MILLER, Milton. "Definition by Comparison: Chaucer, Lawrence and Joyce." *EIC,* 3 (1953), 369–381.

527 MITCHELL, Jerome. "Hoccleve's Tribute to Chaucer." 54, pp. 275–285.

528 MITCHELL, Jerome, and William PROVOST, eds. *Chaucer the Love Poet.* Athens, Ga.: Univ. of Georgia Press, [1973]. (General intro. by William Provost)

529 MOGAN, Joseph J., Jr. *Chaucer and the Theme of Mutability.* The Hague: Mouton, 1969.

530 MOORE, Arthur K. "Chaucer's Use of Lyric as an Ornament of Style." *CL,* 3 (1951), 32–46.

531 MOSSÉ, F. "Chaucer et la liturgie." *Revue Germanique,* 14 (1923), 283–289.

532 MOSSÉ, F. "Chaucer et le métier de l'écrivain." *EA,* 7 (1954), 395–401.

533 MURPHY, James J. "A New Look at Chaucer and the Rhetoricians." *RES,* n.s. 15 (1964), 1–20.

534 MURTAUGH, Daniel M. "Women and Geoffrey Chaucer." *ELH,* 38 (1971), 473–492.

CRITICISM

535 Muscatine, Charles. *Chaucer and the French Tradition: A Study in Style and Meaning.* Berkeley and Los Angeles: Univ. of Calif. Press, 1957. [Cal-104]*

536 Muscatine, Charles. "Chaucer in an Age of Criticism." *MLQ,* 25 (1964), 473–478.

537 Muscatine, Charles. *The Book of Geoffrey Chaucer: An Account of the Publication of Geoffrey Chaucer's Works from the Fifteenth Century to Modern Times.* [San Francisco:] Book Club of California, 1963.

538 Naunin, Traugott. *Der Einfluss der mittelalterlichen Rhetorik auf Chaucers Dichtung.* Bonn, 1929 (diss.).

539 Newbolt, Henry. "The Poetry of Chaucer." *English Rev.,* 15 (1913), 170–189.

540 Nist, John. "The Art of Chaucer: *Pathedy.*" *TSL,* 11 (1966), 1–10.

541 North, J. D. "Kalenderes Enlumyned Ben They: Some Astronomical Themes in Chaucer." *RES,* 20 (1969), 129–154, 257–283, 418–444.

542 Norton-Smith, J. "Chaucer's Epistolary Style." In *Essays on Style and Language,* ed. Roger Fowler, pp. 157–165. London: Routledge and Kegan Paul; New York: Humanities Press, 1966.

543 Novelli, Cornelius. "The Demonstrative Adjective *This:* Chaucer's Use of a Colloquial Narrative Device." *MS,* 19 (1957), 246–249.

544 Olson, Clair C. "Chaucer and the Music of the Fourteenth Century." *Speculum,* 16 (1941), 64–91.

545 Ono, Shigeru. "Chaucer's Variants and What They Tell Us: Fluctuation in the Use of Modal Auxiliaries." *SELit,* English Number (1969), 51–74.

546 Owen, Charles A., Jr. "The Problem of Free Will in Chaucer's Narratives." *PQ,* 46 (1967), 433–456.

547 Pace, George B. "Speght's Chaucer and MS. Gg.4.27 [Cambridge Univ. Library]." *SB,* 21 (1968), 225–235.

548 Patch, Howard R. "Chaucer and the Common People." *JEGP,* 29 (1930), 376–384.

549 Patch, Howard R. "Chaucer and Lady Fortune." *MLR,* 22 (1927), 377–388.

550 Patch, Howard R. "Chaucer and Mediaeval Romance." *Essays in Memory of Barrett Wendell,* pp. 93–108. Cambridge, Mass.: Harvard Univ. Press, 1926.

551 Patch, Howard R. "Chauceriana." *ESt,* 65 (1930–31), 351–359.

552 Patch, Howard R. "Geoffrey Chaucer and Youth." *CE,* 11 (1949), 14–22.

553 Patch, Howard R. "The Subjects of Chaucer's Poetry." *Franciplegius: Medieval and Linguistic Studies in Honor of Francis Peabody Magoun, Jr.,* pp. 255–264. New York: New York Univ. Press, 1965.

554 Payne, Robert O. *The Key of Remembrance: A Study of Chaucer's Poetics.* New Haven: Yale Univ. Press, for the Univ. of Cincinnati, 1963.

555 Payne, Robert O. "Chaucer and the Art of Rhetoric." 296, 38–57.

556 Plimpton, George A. *The Education of Chaucer Illustrated from the Schoolbooks in Use in His Time.* London and New York: Oxford Univ. Press, 1935.

557 Pratt, Robert A. "Chaucer and the Hand That Fed Him." *Speculum,* 41 (1966), 619–642.

558 Pratt, Robert A. "Chaucer and the Visconti Libraries." *ELH,* 6 (1939), 191–199.

CRITICISM

559 PRATT, Robert A. "Chaucer Borrowing from Himself." *MLQ* 7 (1946), 259–264.

560 PRATT, Robert A. "Conjectures Regarding Chaucer's Manuscript of the *Teseida.*" *SP,* 42 (1945), 745–763.

561 PRATT, Robert A. "The Importance of Manuscripts for the Study of Medieval Education, as Revealed by the Learning of Chaucer." In *Progress of Medieval and Renais. Stud.,* Bull. No. 20 (1949), pp. 43–51.

562 PRATT, Robert A. "Karl Young's Work on the Learning of Chaucer." In *A Memorial of Karl Young,* pp. 45–55. New Haven: Privately printed, 1946.

563 PRESTON, Raymond. "Chaucer and the *ballades notees* of Guillaume de Machaut." *Speculum,* 26 (1951), 615–623.

564 RAJIVA, Stanley F. "The Eternal Anti-feminine: An Essay on Femininism and Anti-Femininism in Chaucer." *IJES,* 12 (1971), 1–21.

565 RAMSON, W. S. "In Praise of Chaucer." *Australasian Universities Lang. and Lit. Assoc.: Proc. . . . Twelfth Congress,* (Sydney: AAULA, [1970]), pp. 456–476.

566 REGAN, Charles L. "Chaucer's 'I passe.'" *Greyfriar,* 14 (1973), 3–14.

567 REINECKE, George F. "Speculation, Intention, and the Teaching of Chaucer." 57, pp. 81–93.

568 REISS, Edmund. "Chaucer's Courtly Love." 57, pp. 95–111.

569 REISS, Edmund. "Chaucer's Parodies of Love." 528, pp. 27–44.

570 RENOIR, Alain. "A Note on Chaucer's Women." *N&Q,* 203 (1958), 283–284.

571 RENOIR, Alain. "Tradition and Moral Realism: Chaucer's Conception of the Poet." *SN,* 35 (1963), 199–210.

572 RHYS, Brinley. "A Preface to Chaucer." *SR,* 72 (1964), 335–341. [A review article on 575.]

573 RICHARDSON, Janette. *Blameth Nat Me: A Study of Imagery in Chaucer's Fabliaux.* The Hague: Mouton, 1970. (*Studies in English Lit.,* 58)

574 RICKERT, Edith. "Are There More Chaucer Manuscripts?" *TLS,* Dec. 17, 1931, p. 1028.

575 ROBERTSON, D. W., Jr. *A Preface to Chaucer: Studies in Medieval Perspectives.* Princeton: Princeton Univ. Press, 1963.

576 ROBERTSON, D. W., Jr. "The Doctrine of Charity in Medieval Literary Gardens: A Topical Approach through Symbolism and Allegory." *Speculum,* 26 (1951), 24–49.

577 ROBINSON, Ian. *Chaucer and the English Tradition.* Cambridge: Cambridge Univ. Press, 1972.

578 ROSE MARIE, Sister. "Chaucer and His Mayde Bright." *Commonweal,* 33 (1940), 225–227.

579 ROSS, Thomas W. *Chaucer's Bawdy.* New York: Dutton, [1972]. [D 317]

580 ROWLAND, Beryl. "Aspects of Chaucer's Use of Animals." *Archiv,* 201 (1964), 110–114.

581 ROWLAND, Beryl. "Chaucer and the Unnatural History of Animals." *MS,* 25 (1963), 367–372.

582 ROWLAND, Beryl. "The Horse and Rider Figure in Chaucer's Works." *UTQ,* 35 (1966), 246–259.

CRITICISM

583 ROWLAND, Beryl. "Chaucer's Imagery." 296, pp. 103–122.

584 RUGGIERS, Paul G. "Notes towards a Theory of Tragedy in Chaucer." *ChauR*, 8 (1973), 89–99.

585 SARNO, Ronald A. "Chaucer and the Satirical Tradition." *Classical Folia*, 21 (1967), 41–61.

586 SCHAAR, Claes. "A Postscript to Chaucer Studies." *ES*, 42 (1961), 153–156.

587 SCHAAR, Claes. *The Golden Mirror: Studies in Chaucer's Descriptive Technique and Its Literary Background.* Lund: Gleerup, 1955 (*Skrifter k. humanistika Vetenskapssamfundet i Lund*, 54).

588 SCHAAR, Claes. *Some Types of Narrative in Chaucer's Poetry.* Lund, 1954 (*Lund Stud. in English*, 25).

589 SCHLAUCH, Margaret. "The Art of Chaucer's Prose." in 339, pp. 140–163.

590 SCHLAUCH, Margaret. "Chaucer's Doctrine of Kings and Tyrants." *Speculum*, 20 (1945), 133–156.

591 SCHLAUCH, Margaret. "Chaucer's Prose Rhythms," *PMLA*, 65 (1950), 568–589.

592 SCHLESS, Howard. "Transformations: Chaucer's Use of Italian." 260, pp. 184–223.

593 SCHOECK, Richard J., and Jerome TAYLOR, eds. *Chaucer Criticism*, Vol. II: *Troilus and Criseyde & the Minor Poems.* Notre Dame, Ind.: Univ. of Notre Dame Press, 1961. [NDP-2]

594 SEVERS, J. Burke. "Chaucer's Clerks." 53, pp. 140–152.

595 SHARMA, Govind N. "Dreams in Chaucer." *IJES*, 6 (1965), 1–18.

596 SHEPHERD, Geoffrey. "Religion and Philosophy in Chaucer." 260, pp. 262–289.

597 SILVIA, D. S. "Geoffrey Chaucer on the Subject of Men, Women, Marriage, and Gentillesse." *Revue des Langues Vivantes*, 33 (1967), 228–236.

599 SLAUGHTER, Eugene E. *Love and the Virtues and Vices in Chaucer.* Nashville: Joint Univ. Libraries, 1946. [A condensed form of 600.]

600 SLAUGHTER, Eugene E. *Virtue According to Love—In Chaucer,* New York: Bookman Associates, 1957. Reprinted 1972.

601 SMITH, Roland M. "Five Notes on Chaucer and Froissart." *MLN*, 66 (1951), 27–32. [*KnT, PF, LGW, Purse*]

602 SMITH, Roland M. "Two Chaucer Notes." *MLN*, 51 (1936), 314–317.

603 SMYSER, H. M. "A View of Chaucer's Astronomy." *Speculum*, 45 (1970), 359–373.

604 SPENCER, Theodore. "Chaucer's Hell: A Study in Mediaeval Convention." *Speculum*, 2 (1927), 177–200.

605 SPURGEON, Caroline F. E. *Chaucer devant la critique en Angleterre et en France.* Paris: Hachette, 1911.

606 SPURGEON, Caroline F. E. *Five Hundred Years of Chaucer Criticism and Allusion, 1357–1900.* 7 parts, London, 1914–24 (Chaucer Soc., 2nd Ser., Nos. 48–50, 52–56); also 3 vols., Cambridge, 1925; reprinted New York: Russell, 1961. See 312, and for other allusions, since reported, consult Griffith (12) and Crawford (8).

607 STARR, Herbert W. "Oaths in Chaucer's Poems." *WVUPP*, 4 (1943), 44–63.

608 STAVROU, G. N. "Some Implications of Chaucer's Irony." *SAQ*, 56 (1957), 454–461.

CRITICISM

609 STEARNS, Marshall W. "Chaucer Mentions a Book." *MLN,* 57 (1942), 28–31.

610 STEARNS, Marshall W. "A Note on Chaucer's Use of Aristotelian Psychology." *SP,* 43 (1946), 15–21.

611 STEWART, George R., Jr. "The Moral Chaucer." *Essays in Criticism,* pp. 89–109 (*Univ. of Calif. Pub. in English,* No. 1, 1929).

612 STROHM, Paul. "Jean of Angouleme: A Fifteenth Century Reader of Chaucer." *NM,* 72 (1971), 69–76.

613 STROUD, Theodore A. "A Chaucer Scribe's Concern with Page Format." *Speculum,* 23 (1948), 683–687.

614 SULLIVAN, Sheila, ed. *Critics on Chaucer.* London: Allen and Unwin; Coral Gables, Fla.: Univ. of Miami Press, 1970. [Extracts from Dryden to the present]

615 TATLOCK, John S. P. "Chaucer and Wyclif." *MP,* 14 (1916), 257–268.

616 TATLOCK, John S. P. "Notes on Chaucer: Earlier and Minor Poems." *MLN,* 29 (1914), 97–101.

617 TATLOCK, John S. P. "Puns in Chaucer." *Flügel Memorial Volume,* pp. 228–232. Stanford, Calif.: Stanford Univ., 1916.

618 THOMAS, Mary E. *Medieval Skepticism and Chaucer.* New York: William-Frederick Press, 1950.

619 THOMPSON, W. Meredith. "Chaucer's Translation of the Bible." In *English and Medieval Studies Presented to J. R. R. Tolkien,* pp. 183–199. London: Allen & Unwin, 1962.

620 THOMPSON, Meredith. "Current and Recurrent Fallacies in Chaucer Criticism." *Essays in American and English Literature Presented to Bruce Robert McElderry, Jr.,* ed. Max F. Schulz, *et al.,* pp. 141–164. Athens, Ohio: Ohio Univ. Press, [1968].

621 *Three Chaucer Studies:* I. Chaucerian Problems: Especially the Petherton Forestership and the Question of Thomas Chaucer, by Russell Krauss; II. The *Parlement of Foules* in Its Relation to Contemporary Events, by Haldeen Braddy; III. Observations on the Shifting Position of Groups G and DE in the Manuscripts of the *Canterbury Tales,* by C. Robert Kase. New York: Oxford Univ. Press, 1932. No. II reprinted with additions, New York: Farrar, Straus, and Giroux, 1969.

621a THUNDYLL, Zacharias. "The *Moral* Chaucer." *Christianity and Literature,* 20, iii (1971), 12–16.

622 TOWNE, Frank. "Wyclif and Chaucer on the Contemplative Life." *Essays Critical and Historical Dedicated to Lily B. Campbell,* pp. 3–14. Berkeley and Los Angeles: Univ. of Calif. Press, 1950.

623 TWYCROSS, Meg. *The Medieval Anadyomene: A Study in Chaucer's Mythography.* (*Medium Ævum Monographs,* n.s. 1) Oxford: Blackwell, 1972.

624 UENO, Naozo. *The Religious View of Chaucer in His Italian Period.* Tokyo: Nanundo, 1958.

625 UTLEY, Francis L. "Robertsonianism Redivivus." *RPh,* 19 (1965), 250–260. [Review article.] Reprinted in 264.

626 VALLESE, Tarquinio. *Goffredo Chaucer vista da un italiano.* Roma: Albrighi e Segati, 1930.

627 VALLESE, Tarquinio. *La poesia di Chaucer.* 2nd ed. Napoli: Pironti, 1946.

628 WAGENKNECHT, Edward, ed. *Chaucer: Modern Essays in Criticism.* New York: Oxford Univ. Press, 1959. [GB 24]

629 WATTS, Ann C. "Chaucerian Selves—Especially Two Serious Ones." *ChauR,* 4 (1970), 229–241.

630 WEBSTER, C. M. "Chaucer's Turkish Bows." *MLN,* 47 (1932), 260.

631 WELLS, Whitney H. "Chaucer as a Literary Critic." *MLN,* 39 (1924), 255–268.

632 WENTERSDORF, Karl P. "Chaucer and the Lost Tale of Wade." *JEGP,* 65 (1966), 274–286.

633 WEST, Michael D. "Dramatic Time, Setting, and Motivation in Chaucer." *ChauR,* 2 (1968), 172–187.

634 WHITMAN, F. H. "Exegesis and Chaucer's Dream Visions." *ChauR,* 3 (1969), 229–238.

635 WILKS, Michael. "Chaucer and the Mystical Marriage in Medieval Political Thought." *BJRL,* 44 (1962), 489–530.

636 WILLIAMS, Arnold. "Chaucer and the Friars." *Speculum,* 28 (1953), 499–513.

637 WILSON, George P. "Chaucer and Oral Reading." *SAQ,* 25 (1926), 283–299.

638 WILSON, William S. "Days and Months in Chaucer's Poems." *AN&Q,* 4 (1966), 83–84.

639 WIMSATT, James I. "Chaucer and French Poetry." 260, pp. 109–136.

640 WIMSATT, James I. "Chaucer and the Canticle of Canticles." 528, pp. 66–90.

641 WINNY, James. *Chaucer's Dream Poems.* New York: Barnes & Noble, 1973.

642 WOOD, Chauncey. *Chaucer and the Country of the Stars: Poetical Uses of Astrological Imagery.* Princeton: Princeton Univ. Press, 1970.

643 WOOD, Chauncey. "Chaucer and Astrology." 296, pp. 176–191.

644 WORK, James A. "Echoes of the Anathema in Chaucer." *PMLA,* 47 (1932), 419–430.

645 YOUNG, Karl. "Chaucer and Aulus Gellius." *MLN,* 52 (1937), 347–351.

646 YOUNG, Karl. "Chaucer's Aphorisms from Ptolemy." *SP,* 34 (1937), 1–7.

Language and Versification

Language

647 BAUER, Gero. *Studien zum System und Gebrauch der 'Tempora' in der Sprache Chaucers und Gowers.* Wien: Braumüller, [1970]. (*Wiener Beiträge zur englischen Philologie,* 73)

648 BAUGH, Albert C. *A History of the English Language.* 2nd ed., New York: Appleton-Century-Crofts, 1957; since 1974 Prentice-Hall. [The standard works on Middle English are listed on p. 285.]

649 BENSON, L. D. "Chaucer's Historical Present: Its Meaning and Uses." *ES,* 42 (1961), 65–77.

LANGUAGE AND VERSIFICATION

650 BIGGINS, D. "A Chaucerian Crux: *Spiced Conscience, CT* I (A) 526, III (D) 435."
ES, 47 (1966), 169–180.

651 BOYS, Richard C. "An Unusual Meaning of 'Make' in Chaucer." *MLN,* 52 (1937),
251–253.

652 BRADDY, Haldeen. "Chaucer's Bilingual Idiom." *SFQ,* 32 (1968), 1–6. In 258.

653 BROWN, Carleton. "*Shul* and *shal* in the Chaucer MSS." *PMLA,* 26 (1911), 6–30.

654 CLOYD, Manie G. "Chaucer's Romance Element." *PQ,* 11 (1932), 89–91.

655 CROSS, James E. "On the Meaning of 'a-blakeberyed' (*Canterbury Tales,* C 406)."
RES, n.s. 2 (1951), 372–374.

656 CROSS, James E. "A Point of Chaucer's Syntax." *N&Q,* 197 (1952), 468. [*Of* +
noun as an adjective.]

657 DAVIS, Norman. "Chaucer and Fourteenth Century English." 260, pp. 58–84.

658 DEAN, Christopher. "Chaucer's Use of Function Words with Substantives." *CJL,*
9 (1964), 67–74.

659 DIECKMANN, Emma P. M. "The Meaning of *burdoun* in Chaucer." *MP,* 26
(1928–29), 279–282.

660 DUSTOOR, P. E. "Chaucer's Use of *discreet.*" *RES,* 13 (1937), 206–209.

661 EMONDS, Joseph. "The Derived Nominals, Gerunds, and Participles in Chaucer's
English." in *Issues in Linguistics: Papers in Honor of Henry and Renee Kahane,*
ed. Braj B. Kachru, *et al.,* pp. 185–198. Chicago: Univ. of Illinois Press, 1973.

662 FAUST, George P. "Two Notes on Chaucer." *MLN,* 47 (1932), 365–367. [*To-nyght*
and *undern.*]

663 FISHER, John H. "Chaucer's Use of *swete* and *swote.*" *JEGP,* 50 (1951), 326–331.

664 FISIAK, Jacek. *Morphemic Structure of Chaucer's English.* University, Ala.: Univ.
of Alabama Press, 1965. (*Alabama Ling. and Phil. Ser.,* 10.)

665 FLÜGEL, Ewald. "Specimen of the Chaucer Dictionary: Letter E." *Anglia,* 37
(1913), 497–532.

666 FOSTER, C. H. "A Note on Chaucer's Pronunciation of *ai, ay, ei, ey.*" *MLN,* 26
(1911), 76–77.

667 GERIKE, Fritz. *Das Partizipium Präsentis bei Chaucer.* Potsdam, 1911 (Kiel diss.).

668 GRIFFITH, D. D. "On Word-Studies in Chaucer." *Philologica: The Malone Anniversary Studies,* pp. 195–199. Baltimore: Johns Hopkins Press, 1949.

669 HANKEY, Clyde T. "Defining-Context, Association Sets, and Glossing Chaucer."
Studies in Medieval Culture, ed. John R. Sommerfeldt, pp. 69–73. [Kalamazoo]:
Western Michigan Univ., 1964.

670 HEUER, Hermann. *Studien zur syntaktischen und stilistischen Funktion des Ad-
verbs bei Chaucer und im Rosenroman.* Heidelberg, 1932 (*Anglistische Forsch.,*
75).

671 HOLMES, Urban T. "Chaucer's *tydif* 'a small bird.' " *PQ,* 16 (1937), 65–67. Cf.
ibid., 17 (1938), 216–218 (F. P. Wilson).

672 HOMANN, Elizabeth R. "Chaucer's Use of *gan.*" *JEGP,* 53 (1954), 389–398.

673 HULBERT, James R. "Chaucer's Romance Vocabulary." *PQ,* 26 (1947), 302–306.

674 ISAACS, Neil D. " 'Furlong Wey' in Chaucer." *N&Q,* 206 (1961), 328–329.

LANGUAGE AND VERSIFICATION

675 JACOBSON, R. *The London Dialect of the Late Fourteenth Century: A Transformational Analysis in Historical Linguistics.* The Hague: Mouton, 1970. (*Janua linguarum, series practica,* 97.)

676 KARPF, Fritz. *Studien zur Syntax in den Werken Geoffrey Chaucers.* Teil I. Wien, 1930 (*Wiener Beiträge zur engl. Phil.,* 55).

677 KARPF, Fritz. "Zur Kontamination bei Chaucer." *ESt,* 64 (1929), 252–260. Nachträge, *ibid.,* 66 (1931–32), 467–468.

678 KENYON, John S. *The Syntax of the Infinitive in Chaucer.* London, 1909 (Chaucer Soc., 2nd Ser., No. 44).

679 KERKHOF, J. *Studies in the Language of Geoffrey Chaucer.* Leiden, 1966. (*Leidse germanistische en anglistische Reeks van de Rijksuniv. te Leiden,* No. 5)

680 KITTREDGE, George L. *Observations on the Language of Chaucer's Troilus.* London, 1891 (Chaucer Soc., 2nd Ser., No. 28). [The preface is dated 1894.]

681 KIVIMAA, Kirsti. *The Pleonastic* That *in Relative and Interrogative Constructions in Chaucer's Verse.* Helsinki, 1966 (*Commentationes Humanarum Litterarum: Societas Scientiarum Fennica,* 39, No. 3).

682 KIVIMAA, Kirsti. *Clauses in Chaucer Introduced by Conjunctions with Appended* that. Helsinki, 1968. (*Commentationes Humanarum Litterarum: Societas Scientiarum Fennica,* 43, No. 1).

683 KÖKERITZ, Helge. *A Guide to Chaucer's Pronunciation.* Stockholm: Almqvist and Wiksel; New Haven: Whitlock, 1954.

684 KOZIOL, Herbert. "Die Anredeform bei Chaucer." *ESt,* 75 (1942–43), 170–174.

685 LANGHANS, Viktor. "Rer Reimvokal *e* bei Chaucer." *Anglia,* 45 (1921), 221–282, 297–392.

686 LOTSPEICH, C. M. "The Type OE *Lōca hwā,* ME *Looke who.*" *JEGP,* 37 (1938), 1–2.

687 LUMIANSKY, R. M. "Chaucer's 'For the nones.'" *Neophil,* 35 (1951), 29–36.

688 MALONE, Kemp. "Chaucer's Double Consonants and the Final *E.*" *MS,* 18 (1956), 204–207.

689 MALONE, Kemp. "Studies in English Phonology, II: *AI.*" *MP,* 23 (1925–26), 483–490.

690 MANLY, John M. "Observations on the Language of Chaucer's Legend of Good Women." [Harvard] *Stud. and Notes in Phil. and Lit.,* 2 (1893), 1–120.

691 MASUI, Michio. *The Structure of Chaucer's Rime Words: An Exploration into the Poetic Language of Chaucer.* Tokyo: Kenkyusha, 1964.

692 MASUI, Michio. "A Mode of Word-Meaning in Chaucer's Language of Love." *SELit,* English Number (1967), pp. 113–126.

693 McJIMSEY, Ruth B. *Chaucer's Irregular -e: A Demonstration among Monosyllabic Nouns of the Exceptions to Grammatical and Metrical Harmony.* New York: King's Crown Press, 1942.

694 MERSAND, Joseph. *Chaucer's Romance Vocabulary.* Brooklyn: Comet Press, 1937. Reprinted, New York: Kennikat Press, 1968.

695 MIRUA, Tsuneshi. "Arrangement of Two or More Attributive Adjectives in Chaucer, I." *Anglica* (Osaka), 6, i–ii (1966), 1–23.

696 MUSTANOJA, Tauno F. *The English Syntactical Type* One the best man *and Its Occurrence in Other Germanic Languages.* Helsinki, 1958 (*Mémoires de la Soc. Néophil. de Helsinki,* 20, 5).

697 MUSTANOJA, Tauno F. *A Middle English Syntax. Part I: Parts of Speech.* Helsinki, 1960 (*Mémoires de la Soc. Néophil. de Helsinki,* 23).

698 NATHAN, Norman. "Pronouns of Address in the *Canterbury Tales.*" *MS,* 21 (1959), 193–201.

699 NÖJD, Ruben. *The Vocalism of Romanic Words in Chaucer.* Uppsala: Appleberg, 1919.

700 POTTER, Simeon. "Chaucer's Untransposable Binomials." 52, pp. 309–314.

701 PRINS, A. A. *"Loke who, what, how, when."* *ES,* 43 (1962), 165–169.

702 REMUS, Hans. *Die kirchlichen und speziell-wissenschaftlichen romanischen Lehnworte Chaucers.* Halle, 1906 (*Studien zur engl. Phil.,* 14).

703 SAMUELS, M. L. "Chaucerian Final '-e'." *N&Q,* 217 (1972), 445–448.

704 SCHLAUCH, Margaret. "Chaucer's Colloquial English: Its Structural Traits." *PMLA,* 67 (1952), 1103–1116.

705 SHIMOSE, Michiro. See 1369.

706 SMYSER, H. M. "Chaucer's Use of *Gin* and *Do.*" *Speculum,* 42 (1967), 68–83.

707 SPITZER, Leo. "Le Type moyen anglais *I was weary for wandred* et ses parallèles romans." *NM,* 55 (1954), 161–177.

708 STORMS, G. "A Note on Chaucer's Pronunciation of French *u.*" *ES,* 41 (1960), 305–308.

709 SUDO, Jun. "A Preliminary Note on the Language of Chaucer's *House of Fame.*" *Kobe City Univ. Jour.,* 19, No. 6 (1969), 25–42; 24, No. 6 (1973), 21–35. (to be continued)

710 SVARTVIK, Jan, and Randolph QUIRK. "Types and Uses of Non-finite Clause in Chaucer." *ES,* 51 (1971), 393–411.

711 TEN BRINK, Bernard. *The Language and Metre of Chaucer,* trans. M. B. Smith. London: Macmillan, 1921.

712 TOPLIFF, Delores E. "Analysis of Singular Weak Adjective Inflection in Chaucer's Works." *Jour. of English Linguistics,* 4 (1970), 78–89.

713 TROUNCE, A. M. "Chaucer's Imperative with *As.*" *MÆ,* 2 (1933), 68–70.

714 WILD, Friedrich. *Die sprachlichen Eigentümlichen der wichtigeren Chaucer-Handschriften und die Sprache Chaucers.* Wien, 1915 (*Wiener Beiträge zur engl. Phil.,* 44).

Versification

715 ADAMS, Percy G. "Chaucer's Assonance." *JEGP,* 71 (1972), 526–539.

716 BABCOCK, Charlotte F. "A Study of the Metrical Use of the Inflectional *E* in Middle English, with particular Reference to Chaucer and Lydgate." *PMLA,* 29 (1914), 59–92.

717 BAUM, Paull F. *Chaucer's Verse.* Durham, N.C.: Duke Univ. Press, 1961.

LANGUAGE AND VERSIFICATION

718 BUCK, Howard. "Chaucer's Use of Feminine Rhyme." *MP,* 26 (1928-29), 13-14.

719 CHRISTOPHERSON, Paul. "The Scansion of Two Lines in Chaucer." *ES,* 45 (1964), Suppl., pp. 146-150.

720 COWLING, G. H. "A Note on Chaucer's Stanza [*ababbcc*]." *RES,* 2 (1926), 311-317.

721 EMERSON, Oliver F. "The Old French Dipthong *ei (ey)* and Middle English Metrics." *RR,* 8 (1917), 68-76.

722 EVANS, Robert O. "Whan that Aprill(e)?" *N&Q,* 202 (1957), 234-237.

723 EVERETT, Dorothy. "Chaucer's 'Good Ear'." *RES,* 23 (1947), 201-208.

724 FIFIELD, Merle. *Theoretical Techniques for the Analysis of Variety in Chaucer's Metrical Stress.* (*Ball State Monograph* 23; *Pub. in English* 17.) Muncie, Ind.: Ball State Univ., 1973.

725 HALLE, Morris, and Samuel J. KEYSER. "Chaucer and the Study of Prosody." *CE,* 28 (1966), 187-219.

726 MASUI, Michio. "Further Consideration of Chaucer's Rimes." *Hiroshima Univ. Stud.,* 29, No. 2 (1970), 92-124.

727 MAYNARD, Theodore. *The Connection between the Ballade, Chaucer's Modification of it, Rime Royal, and the Spenserian Stanza.* Washington, D.C.: Catholic Univ. of Amer. Press, 1934.

728 McCLUMPHA, Charles F. *The Alliteration of Chaucer.* Leipzig, n.d. (Leipzig diss.).

729 MUSTANOJA, Tauno F. "Chaucer's Prosody." 296, pp. 58-84.

730 MUSTANOJA, Tauno F. "Verbal Rhyming in Chaucer." 53, pp. 104-110.

731 OWEN, Charles A., Jr. " 'Thy Drasty Rymyng . . .'." *SP,* 63 (1966), 533-564.

732 PYLE, Fitzroy. "Chaucer's Prosody." *MÆ,* 42 (1973), 47-56. Review article (mainly on 734).

733 ROBERTSON, Stuart. "Old English Verse in Chaucer." *MLN,* 43 (1928), 234-236.

734 ROBINSON, Ian. *Chaucer's Prosody: A Study of the Middle English Verse Tradition.* London: Cambridge Univ. Press, 1971.

735 SHANNON, Edgar. "Chaucer's Use of the Octosyllabic Verse in the Book of the Duchess and the House of Fame." *JEGP,* 12 (1913), 277-294.

736 SOUTHWORTH, James G. "Chaucer's Final *-e* in Rhyme." *PMLA,* 62 (1947), 910-935. Cf. *ibid.,* 63 (1948), 1101-1124 (E.T. Donaldson); 64 (1949), 601-609 (Southworth); 609 (Donaldson), 609-610 (Southworth).

737 SOUTHWORTH, James G. *The Prosody of Chaucer and His Followers: Supplementary Chapters to Verses of Cadence.* Oxford: Blackwell, 1962.

738 SOUTHWORTH, James G. *Verses of Cadence: An Introduction to the Prosody of Chaucer and His Followers.* Oxford: Blackwell, 1954.

739 SOUTHWORTH, James G. "Chaucer: A Plea for a Reliable Text." *CE,* 26 (1964), 173-179. Reprinted in 264.

740 SUDO, Jun. "Chaucer as a Verse Craftsman." *Kobe City Univ. Jour.,* 14, No. 5 (1964), 35-51.

741 SUDO, Jun. "Some Specific Rime-Units in Chaucer." *SELit,* 45 (1969), 221-236.

742 TEN BRINK, Bernard. See 711.

743 WIMSATT, W. K. "The Rule and the Norm: Halle and Keyser on Chaucer's Meter." *CE*, 31 (1970), 774–788. Also in *Literary Style: A Symposium*, ed. Seymour Chatman, pp. 197–215. New York: Oxford Univ. Press, 1971.

Sources and Influences

Some French, Latin, and Italian Works Known to Chaucer

(other than Dante, Virgil, Ovid, etc.)

Alain de Lille

744 *Anticlaudianus*, ed. R. Bossuat. Paris: Vrin, 1955. Also ed. Thomas Wright, in *Anglo-Latin Satirical Poets and Epigrammatists of the Twelfth Century*. 2 vols. London, 1872 (Rolls Ser.). Trans. William H. Cornog. Philadelphia, 1935 (Univ. of Pennsylvania diss.) *Anticlaudianus or the Good and Perfect Man*, trans. James J. Sheridan. Toronto: Pontifical Institute, 1973.

745 *De Planctu Naturae*, ed. Thomas Wright (as above) trans. Doublas M. Moffat. New Haven, 1908 (*Yale Stud. in English*, 36).

Albertano of Brescia

746 *Albertani Brixiensis Liber Consolationis et Consilii*, ed. Thor Sundby. London, 1873 (Chaucer Soc., 2nd Ser., No. 8).

Benoit de Sainte-Maure

747 *Le Roman de Troie*, ed. L. Constans. 6 vols. Paris, 1904–12 (*SATF*).

Boccaccio

748 *The Filostrato of Giovanni Boccaccio: A Translation with Parallel Text by Nathaniel E. Griffin and Arthur B. Myrick. Philadelphia: Univ. of Pennsylvania Press, 1929. Also a verse trans. by H. M. Cummings. Princeton: Princeton Univ. Press, 1924. Trans. as *The Book of Theseus* by Bernadette M. McCoy, Sea Cliff, N.Y.: Teesdale Pub. Assoc., 1974.

749 *Teseida*, ed. S. Battaglia. Florence, 1938 (Accademia della Crusca).

Boethius

750 *De Consolatione Philosophiae*, ed. H. F. Stewart and E. K. Rand. London, 1918 (Loeb Classical Library).

Deschamps

751 *Oeuvres complètes de Eustache Deschamps,* ed. le Marquis de Saint-Hilaire et G. Raynaud. 11 vols. Paris, 1878–1903 (*SATF*).

Distichs of Cato

752 *Disticha Catonis,* ed. Marcus Boas and H. J. Botschuyver. Amsterdam: North Holland Pub. Co., 1952.

Froissart

753 *Oeuvres de Froissart: Poesies,* ed. A. Scheler. 3 vols. Bruxelles, 1870–1872.

Guido delle Colonne

754 *Guido de Columnis: Historia Destructionis Troiae,* ed. Nathaniel E. Griffin. Cambridge, Mass.: The Mediaeval Academy, 1936.

Guillaume de Lorris and Jean de Meun

755 *Le Roman de la Rose,* ed. E. Langlois. 5 vols. Paris, 1914–24 (*SATF*); ed. Félix Lecoy. 3 vols. Paris: Champion, 1965–70 [in progress], (*CFMA*). Verse trans. by F. S. Ellis. 3 vols. London: Dent, 1900; by Harry W. Robbins. New York: Dutton, 1962; prose trans. by Charles Dahlberg. Princeton: Princeton Univ. Press, 1971.

Machaut

756 *Oeuvres de Guillaume de Machaut,* ed. E. Hoepffner. 3 vols. Paris, 1908–21 (*SATF*).

Macrobius

757 *Commentary on the Dream of Scipio,* trans. with intro. and notes by William H. Stahl. New York: Columbia Univ. Press, 1952 (*Records of Civilization,* No. 48); also *The Dream of Scipio,* ed. and trans. James A. Kleist. New York: Schwartz, Kirwin & Fause, 1915. [The best Latin text is that of L. von Jan (2 vols. Leipzig, 1852).]

Peter of Riga

758 *Aurora, Petri Rigae Biblia Versificata: A Verse Commentary on the Bible,* ed. Paul E. Beichner. 2 vols. Notre Dame, Ind.: Univ. of Notre Dame Press, 1965 (*Pubns. in Mediæval Stud.,* 19).

Statius

759 *Works,* ed. (with English trans.) J. H. Mozley. 2 vols. London: Heinemann, 1928 (Loeb Classical Library).

759a *The Medieval Achilleid of Statius,* ed. Paul M. Clogan. Leiden: Brill, 1968.

Literary Influences

(See also under separate works)

760 AXON, William E. A. "Italian Influence on Chaucer." 360 pp. 83–110.

761 AYRES, Harry M. "Chaucer and Seneca." *RR,* 10 (1919), 1–15.

762 BARDELLI, Maria. *Qualche contributo agli studi sulle relazioni del Chaucer col Boccaccio.* Firenze: Cooperativa, 1911.

763 BENNETT, J. A. W. "Chaucer, Dante, and Boccaccio." *MÆ,* 22 (1953), 114–115.

764 BRADDY, Haldeen. "Chaucer and Graunson: The Valentine Tradition." *PMLA,* 54 (1939), 359–368.

765 BRADDY, Haldeen. *Chaucer and the French Poet Graunson.* Baton Rouge: Louisiana State Univ. Press, 1947. Reprinted Port Washington, N.Y.: Kennikat, 1968.

766 BRADDY, Haldeen. "Messire Oton de Graunson, Chaucer's Savoyard Friend." *SP,* 35 (1938), 515–531.

767 BRADDY, Haldeen. "Sir Oton de Graunson—'Flour of Hem That Make in Fraunce'." *SP,* 35 (1938), 10–24.

768 BRADDY, Haldeen. "The French Influence on Chaucer." 296, pp. 123–138.

769 CLOGAN, Paul M. "Chaucer and the *Thebaid* Scholia." *SP,* 61 (1964), 599–615.

770 CLOGAN, Paul M. "Chaucer's Use of the 'Thebaid'." *EM,* 18 (1967), 9–31.

771 CUMMINGS, H. M. *The Indebtedness of Chaucer's Works to the Italian Works of Boccaccio.* Menasha, Wis., 1916 (*Univ. of Cincinnati Stud.,* 10, pt. 2). Reprinted New York: Haskell House, 1965.

772 DÉDÉYAN, Charles. "Dante en Angleterre." *Les Lettres romanes,* 12 (1958), 367–388; 13 (1959), 45–68; 14 (1960), 41–52; 15 (1961), 39–50.

773 DELANY, Paul. "Constantinus Africanus' *De Coitu.*" *ChauR,* 4 (1970), 55–65.

774 FANSLER, Dean S. *Chaucer and the Roman de la Rose.* New York, 1914 (*Columbia Univ. Stud. in English and Compar. Lit.,* 7). Reprinted Gloucester, Mass: Peter Smith, 1965.

775 FISHER, John H. *John Gower, Moral Philosopher and Friend of Chaucer.* New York: N.Y. Univ. Press, 1964.

776 GARBÁTY, Thomas J. "Pamphilus de Amore: An Introduction and Translation." *ChauR,* 2 (1967), 108–134.

777 GARBÁTY, Thomas J. "The *Pamphilus* Tradition in Ruiz and Chaucer." *PQ,* 46 (1967), 457–470.

778 GARDNER, Averil. "Chaucer and Boethius: Some Illustrations of Indebtedness." *Univ. of Cape Town Stud. in English,* 2 (1971), 31–38.

779 HAZELTON, Richard. "Chaucer and Cato." *Speculum,* 35 (1960), 357–380.

780 HOFFMAN, Richard L. *Ovid and the Canterbury Tales.* Philadelphia: Univ. of Pennsylvania Press, 1967.

781 HOFFMAN, Richard L. "A Newly Acquired Manuscript of Albertano of Brescia." *Library Chronicle* (Univ. of Pennsylvania), 36 (1970), 105–109.

SOURCES AND INFLUENCES

782 HOFFMAN, Richard L. "The Influence of the Classics on Chaucer." 296, pp. 162–175.

783 JEFFERSON, B. L. Chaucer and the Consolation of Philosophy of Boethius. Princeton: Princeton Univ. Press, 1917. Reprinted New York: Haskell House, 1965.

784 KOCH, John. "Chaucers Belesenheit in den römischen Klassikern." ESt, 57 (1923), 8–84.

785 KOCH, John. see 398.

786 KOEPPEL, Emil. "Chaucer und Alanus de Insulis." Archiv, 90 (1893), 149–151.

787 KOEPPEL, Emil. "Chaucer und Albertanus Brixiensis." Archiv, 86 (1891), 29–46.

788 KOEPPEL, Emil. "Chaucer und Innocenz des Dritten Traktat De Contemptu Mundi sive De Miseria Conditionis Humanae." Archiv, 84 (1890), 405–418.

789 KORTEN, Hertha. Chaucers literarische Beziehungen zu Boccaccio: Die kunstlerische Konzeption der Canterbury Tales und das Lolliusproblem. Rostock: Hinstorff, 1920.

790 LANDRUM, Grace W. "Chaucer's Use of the Vulgate." PMLA, 39 (1924), 75–100.

791 LANGE, Hugo. "Chaucer und Mandeville's Travels." Archiv, 174 (1938), 79–81.

792 LOOTEN, C. "Chaucer et Dante." RLC, 5 (1925), 545–571.

793 LOUNSBURY, Thomas R. "The Learning of Chaucer." 498, Chap. 5.

794 LOWES, John L. "Chaucer and the Classics." Nation, 103 (Dec. 21, 1916), Suppl., pp. 2–3.

795 LOWES, John L. "Chaucer and Dante." MP, 14 (1916–17), 705–735.

796 LOWES, John L. "Chaucer and Dante's Convivio." MP, 13 (1915–16), 19–33.

797 LOWES, John L. "Chaucer and the Miroir de Mariage." MP, 8 (1910–11), 165–186, 305–334.

798 LOWES, John L. "Chaucer and the Ovide Moralisé." PMLA, 33 (1918), 302–325.

799 MAKAREWICZ, Sister M. Raynelda. The Patristic Influence on Chaucer. Washington, D.C.: Catholic Univ. of Amer. Press, 1953.

800 MEECH, Sanford B. "Chaucer and an Italian Translation of the Heroides." PMLA, 45 (1930), 110–128.

801 MEECH, Sanford B. "Chaucer and the Ovide Moralisé—A Further Study." PMLA, 46 (1931), 182–204.

802 MORSBACH, L. See 1665, 1666.

803 ORTEGO, Philip D. "A Bibliography of Chaucer's French Sources." Bull. of Bibl., 27 (1970), 72–76.

804 PRATT, Robert A. "Chaucer and Boccaccio." TLS, Feb. 28, 1935, p. 124. Cf. ibid., March 7, p. 143 (E. Hutton), April 11, p. 244 (Pratt).

805 PRATT, Robert A. "Chaucer's Claudian." Speculum, 22 (1947), 419–429.

806 PRATT, Robert A. "Chaucer's Use of the Teseida." PMLA, 62 (1947), 598–621.

807 PRATT, Robert A. "Chaucer and Les Cronicles of Nicholas Trevet." Stud. in Lang. and Culture of the Middle Ages and Later, ed. E. Bagby Atwood and Archibald A. Hill, pp. 303–311. Austin: Univ. of Texas, 1969.

808 PRATT, Robert A. See 2567.

809 Praz, Mario. "Chaucer and the Great Italian Writers of the Trecento." *Monthly Criterion,* 6 (1927), 18–39, 131–157, 238–242. Also in *The Flaming Heart,* pp. 29–89. Garden City: Doubleday, 1958. Also published in Italian in *Machiavelli in Inghilterra ed altri saggi.* Roma, 1942; 2nd ed., 1943.

810 Root, Robert K. "Chaucer's Dares [Joseph of Exeter]." *MP,* 15 (1917–18), 1–22.

811 Ruggiers, Paul G. "The Italian Influence on Chaucer." 296, pp. 139–161.

812 Schirmer, W. F. "Boccaccios Werke als Quelle G. Chaucers." *GRM,* 12 (1924), 288–305.

813 Schless, Howard. "Chaucer and Dante." *Critical Approaches to Medieval Literature.* 380, pp. 134–154, 169–171.

814 Seibert, Harriet. "Chaucer and Horace." *MLN,* 31 (1916), 304–307

815 Shannon, Edgar F. "Chaucer and Lucan's *Pharsalia.*" *MP,* 6 (1918–19), 609–614.

816 Shannon, Edgar F. *Chaucer and the Roman Poets.* Cambridge, Mass.: Harvard Univ. Press, 1929 (*Harvard Stud. in Compar. Lit.,* 7).

817 Steele, Robert. "Chaucer and the *Almagest.*" *Library,* 3rd Ser., 10 (1919), 243–247.

818 Tatlock, John S. P. "Chaucer and Dante." *MP,* 3 (1905–06), 367–372.

819 Tatlock, John S. P. See 616.

820 Trigona, F. P. *Chaucer imitatore del Boccaccio: Saggio di letteratura comparata.* Cantania: Studio editoriale moderno, 1923.

821 Wise, Boyd A. *The Influence of Statius upon Chaucer.* Baltimore: Furst, 1911.

822 Witlieb, Bernard L. "Chaucer and the Ovide Moralisé." *N&Q,* 215 (1970), 202–207.

823 Wrenn, C. L. "Chaucer's Knowledge of Horace." *MLR,* 18 (1923), 286–292.

824 Young, Karl "Chaucer's Use of Boccaccio's *Filocolo.*" *MP,* 4 (1906–07), 169–177.

Major Poems

The Romaunt of the Rose

825 Ando, Shinsuke. "The Language of *The Romaunt of the Rose* (Fragment A), with Particular Reference to Chaucer's Relationship to Middle English Provincial Poetry." *SELit,* English Number (1970), 63–74.

826 Caie, Graham D. "An Iconographic Detail in the *Roman de la Rose* and the Middle English *Romaunt.*" *ChauR,* 8 (1974), 320–323.

827 Cook, Albert S. "Chaucer and Venantius Fortunatus." *MLN,* 39 (1924), 376–378.

828 Huppé, Bernard F. "The Translation of the Technical Terms in the Middle English *Romaunt of the Rose.*" *JEGP,* 47 (1948), 334–342.

829 KITTRIDGE, George L. "The Authorship of the English Romaunt of the Rose." [Harvard] *Stud. and Notes in Phil. and Lit.*, 1 (1892), 1–65.

830 KUNSTMANN, John G. "Chaucer's Archangel." *MLN*, 55 (1940), 259–262.

831 LANGE, Hugo. "Rettungen Chaucers: Neue Beiträge zur Echtheitsfrage von Fragment A des mittelenglischen Rosenromans." *Anglia*, 35 (1912), 338–346; 36 (1912), 479–491; 37 (1913), 146–162; 38 (1914), 477–490.

832 LANGHANS, Viktor. "Roman der Rose—Troilus." 284, pp. 223–228.

833 REEVES, W. P. "*Romance of the Rose*, 1705." *MLN*, 38 (1923), 124.

834 SCHOCH, A. D. "The Differences in the Middle English *Romaunt of the Rose* and Their Bearing upon Chaucer's Authorship." *MP*, 3 (1905–06), 339–358.

835 SKEAT, W. W. "Why 'The Romaunt of the Rose' Is Not Chaucer's." *Essays on Chaucer*, Part V, pp. 437–451 (Chaucer Soc., 2nd Ser., No. 19). Incorporated in 299.

836 SUDO, Jun. "A Preliminary Note on the Language of Chaucer's *Romaunt of the Rose.*" *Kobe City Univ. Jour.*, 16, No. 6 (1966), 73–87.

837 SUTHERLAND, Ronald. "*The Romaunt of the Rose* and Source Manuscripts." *PMLA*, 74 (1959), 178–183.*

838 SUTHERLAND, Ronald. ed. *The Romaunt of the Rose and Le Roman de la Rose: A Parallel-Text Edition.* Oxford: Blackwell, 1967.

839 THOMPSON, D'Arcy W. " 'Archangel' as a Bird-Name in Chaucer." *N&Q*, 175 (1938), 332.

840 WHITTERIDGE, Gweneth. "The Word *archaungel* in Chaucer's *Romaunt of the Rose.*" *English and Germanic Stud.*, 3 (1949–50), 34–36.

The Book of the Duchess

841 ANDERSON, Marjorie. "Blanche, Duchess of Lancaster." *MP*, 45 (1947–48), 152–159.

842 BAKER, Donald C. "The Dreamer Again in *The Book of the Duchess.*" *PMLA*, 70 (1955), 279–282.

843 BAKER, Donald C. "Imagery and Structure in Chaucer's *Book of the Duchess.*" *SN*, 30 (1958), 17–26.

844 BEICHNER, Paul E. *The Medieval Representatives of Music, Jubal or Tubalcain?* Notre Dame, Ind.: Univ. of Notre Dame Press, 1954 (*Texts and Stud. in the Hist. of Mediaeval Educ.*, 2).

845 BRADDY, Haldeen. "Chaucer's *Book of the Duchess* and Two of Granson's Complaintes." *MLN*, 52 (1937), 487–491.

846 BRADDY, Haldeen, See 336.

847 BRONSON, Bertrand H. "*The Book of the Duchess* Re-opened." *PMLA*, 67 (1952), 863–881. Reprinted in 628.

848 BRONSON, Bertrand H. "Concerning 'Houres Twelve'." *MLN*, 68 (1953), 515–521.

849 BROSNAHAN, Leger. "Now (This), Now (That) and *BD* 646." 57, pp. 11–18.

THE BOOK OF THE DUCHESS

850 BROUGHTON, Bradford B. "Chaucer's *Book of the Duchess:* Did John Love Blanche?" In *Twenty-Seven to One: A Potpourri of Humanistic Material presented to Dr. Donald Gale Stillman* . . . , ed. Bradford B. Broughton, [Ogdensburg, N.Y.: Ryan Press, 1970]. pp. 71–84.

851 BROWN, James N. "Narrative Focus and Function in *The Book of the Duchess.*" *Massachusetts Stud. in English,* 2 (1970), 71–79.

851a BURNLEY, J. D. See 2832.

852 CARSON, M. Angela. "Easing of the 'Hert' in the *Book of the Duchess.*" *ChauR.* 1 (1967), 157–160.

853 CARSON, M. Angela. "The Sovereignty of Octovyen in the *Book of the Duchess. AnM,* 8 (1967), 46–58.

855 CARTIER, Normand R. "Froissart, Chaucer and Eclimpostair." *RLC,* 38 (1964), 18–34.

856 CARTIER, Normand R. "*Le Bleu Chevalier* de Froissart et le *Livre de la Duchesse* de Chaucer." *Romania,* 88 (1967), 232–252.

857 CHERNISS, Michael D. "The Boethian Dialogue in Chaucer's *Book of the Duchess.*" *JEGP,* 68 (1969), 655–665.

858 CHERNISS, Michael D. "The Narrator Asleep and Awake in Chaucer's *Book of the Duchess.*" *PLL,* 8 (1972), 115–126.

859 CONDREN, Edward I. "The Historical Context of the *Book of the Duchess:* A New Hypothesis." *ChauR,* 5 (1971), 195–212.

860 COOLEY, Franklin D. "Two Notes on the Chess Terms in *The Book of the Duchess.*" *MLN,* 63 (1948), 30–35.

861 CRAMPTON, Georgia R. "Transitions and Meaning in *The Book of the Duchess.*" *JEGP,* 62 (1963), 436–500.

862 CUSHMAN, L. W. "Chaucer's Book of the Duchess." *Univ. of Calif. Chron.,* 11 (1909), 252–266.

863 DELASANTA, Rodney. "Christian Affirmation in *The Book of the Duchess.*" *PMLA,* 84 (1969), 245–251.

864 DICKERSON, A. Inskip, Jr. "*The Book of the Duchess,* line 480." *Papers of the Bibl. Soc. of America,* 66 (1972), 51–54.

865 DONOVAN, Mortimer J. "The Book of the Duchess, vv. 16–21." *N&Q,* 195 (1950), 333–334.

866 EBEL, Julia G. "Chaucer's *The Book of the Duchess:* A Study in Medieval Iconography and Literary Structure." *CE,* 29 (1967), 197–206.

867 ELDREDGE, Laurence. "The Structure of *The Book of the Duchess.*" *RUO,* 39 (1969), 132–151.

868 EMERSON, O. F. See 396.

869 FINLAYSON, John. "The *Book of the Duchess:* Sources for Lines 174, 203–5, 249–253." *ELN,* 10 (1973), 170–172.

870 FOSTER, Edward E. "Allegorical Consolation in *The Book of the Duchess.*" *Ball State Univ. Forum,* 11, iv (1971), 14–20.

871 FRENCH, W. H. "The Man in Black's Lyric." *JEGP,* 56 (1957), 231–241.

872 FRENCH, W. H. "Medieval Chess and the *Book of the Duchess.*" *MLN,* 64 (1949), 261–264.

873 FRIEDMAN, John B. "The Dreamer, the Whelp, and Consolation in the *Book of the Duchess.*" *ChauR,* 3 (1968), 145–162.

874 GALWAY, Margaret. "Chaucer's Hopeless Love." *MLN,* 60 (1945), 431–439.

875 GARDNER, John. "Style as Meaning in the *Book of the Duchess.*" *Language and Style,* 2 (1969), 143–171.

876 GRENNEN, Joseph E. "*Hert-huntyng* in the *Book of the Duchess.*" *MLQ,* 25 (1964), 131–139.

877 HAMMERLE, Karl. "*The Book of the Duchess,* vv. 599–616." *Anglia,* 66 (1942), 70–72.

878 HARRISON, Benjamin S. "Medieval Rhetoric in the *Book of the Duchess.*" *PMLA,* 49 (1934), 428–442.

879 HINTON, Norman D. "The Black Death and The Book of the Duchess." *His Firm Estate: Essays in Honor of Franklin James Eikenberry by Former Students,* ed. Donald E. Hayden, pp. 72–78. Tulsa, Okla.: Univ. of Tulsa, 1967.

881 HUPPÉ, Bernard F., and D. W. ROBERTSON, Jr. See 444.

882 KELLOGG, Alfred L. "Amatory Psychology and Amatory Frustration in the Interpretation of the 'Book of the Duchess'." 456, pp. 59–107.

883 KITCHEL, Anna T. "Chaucer and Machaut's *Dit de la Fontaine Amoureuse.*" *Vassar Medieval Studies,* pp. 217–231. New Haven: Yale Univ. Press, 1923.

884 KITTREDGE, George L. "Chaucer and Froissart (with a discussion of the date of the Méliador)." *ESt,* 26 (1899), 321–336.

885 KITTREDGE, George L. "Guillaume de Machaut and *The Book of the Duchess.*" *PMLA,* 30 (1915), 1–24.

886 KREUZER, James R. "The Dreamer in the *Book of the Duchess.*" *PMLA,* 66 (1951), 543–547.

887 LACKEY, Allen D. "Chaucer's *Book of the Duchess,* 330." *Explicator,* 32 (1974), item 74.

888 LANGHANS, Viktor, See 284, pp. 253–302.

889 LAWLOR, John. "The Pattern of Consolation in *The Book of the Duchess.*" *Speculum,* 31 (1956), 626–648. Reprinted in 593.

890 LEWIS, N. B. "The Anniversary Service for Blanche, Duchess of Lancaster, 12th September, 1374." *BJRL,* 21 (1937), 176–192.

891 LOOMIS, Roger S. "Chaucer's Eight Years Sickness." *MLN,* 21 (1944), 178–180.

892 LOWES, John L. "The Dry Sea and the Carrenare." *MP,* 3 (1905–06), 1–46.

893 LUISI, David. "The Hunt Motif in *The Book of the Duchess.*" *ES,* 52 (1971), 309–311.

894 LUMIANSKY, R. M. "The Bereaved Narrator in Chaucer's *The Book of the Duchess.*" *TSE,* 9 (1959), 5–17.

895 MALONE, Kemp. "Chaucer's 'Book of the Duchess': A Metrical Study." 54, pp. 71–95.

896 MANNING, Stephen. "Chaucer's Good Fair White: Woman and Symbol." *CL,* 10 (1958), 97–105.

897 MANNING, Stephen. "That Dreamer Once More." *PMLA,* 71 (1956), 540–541.

898 MATHEWS, Johnye E. "The Black Knight as King of the Castle in *The Book of the Duchess.*" *South Central Bull.*, 31 (1971), 200–201.

899 MORETON, Rebecca L. "Literary Convention in *The Book of the Duchess.*" *UMSE*, 4 (1963), 69–78.

900 NAULT, Clifford A., Jr. "'Foure and Twenty Yer' Again." *MLN*, 71 (1956), 319–321.

901 PALMER, John J. N. "The Historical Context of the *Book of the Duchess:* A Revision." *ChauR*, 8 (1974), 253–261.

902 PECK, Russell A. "Theme and Number in Chaucer's *Book of the Duchess.*" *Silent Poetry: Essays in Numerological Analysis,* ed. Alastair Fowler, pp. 73–115. New York: Barnes & Noble; London: Routledge & Kegan Paul, 1970.

903 PETERS, E. J. J. "*Bo D:* Line 47." *AN&Q,* 8 (1970), 135.

904 ROBERTSON, D. W., Jr. "The Historical Setting of Chaucer's *Book of the Duchess.*" *Medieval Studies in Honor of Urban Tigner Holmes, Jr.,* ed. J. Mahoney and J. E. Keller, pp. 169–195. Chapel Hill, 1966 (*Univ. of No. Carolina Stud. in Romance Lang. and Lit.,* 56).

905 ROBERTSON, D. W., Jr. "The Book of the Duchess." 296, pp. 332–340.

906 ROSENTHAL, Constance L. "A Possible Source of Chaucer's *Booke of the Duchesse —Li Regret de Guillaume* by Jehan de la Mote." *MLN,* 48 (1933), 511–514.

907 ROWLAND, Beryl. "Chaucer's 'Mistake': *The Book of the Duchess,* line 455." *AN&Q,* 4 (1966), 99–100.

908 ROWLAND, Beryl. "The Chess Problem in Chaucer's *Book of the Duchess.*" *Anglia,* 80 (1962), 384–389.

909 ROWLAND, Beryl. "'A Round Tour of Yvoyre' (*The Book of the Duchess,* 946)." *N&Q,* 208 (1963), 9.

910 ROWLAND, Beryl. "The Whelp in Chaucer's *Book of the Duchess.*" *NM,* 46 (1965), 148–160.

911 ROWLAND, Beryl. "Chaucer as a Pawn in *The Book of the Duchess.*" *AN&Q,* 6 (1967), 3–5.

912 SADLER, Lynn V. "Chaucer's *The Book of the Duchess* and the 'Law of Kinde'." *AnM,* 11 (1970), 51–64.

913 SAVAGE, Howard J. "Chaucer's 'Long Castel'." *MLN,* 31 (1916), 442–443.

914 SCHAAR, Claes. "An Emendation in Chaucer's *Book of the Duchess.*" *ES,* 35 (1954), 16.

915 SCHOENBAUM, Samuel. "Chaucer's Black Knight." *MLN,* 68 (1953), 121–122.

916 SEVERS, J. Burke. "Chaucer's Self-Portrait in the *Book of the Duchess.*" *PQ,* 43 (1964), 27–39.

917 SEVERS, J. Burke. "The Sources of *The Book of the Duchess.*" *MS,* 25 (1963), 355–362.

918 SPITZER, Leo. "Eng. *dismal*—O.F. **dism-al.*" *MLN,* 57 (1942), 602–613.

919 STEADMAN, John M. "Chaucer's 'whelp': A Symbol of Marital Fidelity?" *N&Q,* 201 (1956), 374–375.

920 STEARNS, M. W. "A Note on Chaucer's Attitude toward Love." *Speculum,* 17 (1942), 570–574.

921 STEVENS, Martin. "Narrative Focus in *The Book of the Duchess:* A Critical Revaluation." *AnM,* 7 (1966), 16–32.

922 STEVENSON, S. W. "Chaucer's Ferses Twelve." *ELH,* 7 (1940), 215–222.

923 SUDO, Jun. "A Preliminary Note on the Language and Style of Chaucer's *Book of the Duchess.*" *Kobe City Univ. Jour.,* 18, No. 4 (1967), 1–28.

924 SYPHERD, W. O. "Chaucer's Eight Years' Sickness." *MLN,* 20 (1905), 240–243.

925 SYPHERD, W. O. "*Le Songe Vert* and Chaucer's Dream-Poems." *MLN,* 24 (1909), 46–47.

926 TISDALE, Charles P. "Boethian 'Hert-Huntyng': The Elegiac Pattern of the *Book of the Duchess.*" *American Benedictine Rev.,* 24 (1973), 365–380.

927 TUPPER, Frederick. "Chaucer and Richmond." *MLN,* 31 (1916), 250–252. Cf. *ibid.,* 32 (1917), 54.

928 WILSON, G. R., Jr. "The Anatomy of Compassion: Chaucer's *Book of the Duchess.*" *TSLL,* 14 (1972), 381–388.

929 WIMSATT, James I. "The Apotheosis of Blanche in *The Book of the Duchess.*" *JEGP,* 66 (1967), 26–44.

930 WIMSATT, James I. "The Sources of Chaucer's 'Seys and Alcyone'." *MÆ,* 36 (1967), 231–241.

931 WIMSATT, James I. *Chaucer and the French Love Poets: The Literary Background of* The Book of the Duchess. Chapel Hill, N.C.: Univ. of No. Carolina Press, 1968 (*Univ. of N. C. Stud. in Compar. Lit.,* 43).

932 YOUNG, Karl. "Chaucer and Peter Riga." *Speculum,* 12 (1937), 299–303.

The Hous of Fame

933 ALLEN, Robert J. "A Recurring Motif in Chaucer's *House of Fame.*" *JEGP,* 55 (1956), 393–405.

934 BAKER, Donald C. "Recent Interpretations of Chaucer's *Hous of Fame* and a New Suggestion." *UMSE,* 1 (1960), 97–104.

935 BAUGH, Albert C. "Chaucer and the *Panthere d'Amours.*" *Britannica: Festschrift für Hermann M. Flasdieck,* pp. 51–60. Heidelberg, 1960.

936 BAUM, Paull F. "Chaucer's *The House of Fame.*" *ELH,* 8 (1941), 248–256.

937 BENNETT, J. A. W. *Chaucer's* Book of Fame: *An Exposition of the* House of Fame. Oxford: Clarendon Press, 1968.

938 BERRY, Reginald. "Chaucer's Eagle and the Element of Air." *UTQ,* 43 (1974), 285–297.

939 BESSER, Ingeborg. *Chaucer's 'Hous of Fame': Eine Interpretation.* Hamburg, 1941 (*Britannica,* Heft 20).

940 BEVINGTON, David M. "The Obtuse Narrator in Chaucer's *House of Fame.*" *Speculum,* 36 (1961), 288–298.

941 BEVINGTON, David M. "On Translating Ovid in Chaucer's *House of Fame,*" *N&Q,* 205 (1960), 206–207.

942 Bronson, Bertrand H. *Chaucer's Hous of Fame: Another Hypothesis.* Berkeley, 1934.(*Univ. of Calif. Pub. in English,* 3, No. 4, pp. 171–192). Reprinted Folcroft, Pa.: Folcroft Library Editions, 1973.

943 Brown, Margery L. "The *House of Fame* and the *Corbaccio.*" *MLN,* 32 (1917), 411–415.

944 Brunner, Karl. "Chaucer's *House of Fame.*" *Atti del quinto congresso internazionale di lingue e letterature moderne* (Firenze, 1955), pp. 55–62. Also in *Rivista di letterature moderne,* 2 (1951), 344–350.

945 Carr, John. "A Borrowing from Tibullus in Chaucer's *House of Fame.*" *ChauR,* 8 (1974), 191–197.

946 Carswell, Catherine. " 'Lollius myn autour'." *TLS,* Dec. 28, 1935, p. 899.

947 Cawley, A. C. "Chaucer, Pope, and Fame." *REL* 3, No. 2 (1962), 9–19.

948 Chiarini, Cino. *Di una imitazione inglese della Divina Commedia: La Casa della Fama di G. Chaucer.* Bari: Laterza, 1902. See 1000.

949 Cigada, Sergio. "Il tema arturiano del 'Château Tournant': Chaucer e Christine de Pisan." *SMed,* 2 (1961), 576–606.

950 Colvert, James B. "A Reference to Music in Chaucer's *House of Fame.*" *MLN,* 69 (1954), 239–241.

951 David, Alfred. "Literary Satire in the *House of Fame.*" *PMLA,* 75 (1960), 333–339.

952 David, Alfred. "How Marcia Lost Her Skin: A Note on Chaucer's Mythology." 57, pp. 19–29.

953 Dean, Nancy. "Ovid's Elegies from Exile and Chaucer's *House of Fame.*" *Hunter Coll. Stud.,* 3 (1966), 75–90.

954 Delany, Sheila. " 'Phantom' and the *House of Fame.*" *ChauR,* 2 (1967), 67–74.

955 Delany, Sheila. "Chaucer's *House of Fame* and the *Ovide moralisé.*" *CL,* 20 (1968), 254–264.

956 Delany, Sheila. *Chaucer's House of Fame: The Poetics of Skeptical Fideism.* Chicago: Univ. of Chicago Press, 1972.

957 Delany, Sheila. " 'Ars Simia Naturae' and Chaucer's *House of Fame.*" *ELN,* 11 (1973), 1–5.

958 Dilts, Dorothy A. "Observations on Dante and the *Hous of Fame.*" *MLN,* 57 (1942), 26–28.

959 Eldredge, Laurence. "Chaucer's *Hous of Fame* and the *Via Moderna.*" *NM,* 71 (1970), 105–119.

960 Epstein, Hans J. "The Identity of Chaucer's 'Lollius'." *MLQ,* 3 (1942), 391–400.

961 Estrich, Robert M. "A Possible Provençal Source for Chaucer's *Hous of Fame,* 300–310." *MLN,* 55 (1940), 342–349.

962 Francis, W. Nelson. "Chaucer's 'Airish Beasts'." *MLN,* 64 (1949), 339–341.

963 Friend, Albert C. "Chaucer's Version of the Aeneid." *Speculum,* 28 (1953), 317–323.

964 Goffin, R. C. "Chaucer's Lollius." *TLS,* Aug. 26, 1926, p. 564; April 21, 1927, p. 280.

965 Goffin, R. C. "Quiting by Tidings in *The Hous of Fame,*" *MÆ,* 12 (1943), 40–44.

966 GOFFIN, R. C. " 'Tidings' in the *Hous of Fame.*" *N&Q,* 206 (1961), 246.

967 GRENNEN, Joseph E. "Science and Poetry in Chaucer's *House of Fame.*" *AnM,* 8 (1967), 38–45.

968 HALL, Louis B. "Chaucer and the Dido-and-Aeneas Story." *MS,* 25 (1963), 148–159.

969 HAMILTON, George L. "On a Note to *Hous of Fame,* 358." *MLN,* 23 (1908), 63.

970 HATHAWAY, Charles M., Jr. "Chaucer's Lollius." *ESt,* 44 (1911–12), 161–164.

971 HENKIN, Leo J. "The Apochrypha [*sc.* Apocalypse] and Chaucer's *House of Fame.*" *MLN,* 56 (1941), 583–588.

972 HORNSTEIN, Lillian H. "Petrarch's Laelius, Chaucer's Lollius?" *PMLA,* 63 (1948), 64–84.

973 IMELMANN, Rudolf. "Chaucers *Haus der Fama.*" *ESt,* 45 (1912), 397–431.

974 JONES, H. Lloyd, Jr. "The Date of Chaucer's *House of Fame.*" *Delaware Notes,* 19th Ser. (1946), 47–55.

975 JOYNER, William. "The Journey Motif in Chaucer's *House of Fame.*" *English Rev.,* 50, ii (1973), 28–41.

976 KITTREDGE, George L. "Chaucer's Lollius." *Harvard Stud. in Classical Phil.,* 28 (1917), 47–133.

977 KOCH, John. "Nochmals: Die Bedeutung von Chaucers *Hous of Fame.*" *ESt,* 50 (1916–17), 359–382.

978 KOCH, John. "Textkritische bemerkungen zu Chaucers *Hous of Fame.*" *Anglia Beiblatt,* 27 (1916), 139–153.

979 KOONCE, B. G. *Chaucer and the Tradition of Fame: Symbolism in* The House of Fame. Princeton: Princeton Univ. Press, 1966.

980 KREUZER, James R. "An Alleged Crux in Chaucer [Lollius]." *N&Q,* 202 (1957), 409; cf. *ibid.,* 238–239 (W. Morel).

981 LANGE, Hugo. "Chaucers 'Myn Auctour Called Lollius' und die Datierung des Hous of Fame." *Anglia,* 42 (1918), 345–351.

982 LANGE, Hugo. "Der Heliakische Aufgang der Fixsterne bei Dante und Chaucer." *Deutsches Dante-Jahrbuch,* 21 (1939), 19–41.

983 LANGHANS, Viktor. "Das Haus der Fama." 284, pp. 71–74.

984 LEWIS, R. W. B. "On Translating the *Aeneid: Yif That I Can.*" *YCGL,* 10 (1961), 7–15.

985 LEYERLE, John. "Chaucer's Windy Eagle." *UTQ,* 40 (1971), 247–265.

986 LOWES, John L. See 798.

987 MacCRACKEN, Henry N. " 'Dant in English': A Solution." *Nation,* 89 (1909), 276–277.

988 MANLY, John M. "What is Chaucer's *Hous of Fame?*" 51, 73–81.

989 MANZALAOUI, M. A. "Three Notes on Chaucer's *Hous of Fame.*" *N&Q,* 207 (1962), 85–86.

990 McCOLLUM, John I., Jr. "The House of Fame Revisited." In *A Chaucerian Puzzle* ... (2297), pp. 71–85.

991 MILLER, Amanda H. "Chaucer's 'secte Saturnyn'." *MLN,* 47 (1932), 99–102.

992 Neville, Maria. "Chaucer and St. Clare." *JEGP,* 55 (1956), 423–430.

993 Newman, Francis X. *"House of Fame,* 7–12" *ELN,* 6 (1968), 5–12.

994 Patch, Howard R. "Chaucer's Desert," *MLN,* 34 (1919), 321–328.

995 Patch, Howard R. "Precious Stones in *The House of Fame." MLN,* 50 (1935), 312–317.

996 Pratt, Robert A. "A Note on Chaucer's Lollius." *MLN,* 65 (1950), 183–187.

997 Quinn, Betty N. "Venus, Chaucer, and Peter Bersuire." *Speculum,* 38 (1963), 479–480.

998 Rand, E. K. "Chaucer in Error." *Speculum,* 1 (1926), 222–225.

999 Riedel, Frederick C. "The Meaning of Chaucer's *House of Fame." JEGP,* 27 (1928), 441–469.

1000 Robinson, F. N. "Chaucer and Dante." *Jour. of Compar. Lit.,* 1 (1903), 292–297. [Review article on 948.]

1001 Royster, James F. "Chaucer's 'Colle Tregetour'." *SP,* 23 (1926), 380–384.

1002 Ruggiers, Paul G. "The Unity of Chaucer's *House of Fame." SP,* 50 (1953), 16–29, Reprinted in 593 and 628.

1003 Ruggiers, Paul G. "Words into Images in Chaucer's *Hous of Fame:* A Third Suggestion." *MLN,* 69 (1954), 34–37.

1004 Samuels, M. L. "Middle English 'wery forwandred': A Rejoinder." *ES,* 36 (1955), 310–313.

1005 Sanders, Barry. "Love's Crack-up: *The House of Fame." PLL,* 3, Summer Suppl. (1967), 3–13.

1006 Schoeck, R. J. "Legal Reading of Chaucer's *Hous of Fame." UTQ,* 23 (1954), 185–192. Cf. *N&Q,* 200 (1955), 140 (Schoeck) and 271–272 (H. S. London).

1007 Shackford, Martha H. "The Date of Chaucer's *Hous of Fame." MLN,* 31 (1916), 507–508.

1008 Shook, Laurence K. "The House of Fame." 296, pp. 341–354.

1009 Simmons, J. L. "The Place of the Poet in Chaucer's *House of Fame." MLQ,* 27 (1966), 125–135.

1010 Smith, Roland M. "Chaucer's 'Castle in Spain' (HF 1117)." *MLN,* 60 (1945), 39–42.

1011 Smith, Roland M. " 'Mynstralcie and noyse' in the *House of Fame." MLN,* 65 (1950), 521–530.

1012 Smyser, H. M. "Chaucer's Two-Mile Pilgrimage." *MLN,* 56 (1941), 205–207.

1013 Solari, Marta S. "Sources of the Invocations in the 'House of Fame'." *Revista de literaturas modernas* (Mendoza, Argentina), 1 (1956), 217–225.

1014 Steadman, John M. "Chaucer's 'Desert of Libye,' Venus, and Jove (The House of Fame, 486–487)." *MLN,* 76 (1961), 196–201.

1015 Steadman, John M. "Chaucer's Eagle: A Contemplative Symbol." *PMLA,* 75 (1960), 153–159.

1016 Steadman, John M. " 'Goddes Boteler' and 'Stellifye' (*The House of Fame,* 581, 592)." *Archiv,* 197 (1960), 16–18.

1017 Stillwell, Gardiner. "Chaucer's 'O Sentence' in the *Hous of Fame." ES,* 37 (1956), 149–157.

1018 SYPHERD, W. O. "The Completeness of Chaucer's *Hous of Fame.*" *MLN,* 30 (1915), 65–68.

1019 SYPHERD, W. O. *Studies in Chaucer's Hous of Fame.* (Chaucer Soc., 2nd Ser., No. 39). London, 1907.

1020 TATLOCK, John S. P. "Chaucer's 'Eleanor'." *MLN,* 36 (1921), 95–97.

1021 TEAGER, Florence E. "Chaucer's Eagle and the Rhetorical Colors." *PMLA,* 47 (1932), 410–418.

1022 TISDALE, Charles P. R. "*The House of Fame:* Virgilian Reason and Boethian Wisdom." *CL,* 25 (1973), 247–261.

1023 TRIPP, Raymond P., Jr. "Chaucer's Psychologizing of Virgil's Dido." *Bull. Rocky Mountain Mod. Lang. Assoc.,* 24 (1970), 51–59.

1024 TUVE, Rosemund. "Guillaume's Pilgrim and the *Hous of Fame.*" *MLN,* 45 (1930), 518–522.

1025 WATTS, Ann C. " 'Amor gloriae' in Chaucer's *House of Fame.*" *JMRS,* 3 (1973), 87–113.

1026 WHITING, B. J. "*The Hous of Fame* and Renaud de Beaujeu's *Li Biaus Desconeüs.*" *MP,* 31 (1933–34), 196–198.

1027 WILKINS, Ernest H. "Descriptions of Pagan Divinities from Petrarch to Chaucer." *Speculum,* 32 (1957), 511–522.

1028 WILLIAMS, George G. "*The Hous of Fame* and the House of the Musicians." *MLN,* 72 (1957), 6–9.

1029 WILLIAMS, Jerry T. "Words into Images in Chaucer's *Hous of Fame.*" *MLN,* 62 (1947), 488–490. Cf. *ibid.,* 64 (1949), 73–76 (J. Ziegler).

1030 WILSON, William S. "The Eagle's Speech in Chaucer's *House of Fame.*" *QJS,* 50 (1964), 153–158.

1031 WILSON, William S. "Exegetical Grammar in the *House of Fame,*" *ELN,* 1 (1964), 244–248.

1032 WILSON, William S. "Scholastic Logic in Chaucer's *House of Fame.*" *ChauR,* 1 (1966), 181–184.

1033 ZUCKER, David H. "The Detached and Judging Narrator in Chaucer's *House of Fame,*" *Thoth,* 8 (1967), 3–22.

The Parlement of Foules

Edition

1034 *The Parlement of Foules,* ed. D. S. Brewer. London: Nelson, 1960 (*Nelson's Medieval and Renais. Library*); 2nd ed., Manchester Univ. Press, 1972.

Discussions

1035 BAKER, Donald C. "The Poet of Love and the *Parlement of Foules.*" *UMSE,* 2 (1961), 79–110.

1036 BAKER, Donald C. "The Parliament of Fowls." 296, pp. 355–369.

1037 BENNETT, J. A. W. *The Parlement of Foules: An Interpretation.* Oxford: Clarendon Press, 1957.

1038 BETHURUM, Dorothy. "The Center of the *Parlement of Foules."* *Essays in Honor of Walter Clyde Curry,* pp. 39–50. Nashville: Vanderbilt Univ. Press, 1954.

1039 BRADDY, Haldeen. "Chaucer's Comic Valentine." *MLN,* 68 (1953), 232–234.

1040 BRADDY, Haldeen. "The Historical Background of the *Parlement of Foules."* *RES,* 11 (1935), 204–209. Reprinted in 258.

1041 BRADDY, Haldeen. "The Parlement of Foules: A New Proposal." *PMLA,* 46 (1931), 1007–1019. Reprinted in 258.

1042 BRADDY, Haldeen. *The* Parlement of Foules *in Its Relation to Contemporary Events.* See 621, expanded ed. New York: Octagon, 1969.

1043 BREWER, D. S. "The Genre of the *Parlement of Foules."* *MLR,* 53 (1958), 321–326.

1044 BRONSON, Bertrand H. *In Appreciation of Chaucer's Parlement of Foules.* Univ. of Calif. Pub. in English, 3, No. 5, pp. 193–223. Berkeley, 1935.

1045 BRONSON, Bertrand H. "The *Parlement of Foules* Revisited." *ELH,* 15 (1948), 247–260.

1046 CASIERI, Sabino. "Osservasioni su *The Parlement of Foules."* *Studi e ricerche di letteratura inglese e americana,* ed. Agostino Lombardo, pp. 7–19. Milan, 1967.

1047 CAWLEY, A. C. "Chaucer's Valentine: The *Parlement of Foules."* 264, pp. 125–139.

1048 CHAMBERLAIN, David. "The Music of the Spheres and *The Parlement of Foules."* *ChauR,* 5 (1970), 32–56.

1049 DAMON, Phillip W. "The *Parlement of Foules* and the *Pavo."* *MLN,* 67 (1952), 520–524.

1050 DELIGIORGIS, S. See 372.

1051 DEVEREUX, E. J. "John Rastell's Text of *The Parliament of Fowls."* *Moreana,* 27–28 (1970), 115–120.

1052 DOUGLAS, Theodore W. "What Is the *Parlement of Foules?"* *MLN,* 43 (1928), 378–384.

1053 ECONOMOU, George D. See 176, chap. 5.

1054 ELDREDGE, Laurence. "Poetry and Philosophy in *The Parlement of Foules."* *RUO,* 40 (1970), 441–459.

1056 EMERSON, O. F. "The Suitors in Chaucer's *Parlement of Foules."* *MP,* 8 (1910), 45–62. Reprinted in 395.

1057 EMERSON, O. F. "The Suitors in the *Parlement of Foules* Again." *MLN,* 26 (1911), 109–111. Reprinted in 395.

1058 EMERSON, O. F. "What is the Parlement of Foules?" *JEGP,* 13 (1914), 566–582. Reprinted in 395.

1059 EMERSON, O. F. See 396.

1060 EMSLIE, Macdonald. "Codes of Love and Class Distinctions." *EIC,* 5 (1955), 1–17. Cf. *ibid.,* 405–407 (C. Clark), 407–413 (D. Brewer), 413–418 (Emslie); 6 (1956), 248 (Brewer).

1061 EVERETT, Dorothy. "Chaucer's Love Visions, with Particular Reference to the *Parlement of Foules.*" *Essays on Middle English Literature* [178], pp. 97–114.

1062 FARNHAM, Willard E. "The Contending Lovers." *PMLA,* 35 (1920), 247–323.

1063 FARNHAM, Willard E. "The Fowls in Chaucer's Parlement." *Univ. of Wisconsin Stud. in Lang. and Lit.,* 2 (1919), 340–366.

1064 FARNHAM, Willard E. "The Sources of Chaucer's *Parlement of Foules.*" *PMLA,* 32 (1917), 492–518.

1064a FRANÇON, Marcel. See 3171.

1065 FRANK, Robert W., Jr. "Structure and Meaning in the *Parlement of Foules.*" *PMLA,* 71 (1956), 530–539.

1066 FRIEDMAN, William F. and Elizabeth S. "Acrostics, Anagrams, and Chaucer," *PQ,* 38 (1959), 1–20.

1067 GARBÁTY, Thomas J. "Andreas Capellanus and the Gate in the *Parlement of Foules.*" *Romance Notes,* 9 (1968), 325–330.

1068 GIFFIN, Mary. " 'The Pekok with His Aungels Fetheres Bryghte'." See 413, pp. 49–66.

1069 GILBERT, A. J. "Chaucer, Grandson and the 'Turtil Trewe'." *N&Q,* 19 (1972), 165.

1070 GOFFIN, R. C. "Heaven and Earth in the 'Parlement of Foules'." *MLR,* 31 (1936), 493–499.

1071 HUPPÉ, Bernard F., and D. W. ROBERTSON, Jr. See 444.

1072 JONES, H. S. V. "Parliament of Fowls 693f." *MLN,* 27 (1912), 95.

1073 KELLOGG, Alfred L., and Robert C. Cox. See 457.

1074 KOCH, John. See 464, pp. 287–289; 398.

1075 KREISLER, Nicolai von. "Bird Lore and the Valentine's Day Tradition in Chaucer's *Parlement of Foules.*" *ChauR,* 3 (1968), 60–64.

1076 KREISLER, Nicolai von. "The *Locus Amoenus* and Eschatological Lore in the *Parliament of Fowls* 204–10." *PQ,* 50 (1971), 16–22.

1077 LANGE, H., and A. NIPPOLDT. "Die Deklination am 20. Mai 1380 in London." *Quellen und Studien zur Geschichte der Naturwissenschaften und der Medizin,* 5, No. 4 (1936), 38–56.

1078 LANGE, Hugo. "Ein neuer Chaucerfund: Zu John Kochs Richard-Anna-Theorie (Vogelparlament)." *ESt,* 68 (1933–34), 174–187.

1079 LANGE, Hugo. "Die Nordnordwest-Stellung der Venus und der Nordwestwind in Chaucers *Vogelparlament.*" *Anglia,* 64 (1940), 196–204.

1080 LANGE, Hugo. "What is the Parlement of Foules? (Eine Chaucer-notiz)." *Anglia,* 40 (1916), 394–396.

1081 LANGE, Hugo. "Zu Chaucers *Vogelparlament.*" *Anglia,* 60 (1936), 397–400.

1082 LANGE, Hugo. See 479.

1083 LANGHANS, Viktor. "Altes und neues zu Chaucers Parlement of Foules." *Anglia,* 54 (1930), 25–66.

1084 LANGHANS, Viktor. "Das Parlament der Vögel." 284, pp. 17–70.

1085 LUMIANSKY, Robert M. "Chaucer's *Parlement of Foules:* A Philosophical Interpretation." *RES,* 24 (1948), 81–89.

1086 MALONE, Kemp. "Chaucer's Daughter of Cupid." *MLR,* 45 (1950), 63.

1087 MANLY, John M. "What Is the Parlement of Foules?" *Festschrift für Lorenz Morsbach* (Halle, 1913; *Studien zur engl. Phil.,* 50), pp. 278–290.

1088 MANZALAOUI, Mahmoud. "Ars Longa, Vita Brevis." *EIC,* 12 (1962), 221–224. Cf. *ibid.,* 11 (1961), 255–263 (F. W. Bateson).

1089 McCALL, John P. "The Harmony of Chaucer's *Parliament.*" *ChauR,* 5 (1970), 22–31.

1090 McDONALD, Charles O. "An Interpretation of Chaucer's *Parlement of Foules.*" *Speculum,* 30 (1955), 444–457. Reprinted in 593 and 628.

1091 MOORE, Arthur K. " Somer' and 'Lenten' as Terms for Spring." *N&Q,* 194 (1949), 82–83.

1092 MOORE, Samuel. "A Further Note on the Suitors in the *Parlement of Foules.*" *MLN,* 26 (1911), 8–12.

1093 MORRIS, FRANCIS J. "Platonic Elements in the Parliament of Fowls." *Penna. Council of Teachers of English, Bulletin,* Feb. 1967, no. 14, pp. 28–41.

1094 OWEN, Charles A., Jr. "The Role of the Narrator in the *Parlement of Foules.*" *CE,* 14 (1953), 264–269.

1095 PATRICK, David. "The Satire in Chaucer's *Parliament of Birds.*" *PQ,* 9 (1930), 61–65.

1096 PRATT, Robert A. See 559 and 806.

1097 RAYMO, R. R. "*The Parlement of Foules* 309–15." *MLN,* 71 (1956), 159–160.

1098 REID, Mary E. "The Historical Interpretations of the Parlement of Foules." *Univ. of Wisconsin Stud. In Lang. and Lit.,* 18 (1923), 60–70.

1099 RICKERT, Edith. "A New Interpretation of *The Parlement of Foules.*" *MP,* 18 (1920–21), 1–29.

1100 ROWLAND, Beryl. "Chaucer's 'Throstil Old' and Other Birds." *MS,* 24 (1962), 381–384.

1101 SAMUEL, Irene. "Semiramis in the Middle Ages: the History of a Legend." *M&H,* 2 (1944), 32–44. [*PF* 279–294]

1102 SEATON, Ethel. "*The Parlement of Foules* and Lionel of Clarence." *MÆ,* 25 (1956), 168–174. Cf. *ibid.,* 26 (1957), 107–109 (K. T. Emerson); 109–111 (Seaton). See also 1066.

1103 SELVIN, Rhoda H. "Shades of Love in the *Parlement of Foules.*" *SN,* 37 (1965), 146–160.

1104 SILVERSTEIN, Theodore. "Chaucer's Modest and Homely Poem: The *Parlement.*" *MP,* 56 (1958–59), 270–276. [Review article.]

1105 SLAUGHTER, E. E. " 'Every Vertu at his Reste'." *MLN,* 46 (1931), 448–453.

1106 SMITH, Roland M. See 601.

1107 STILLWELL, Gardiner. "Chaucer's Eagles and Their Choice on February 14." *JEGP,* 53 (1954), 546–561.

1108 STILLWELL, Gardiner. "Unity and Comedy in the *Parlement of Foules.*" *JEGP,* 49 (1950), 470–495.

1109 SUDO, Jun. "A Preliminary Note on the Language of Chaucer's *Parliament of Fowls.*" *Kobe City Univ. Jour.,* 21, No. 6 (1971), 69–84.

1110 UPHAUS, Robert W. "Chaucer's *Parlement of Foules:* Aesthetic Order and Individual Experience." *TSLL,* 10 (1968), 349–358.

1111 WILHELM, James J. "The Narrator and His Narrative in Chaucer's *Parlement.*" *ChauR,* 1 (1967), 201–206.

Boece

1112 CLINE, James M. "Chaucer and Jean de Meun: *De Consolatione Philosophiae.*" *ELH,* 3 (1936), 170–181.

1113 DEDECK-HÉRY, V. L. "Jean de Meun et Chaucer, Traducteurs de la Consolation de Boèce." *PMLA,* 52 (1937), 967–991.

1114 DEDECK-HÉRY, V. L. "Le Boèce de Chaucer et les Manuscrits français de la *Consolatio* de J. de Meun." *PMLA,* 59 (1944), 18–25.

1115 DUNLEAVY, Gareth W. "The Wound and the Comforter: The Consolations of Geoffrey Chaucer." *PLL,* 3, Summer Suppl. (1967), 14–27.

1116 HOLLANDER, John. " 'Moedes or Prolaciouns' in Chaucer's *Boece.*" *MLN,* 71 (1956), 397–399.

1117 KOCH, John. "Chaucers Boethiusübersetzung: Ein Beitrag zur Bestimmung der Chronologie seiner Werke." *Anglia,* 46 (1922), 1–51.

1118 LOWES, John L. "Chaucer's *Boethius* and Jean de Meun." *RR,* 8 (1917), 383–400.

1119 WITCUTT, W. P. "Chaucer's Boëthius." *Amer. Rev.,* 8 (1936), 61–70.

Anelida and Arcite

1120 BUSH, Douglas. "Chaucer's 'Corinne'." *Speculum,* 4 (1929), 106–107.

1121 CHERNISS, Michael D. "Chaucer's *Anelida and Arcite:* Some Conjectures." *ChauR,* 5 (1970), 9–21.

1122 FABIN, Madeline. "On Chaucer's *Anelida and Arcite.*" *MLN,* 34 (1919), 266–272.

1123 GREEN, A Wigfall. "Meter and Rhyme in Chaucer's *Anelida and Arcite.*" *UMSE,* 2 (1961), 55–63.

1124 KOCH, John. "Ein neues Datum für Chaucers *Quene Anelida and Fals Arcite.*" *ESt,* 56 (1922), 28–35.

1125 KOCH, John. See 398.

1126 LANGHANS, Viktor. "Chaucers Anelida and Arcite." *Anglia,* 44 (1920), 226–244.

1127 PRATT, Robert A. See 806.

1128 SHANNON, E. F. "The Source of Chaucer's *Anelida and Arcite.*" *PMLA,* 27 (1912), 461–485.

1129 SULLIVAN, Frank. "Finished Fragments in Chaucer." *Sat. Rev.,* 26 (1943), 27.

1130 TUPPER, Frederick. "Chaucer's Tale of Ireland." *PMLA,* 36 (1921), 186–222.

1131 WIMSATT, James I. "*Anelida and Arcite:* A Narrative of Complaint and Comfort." *ChauR,* 5 (1970), 1–8.

Troilus and Criseyde

Editions

1132 COOK, Daniel, ed. *Troilus and Criseyde.* New York: Doubleday, 1966 (selections). [A524-Anch]

1133 ROOT, Robert K., ed. *The Book of Troilus and Criseyde by Geoffrey Chaucer.* Princeton: Princeton Univ. Press, 1926. [Princeton Paperback, 26]*

1134 WARRINGTON, John, ed. *Troilus and Criseyde.* London: Dent, 1953 (Everyman's Library).

Modernizations

1135 COGHILL, Nevill. *Troilus and Criseyde, trans. into modern English.* [Harmondsworth:] Penguin, 1971.

1136 KRAPP, George P. *Troilus and Criseyde, Englished Anew.* New York: Random House, 1932; Modern Library, 1940. [V 142-Vin]

1137 LUMIANSKY, Robert M. *Geoffrey Chaucer's Troilus and Criseyde, Rendered into Modern English Prose.* Columbia, S. C.: Univ. of So. Carolina Press, 1952.

1138 STANLEY-WRENCH, Margaret, trans. *Troilus and Criseyde.* London: Centaur Press, 1965.

Criticism

1139 ADAMS, John F. "Irony in Troilus' Apostrophe to the Vacant House of Criseyde." *MLQ,* 24 (1863), 61–65.

1140 ADAMSON, Jane. "The Unity of *Troilus and Criseyde.*" *CR,* 14 (1971), 17–37.

1141 APROBERTS, Robert P. "The Central Episode in Chaucer's *Troilus.*" *PMLA,* 77 (1962), 373–385.

1142 APROBERTS, Robert P. "Notes on *Troilus and Criseyde, IV.* 1397–1414." *MLN,* 57 (1942), 92–97.

1143 APROBERTS, Robert P. "Criseyde's Infidelity and the Moral of the *Troilus.*" *Speculum,* 44 (1969), 383–402.

1144 APROBERTS, Robert P. "The Boethian God and the Audience of the *Troilus.*" *JEGP,* 69 (1970), 425–436.

1145 APROBERTS, Robert P. "Love in the *Filostrato.*" *ChauR,* 7 (1972), 1–26.

1146 ARNTZ, Sister M. Luke. " 'That Fol of Whos Folie Men Ryme'." *AN&Q,* 3 (1965), 151–152.

1147 BARNEY, Stephen A. "Troilus Bound." *Speculum,* 47 (1972), 445–458.

1148 BARON, F. Xavier. "Chaucer's Troilus and Self-Renunciation in Love." *PLL,* 10 (1974), 5–14.

1149 BASS, Eben. "The Jewels of *Troilus.*" *CE,* 23 (1961), 145–147.

1150 BAYLEY, John. "Love and the Code: *Troilus and Criseyde.*" *The Character of Love: A Study in the Literature of Personality,* pp. 49–123. London: Constable, 1960, Chap. 2.

1151 BECHTEL, Robert B. "The Problem of Criseide's Character." *Susquehanna Univ. Stud.,* 7 (1963), 109–118.

1152 BERRYMAN, Charles. "The Ironic Design of Fortune in *Troilus and Criseyde.*" *ChauR,* 2 (1967), 1–7.

✓ 1153 BESSENT, Benjamin R. "The Puzzling Chronology of Chaucer's *Troilus.*" *SN,* 41 (1969), 99–111.   *Studia Neophilogica*

1154 BLOOMFIELD, Morton W. "Distance and Predestination in *Troilus and Criseyde.*" *PMLA,* 42 (1957), 14–26. Reprinted in 593 and 160.

1155 BLOOMFIELD, Morton W. "The Eighth Sphere: a Note on Chaucer's *Troilus and Criseyde,* V. 1809." *MLR,* 53 (1958), 408–410.

1156 BLOOMFIELD, Morton W. "Troilus' Paraclausithyron and Its Setting: *Troilus and Criseyde,* V, 519–602." 52, pp. 15–24.

1157 BOLTON, W. F. "Treason in *Troilus.*" *Archiv,* 203 (1967), 255–262.

1158 BONNARD, G. "A Note on Chaucer's *Troilus and Criseyde,* V. 1637." *RES,* 5 (1929), 323–324.

1159 BORTHWICK, Sister M. Charlotte. "Antigone's Song as 'Mirour' in Chaucer's *Troilus and Criseyde.*" *MLQ,* 22 (1961), 227–235.

1160 BOUGHNER, Daniel C. "Elements of Epic Grandeur in the *Troilus.*" *ELH,* 6 (1939), 200–210. Reprinted in 593.

1161 BOWERS, R. H. "The 'Suttell and Dissayvabull' World of Chaucer's *Troilus.*" *N&Q,* 202 (1957), 278–279.

1162 BOYS, Richard C. "An Unusual Meaning of 'make' in Chaucer." *MLN,* 52 (1937), 351–353. [*TC* V. 1788]

1163 BRADDY, Haldeen. "Chaucer's Playful Pandarus." *SFQ,* 34 (1970), 71–81.

✓ 1164 BRENNER, Gerry. "Narrative Structure in Chaucer's *Troilus and Criseyde.*" *AnM,* 6 (1965), 5–18.   *Annuale Mediaevale*

1165 BREWER, Derek S. "The Ages of Troilus, Criseyde and Pandarus." *SELit,* English Number (1972), pp. 3–13.

1166 BREWER, D. S. "Troilus and Criseyde." 161, pp. 195–228.

1167 BROWN, Carleton. "Another Contemporary Allusion in Chaucer's *Troilus.*" *MLN,* 26 (1911), 208–211.

1168 BÜHLER, Curt F. "Notes on the Campsall Manuscript of Chaucer's *Troilus and Criseyde* Now in the Pierpont Morgan Library." *Speculum,* 20 (1945), 457–460.

1169 BURJORJEE, D. M. "The Pilgrimage of Troilus's Sailing Heart in Chaucer's *Troilus and Criseyde.*" *AnM,* 13 (1972), 14–31.

1170 CAMPBELL, Jackson J. "A New *Troilus* Fragment." *PMLA,* 73 (1958), 305–308.

1171 CARPENTER, Nan C. "Chaucer's *Troilus and Criseyde,* III. 624–628." *Explicator,* 30 (1972), item 51.

1172 CARSON, M. Angela. "To Synge a Fool a Masse." *AN&Q,* 6 (1968), 135–136.

1173 CASSIDY, F. G. " 'Don Thyn Hood' in Chaucer's *Troilus.*" *JEGP,* 57 (1958), 739–742.

1174 CLARK, John W. "Dante and the Epilogue of *Troilus.*" *JEGP,* 50 (1951), 1–10.

1175 CONLEE, John W. "The Meaning of Troilus' Ascension to the Eighth Sphere." *ChauR,* 7 (1972), 27–36.

1176 COOK, Albert S. "The Character of Criseyde." *PMLA,* 22 (1907), 531–547.

1177 COOK, Albert S. "Chaucer: *Troilus and Criseyde* 3. 1–38." *Archiv,* 119 (1907), 40–54.

1178 COOK, Robert G. "Chaucer's Pandarus and the Medieval Ideal of Friendship." *JEGP,* 69 (1970), 407–424.

1179 COPE, Jackson I. "Chaucer, Venus, and the 'Seventte Spere'." *MLN,* 67 (1952), 245–246.

1180 CORRIGAN, Matthew. "Chaucer's Failure with Woman: The Inadequacy of Criseyde." *Western Humanities Rev.,* 23 (1969), 107–120.

1181 CORSA, Helen. "Is This a Mannes Herte?" *L&P,* 16 (1866), 184–191.

1182 CORSA Helen S. "Dreams in *Troilus and Criseyde.*" *American Imago,* 27 (1970), 52–65.

1183 COTTON, Michale E. "The Artistic Integrity of Chaucer's *Troilus and Criseyde.*" *ChauR,* 7 (1972), 37–43.

1184 COVELLA, Sister Francis Dolores. "Audience as Determinant of Meaning in the *Troilus.*" *ChauR,* 2 (1968), 235–245.

1185 CRAIG, Hardin. "From Gorgias to Troilus." 48, pp. 97–107.

1186 CURRY, Walter C. "Destiny in Chaucer's *Troilus.*" *PMLA,* 45 (1930), 129–168. Reprinted in 593.

1187 CURRY, Walter C. "Fortuna Maior." *MLN,* 38 (1923), 94–96.

1188 DALY, Saralyn R. "Criseyde's Blasphemous Aube." *N&Q,* 208 (1963), 442–444.

1189 DAVID, Alfred. "The Hero of Troilus." *Speculum,* 37 (1962), 566–581.

1190 DAVIS, Norman. "The *Litera Troili* and English Letters," *RES,* n.s. 16 (1965), 233–244.

1191 DAY Mabel. "Chaucer's *Troilus and Criseyde,* V. 1637." *RES,* 6 (1930), 73.

1192 DENOMY, Alex. J. "The Two Moralities of Chaucer's *Troilus and Criseyde.*" *PTRSC,* 3rd Ser., 44, Section 2 (1950), 35–46. Reprinted in 593.

1193 DESELINCOURT, E. See 376.

1194 D'EVELYN, Charlotte. "Pandarus a Devil?" *PMLA,* 71 (1956), 275–279.

1195 DEVEREAUX, James A. "A Note on *Troilus and Criseyde,* Book III, line 1309." *PQ,* 44 (1965), 550–552.

1196 DE VRIES, F. G. "*Troilus and Criseyde,* Book III, Stanza 251, and Boethius." *ES,* 52 (1971), 502–507.

1197 DIPASQUALE, Pasquale, Jr. " 'Sikernesse' and Fortune in *Troilus and Criseyde.*" *PQ,* 49 (1970), 152–163.

1198 DOBSON, E. J. "Notes on Middle English Texts." *English and Germanic Stud.,* 1 (1947–48), 46–62. [*TC* V. 1807–27]

1199 DONALDSON, E. Talbot. "The Ending of Chaucer's *Troilus.*" *Early English and Norse Studies, presented to Hugh Smith . . . ,* pp. 26–45. London: Methuen, 1963. Reprinted in 273.

1200 DONALDSON, E. Talbot. "Criseide and Her Narrator." 273, pp. 65–83.

1201 DOOB, Penelope B. R. "Chaucer's 'corones tweyne' and the Lapidaries." ChauR, 7 (1972), 85–96.

1202 DRONKE, Peter. "The Conclusion of Troilus and Criseyde." MÆ, 33 (1964), 47–52.

1203 DUNNING, T. P. "God and Man in Troilus and Criseyde." English and Medieval Studies Presented to J. R. R. Tolkien, pp. 164–182, London: Allen and Unwin, 1962.

1204 DURHAM, Lonnie J. "Love and Death in Troilus and Criseyde." ChauR, 3 (1968), 1–11.

1205 EBEL, Julia. "Troilus and Oedipus: The Genealogy of an Image." ES, 55 (1974), 15–21.

1206 EDMUNDS, Paul E. "A Defense of Chaucer's Diomede." Classical Folia, 16 (1962), 110–123.

1207 ELBOW, Peter. "Two Boethian Speeches in Troilus and Criseyde and Chaucerian Irony." Literary Criticism and Historical Understanding: Selected Papers from the English Institute, ed. Phillip Damon, pp. 85–107. New York: Columbia Univ. Press, 1967.

1208 EMERSON, O. F. See 396.

1209 ERZGRÄBER, Willi. "Tragik und Komik in Chaucers Troilus and Criseyde." Festschrift für Walter Hübner, pp. 139–163. Berlin: Schmidt, 1964.

1210 EVANS, L. G. "A Biblical Allusion in Troilus and Criseyde." MLN, 74 (1959), 584–587. Cf. ibid., 76 (1961), 1–4 (Baugh), 4–5 (Donaldson).

1211 EVERETT, Dorothy. "Troilus and Criseyde." Essays on Middle English Literature (178), pp. 115–138.

1212 FARINA, Peter M. See 1595.

1213 FARNHAM, Anthony E. "Chaucerian Irony and the Ending of the Troilus." ChauR, 1 (1967), 207–216.

1214 FOWLER, David C. "An Unusual Meaning of 'win' in Chaucer's Troilus and Criseyde." MLN, 69 (1954), 313–315.

1215 FRANK, Robert W., Jr. "Troilus and Criseyde: The Art of Amplification." 56, pp. 155–171.

1216 FREIWALD, Leah R. "Swych Love of Frendes: Pandarus and Troilus." ChauR, 6 (1971), 120–129.

1217 FRENCH, J. Milton. "A Defense of Troilus." PMLA, 44 (1929), 1246–1251.

1218 FRY, Donald K. "Chaucer's Zanzis and a Possible Source for Troilus and Criseyde, IV, 407–413." ELN, 9 (1971), 81–85.

1219 GALLAGHER, Joseph E. "Theology and Intention in Chaucer's Troilus." ChauR, 7 (1972), 44–66.

1220 GALAWAY, Margaret. "The Troilus Frontispiece." MLR, 44 (1949), 161–177.

1221 GAYLORD, Alan T. "Chaucer's Tender Trap: The Troilus and the 'yonge, fresshe folkes'." EM, 15 (1964), 25–45.

1222 GAYLORD, Alan T. "Gentilesse in Chaucer's Troilus." SP, 61 (1964), 19–34.

1223 GAYLORD,Alan T. "Uncle Pandarus as Lady Philosophy.'. *PMASAL,* 46 (1961), 571–595.

1224 GAYLORD, Alan T. "Friendship in Chaucer's *Troilus."* *ChauR,* 3 (1969), 239–264.

1225 GILL, Sister Ann Barbara. *Paradoxical Patterns in Chaucer's 'Troilus': An Explanation of the Palinode.* Washington, D.C.: Catholic Univ. or Amer. Press, 1960.

1226 GNERRO, Mark L. " 'Ye, Haselwodes Shaken!'—Pandarus and Divination." *N&Q,* 207 (1962), 164–165.

1227 GOFFIN, R. C. " 'Here and howne' in 'Troilus and Criseyde'." *MLR,* 40 (1945), 208–210.

1228 GORDON, Ida L. "The Narrative Function of Irony in Chaucer's *Troilus and Criseyde."* *Medieval Miscellany Presented to Eugène Vinaver,* pp. 146–156. Manchester, 1965.

1229 GORDON, Ida L. *The Double Sorrow of Troilus: A Study of Ambiguities in* Troilus and Criseyde. Oxford, Clarendon Press, 1970.

1230 GORDON, Ida L. "Processes of Characterization in Chaucer's *Troilus and Criseyde."* *Stud. in Medieval Lit. and Lang. in Memory of Frederick Whitehead,* ed. W. Rothwell, *et. al.,* pp. 117–131. Manchester: Manchester Univ. Press, 1973.

1231 GORDON, R. K. *The Story of Troilus as told by Benoît de Sainte-Maure, Giovanni Boccaccio, Geoffrey Chaucer and Robert Henryson.* London: Dent, 1934, 1964. [Prose translations of Benoit and Boccaccio.]

1232 GRAYDON, Joseph S. "Defense of Criseyde." *PMLA,* 44 (1929), 141–177. Cf. *SP,* 26 (1929), 470–481 (J. M. Beatty) and 1217.

1233 GREEN, Marion N. "Christian Implications of Knighthood and Courtly Love in Chaucer's *Troilus."* *Delaware Notes,* 30 (1957), 47–92.

1234 GREENFIELD, Stanley B. "The Role of Calkas in *Troilus and Criseyde."* *MÆ,* 36 (1967), 141–151.

1235 GRIFFIN, N. E. "Chaucer's Portrait of Criseyde." *JEGP,* 20 (1921), 39–46.

1236 GROSS, Laila. "The Two Wooings of Criseyde." *NM,* 74 (1973), 113–125.

1237 GUNN, Alan M. F. "The Polylithic Romance: With Pages of Illustrations." *Stud. in Medieval, Renaissance, American Lit.: A Festschrift,* ed. Betsy F. Colquitt, pp. 1–18. Fort Worth: Texas Christian Univ. Press, 1971.

1238 HAGOPIAN, John V. "Chaucer as Psychologist in *Troilus and Criseyde."* *L&P,* 5 (1955), 5–11.

1239 HAGOPIAN, John V. "Chaucer's *Troilus and Criseyde,* III. 1744–71." *Explicator,* 10 (1951), item 2.

1240 HAMILTON, George L. *The Indebtedness of Chaucer's Troilus and Criseyde to Guido delle Colonne's Historia Trojana.* (*Columbia Univ. Stud. In Romance Phil. and Lit.,* 15). New York, 1903.

1241 HAMILTON, George L. *"Troilus and Criseyde V, Argumentum in Thebaidem." MLN,* 23 (1908), 127.

1242 HANSON, Thomas B. "Criseyde's Brows Once Again." *N&Q,* 216 (1971), 285–286.

1243 HARADS, Haruo. "A Note on Chaucer's *Troilus and Criseyde,* Bk. IV, 11. 414–415." *HSELL,* 10, i (1963), 90–96.

1244 HARVEY, Patricia A. "ME 'Point' (*Troilus and Criseyde*, III. 695)." *N&Q*, 213 (1968), 243–244.

1245 HASELMAYER, Louis A., Jr. "The Portraits in *Troilus and Criseyde.*" *PQ*, 17 (1933), 220–223.

1246 HASKELL, Ann S. "The *Doppelgängers* in Chaucer's *Troilus.*" *NM*, 72 (1971), 723–734.

1247 HATCHER, Elizabeth R. "Chaucer and the Psychology of Fear: Troilus in Book V." *ELH*, 40 (1973), 307–324.

1248 HEIDTMANN, Peter. "Sex and Salvation in *Troilus and Cryseide.*" *ChauR.*, 2 (1968), 246–253.

1249 HELTERMAN, Jeffrey. "The Masks of Love in *Troilus and Criseyde.*" *CL*, 26 (1974), 14–31.

1250 HILL, Archibald A. "Diomede: The Traditional Development of a Character." In *Essays and Stud. in English and Compar. Lit.,* (*Univ. of Michigan Pub., Lang. and Lit.,* VIII), pp. 1–25. Ann Arbor, 1932.

1251 HILL, Archibald A. "Ilium, the Palace of Priam." *MP*, 30 (1932–33), 94–96.

1252 HOWARD, Donald R. "Courtly Love and the Lust of the Flesh: *Troilus and Criseyde.*" *The Three Temptations: Medieval Man in Search of the World,* pp. 77–160. Princeton: Princeton Univ. Press, 1966.

1253 HOWARD, Donald R. "Literature and Sexuality: Book III of Chaucer's *Troilus.*" *Massachusetts Rev.,* 8 (1967), 443–456.

1254 HOWARD, Donald R. "Experience, Language, and Consciousness: *Troilus and Criseyde,* II, 596–931." 56, pp. 173–192.

1255 HUBER, John. "Troilus' Predestination Soliloquy: Chaucer's Changes from Boethius." *NM*, 66 (1965), 120–125.

1256 HUSSEY, S. S. "The Difficult Fifth Book of *Troilus and Criseyde.*" *MLR*, 67 (1972), 721–729.

1257 HUTSON, Arthur E. "Troilus' Confession." *MLN*, 69 (1954), 468–470.

1258 ISAACS, Neil D. "On Six and Seven (*Troilus* IV, 622)." *AN&Q*, 5 (1967), 85–86.

1259 ISAACS, Neil D. "Further Testimony in the Matter of *Troilus.*" *Stud. in the Literary Imagination* (Georgia State Coll.), 4, ii (1971), 11–27.

1260 JELLIFFE, Robert A. *Troilus and Criseyde: Studies in Interpretation,* Tokyo: Hokuseido Press, 1956.

1261 JOHNSTON, Everett C. "The Pronoun of Address in Chaucer's *Troilus.*" *LangQ*, 1, i (1962), 17–20.

1262 JORDAN, Robert M. "The Narrator in Chaucer's *Troilus.*" *ELH*, 25 (1958), 237–257.

1263 JOSEPH, Bertram. "Troilus and Criseyde—'A Most Admirable and Inimitable Epicke Poeme'." *E&S*, 7 (1954), 42–61.

1264 KASKE, Robert E. "The Aube in Chaucer's *Troilus.*" In 593, pp. 167–179.

1265 KÄSMANN, Hans. " 'I wolde excuse hire yit for routhe': Chaucers Einstellung zu Criseyde." 54, pp. 97–122.

1266 KEAN, P. M. "Chaucer's Dealings with a Stanza of *Il Filostrato* and the Epilogue of *Troilus and Criseyde.*" *MÆ*, 33 (1964), 36–46.

1267 KELLOGG, Alfred L. "On the Tradition of Troilus's Vision of the Little Earth." *MS,* 22 (1960), 204–213. Reprinted in 456.

1268 KELLOGG, Alfred L., and Robert C. Cox. See 458.

1269 KELLY, Edward H. "Myth as Paradigm in *Troilus and Criseyde.*" *PLL,* 3, Summer Suppl. (1967), 28–30.

1270 KELLY, Henry A. "Clandestine Marriage and Chaucer's 'Troilus'." *Viator,* 4 (1973), 435–457.

1271 KIRBY, Thomas A. "As Good Chepe." *MLN,* 48 (1933), 527–528. [*TC* III. 641]

1272 KIRBY, Thomas A. *Chaucer's Troilus: A Study of Courtly Love.* (*Louisiana State Univ. Stud.,* No. 39). University, La., 1940. Reprinted Gloucester, Mass.: Peter Smith, 1959.

1273 KIRBY, Thomas A. "A Note on 'Troilus', II. 1298." *MLR,* 29 (1934), 67–68. Cf. *ibid.,* 42 (1947), 358–359 (E. G. Mason).

1274 KITTREDGE, George L. "Antigone's Song of Love." *MLN,* 25 (1910), 158.

1275 KITTREDGE, George L. "Chaucer's *Troilus* and Guillaume de Machaut." *MLN,* 30 (1915), 69.

1276 KITTREDGE, George L. *The Date of Chaucer's Troilus and Other Matters.* (*Chaucer Soc.,* 2nd Ser., No. 42). London, 1909.

1277 KLEINSTÜCK, Johannes. "Chaucers *Troilus* und die höfische Liebe." *Archiv,* 193 (1956), 1–14.

1278 KORETSKY, Allen C. "Chaucer's Use of the Apostrophe in *Troilus and Criseyde.*" *ChauR,* 4 (1970), 242–266.

1279 KORNBLUTH, Alice F. "Another Chaucer Pun." *N&Q,* 204 (1959), 243.

1280 KOSSICK, S. G. "Troilus and Criseyde: The Aubades." *Unisa English Studies,* 9 (1971), 11–13.

1281 KREUZER, James R. "The Zanzis Quotation in Chaucer's *Troilus and Criseyde,* IV, 415." *N&Q,* 202 (1957), 237.

1282 LACKEY, Allen D. "Chaucer's *Troilus and Criseyde,* IV, 295–301." *Explicator,* 32 (1973), item 5.

1283 LANGHANS, Viktor. "Roman der Rose–Troilus." 284, pp. 223–228.

1284 LANHAM, Richard A. "Opaque Style and Its Uses in *Troilus and Criseide.*" *Stud. in Medieval Culture* (Western Michigan Univ.), 3 (1970), 169–176.

1285 LARSEN, Swen A. "The Boat of Chaucer's 'Connyng': *Troilus and Criseyde,* II. 3–4." *N&Q,* 194 (1949), 332.

1286 LEWIS, C. S. "Chaucer." *The Allegory of Love.* Chap. 4. Oxford: Clarendon Press, 1936; Galaxy Books, 1958, [GB 17]

1287 LEWIS, C. S. "What Chaucer Really Did to *Il Filostrato.*" *E&S,* 17 (1932), 56–75.

1288 LOCKHART, Adrienne. "Semantic, Moral, and Aesthetic Degeneration in *Troilus and Criseyde.*" *ChauR,* 8 (1973), 100–118.

1289 LONGO, Joseph A. "The Double Time Scheme in Book II of Chaucer's *Troilus and Criseyde.*" *MLQ,* 22 (1961), 37–40.

1290 LOWES, John L. "The Date of Chaucer's *Troilus and Criseyde.*" *PMLA,* 23 (1908), 285–306.

1291 LUMANSKY, Robert M. "Calchas in the Early Versions of the Troilus Story." *TSE,* 4 (1954), 5–20.

1292 LUMIANSKY, Robert M. "The Function of the Proverbial Monitory Elements in Chaucer's *Troilus and Criseyde.*" *TSE,* 2 (1950), 5–48.

1293 LUMIANSKY, Robert M. "The Story of Troilus and Briseida according to Benoit and Guido." *Speculum,* 29 (1954), 727–733.

1294 MACEY, Samuel L. "Dramatic Elements in Chaucer's *Troilus.*" *TSLL,* 12 (1970), 307–323.

1295 MAGOUN, F. P., Jr. "Chaucer's Summary of Statius' *Thebaid* II–XII." *Traditio,* 11 (1955), 409–420.

1296 MAGOUN, F. P., Jr. "Hymselven like a pilgrym to desgise': *Troilus,* V. 1577." *MLN,* 59 (1941), 176–178.

1297 MAGUIRE, John. "The Clandestine Marriage of Troilus and Criseyde." *ChauR,* 8 (1974), 262–278.

1298 MALARKEY, Stoddard. "The 'Corones Tweyne': An Interpretation." *Speculum,* 38 (1963), 473–478.

1299 MANZALAOUI, M. "Roger Bacon's 'in convexitate' and Chaucer's 'in convers' (Troilus and Criseyde, V. 1810)." *N&Q,* 209 (1964), 165–166.

1300 MARKLAND, Murray F. "Pilgrims Errant: The Doubleness of *Troilus and Criseyde.*" *Research Stud., Washington State Univ.* 33 (1965), 64–77.

1301 MARKLAND, Murray F. "*Troilus and Criseyde:* The Inviolability of the Ending." *MLQ,* 31 (1970), 147–159.

1302 MARTIN, June H. Love's Fools: *Aucassin, Troilus, Calisto, and the Parody of the Courtly Lover.* (Colección Támesis, Serie A: Monografías, 21). London: Támesis, [1972].

1303 MASI, Michael. "Troilus: A Medieval Psychoanalysis." *AnM,* 11 (1970), 81–88.

1304 MASUI, Michi. "The Development of Mood in Chaucer's *Troilus:* An Approach." 55, pp. 245–254.

1305 MAYHEW, A. L. " 'Dulcarnon' in Chaucer." *N&Q,* 11 Ser. I (1910), 505–506.

1306 MAYO, Robert D. "The Trojan Background of the *Troilus.*" *ELH,* 9 (1942), 245–256.

√ 1307 MCCALL, John P. "Five-Book Structure in Chaucer's *Troilus.*" *MLQ,* 23 (1962), 297–308.

1308 MCCALL, John P. "The Trojan Scene in Chaucer's *Troilus.*" *ELH,* 29 (1962), 263–275.

1309 MCCALL, John P., and George RUDISILL, Jr. "The Parliament of 1386 and Chaucer's Trojan Parliament." *JEGP,* 58 (1959), 276–288.

1310 MCCALL, John P. "Troilus and Criseyde." 296, 370–384.

1311 MCCORMICK, W. S. "Another Chaucer Stanza?" 50, pp. 296–300.

1312 MCNALLY, John J. "Chaucer's Topsy-Turvy Dante." *Stud. in Medieval Culture II,* ed. John R. Sommerfeldt, pp. 104–110. Kalamazoo, Mich.: Western Michigan Univ., 1966.

1313 MEECH, Stanford B. *Design in Chaucer's* Troilus. [Syracuse]: Syracuse Univ. Press, 1959. Reprinted New York: Greenwood, 1970.

1314 MEECH, Sanford B. "Figurative Contrasts in Chaucer's *Troilus and Criseyde.*" In *English Institute Essays 1950,* pp. 57–88. New York: Columbia Univ. Press, 1951.

1315 MEHL, Dieter. "The Audience of Chaucer's *Troilus and Criseyde.*" 53, pp. 173–189.

1316 MIESZKOWSKI, Gretchen. *The Reputation of Criseyde: 1155–1500.* (Connecticut Acad., Trans., 43, pp. 71–153.) Hamden, Conn.: Archon, 1971.

1317 MILLER, Ralph N. "Pandarus and Procne." *Studies in Mediæval Culture,* ed. John R. Sommerfeldt, pp. 65–68. Kalamazoo, Mich.: Western Michigan Univ. Press, 1964.

1318 MIZENER, Arthur. "Character and Action in the Case of Criseyde." *PMLA,* 54 (1939), 65–81. Reprinted in 628.

1319 MOGAN, Joseph J., Jr. "Further Aspects of Mutability in Chaucer's *Troilus.*" *Papers on Engl. Lang. and Lit.* (Southern Illinois Univ.) 1 (1965), 72–77.

1320 MOORMAN, Charles. " 'Once More unto the Breach': The Meaning of *Troilus and Criseyde.*" *Stud. in the Literary Imagination* (Georgia State Coll.), 4, ii (1971), 61–71.

1321 MUDRICK, Marvin. "Chaucer's Nightingales." *Hudson Rev.,* 10 (1957), 88–95.

1322 MUSCATINE, Charles. "The Feigned Illness in Chaucer's *Troilus and Criseyde.*" *MLN,* 63 (1948), 372–377.

1323 MUSTANOJA, Tauno F. "*Troilus and Criseyde,* IV, 607: 'Of Fered'." *NM,* 56 (1955), 174–177.

1324 NAGARAJAN, S. "The Conclusion to Chaucer's *Troilus and Criseyde.*" *EIC,* 13 (1963), 1–8.

1325 NEFF, Sherman B. "Chaucer's Cressida, "lufsom lady dere'." *Univ. of Colorado Stud., Ser. B: Studies in the Humanities,* 2, No. 4 (1945), 45–51 (Reynolds Festschrift).

1326 NEFF, Sherman B. "Chaucer's Pandarus." *Western Humanities Rev,* 4 (1950), 343–348.

1327 O'CONNOR, John J. "The Astronomical Dating of Chaucer's *Troilus.*" *JEGP,* 55 (1956), 556–562.

1328 OWEN, Charles A., Jr. "Chaucer's Method of Composition." *MLN,* 72 (1957), 164–165.

1329 OWEN, Charles A., Jr. "Chaucer's *Troilus and Criseyde,* II. 925–31." *Explicator,* 9 (1951), item 26.

1330 OWEN, Charles A., Jr. "The Significance of Chaucer's Revisions of *Troilus and Criseyde.*" *MP,* 55 (1957), 1–5. Reprinted in 593.

1331 OWEN, Charles A., Jr. "Significance of a Day in *Troilus and Criseyde.*" *MS,* 22 (1960), 366–370.

1332 OWEN, Charles A., Jr. "Mimetic Form in the Central Love Scene of *Troilus and Criseyde.*" *MP,* 67 (1969), 125–132.

1333 OWEN, Charles A., Jr. "Minor Changes in Chaucer's *Troilus and Criseyde.*" 53, pp. 303–319.

1334 PATCH, Howard. R. "Troilus on Determinism." *Speculum,* 6 (1931), 225–243. Reprinted in 593.

1335 PATCH, Howard R. "Troilus on Predestination." *JEGP*, 17 (1918), 399–422. Reprinted in 628.

1336 PATCH, Howard R. "Two Notes on Chaucer's *Troilus.*" *MLN*, 70 (1955), 8–12.

1337 PECK, Russell A. "Numerology and Chaucer's *Troilus and Criseyde.*" *Mosaic*, 5, iv (1972), 1–29.

1338 PEED, M. R. "*Troilus and Criseyde:* The Narrator and the 'Olde Bokes'." *AN&Q*, 12 (1924), 143–146.

1339 PRATT, Robert A. "Chaucer and *Le Roman de Troyle et de Criseida.*" *SP*, 53 (1956), 509–539.

1340 PRATT, Robert A. "Chaucer's 'Natal Jove' and 'Seint Jerome . . . agayn Jovinian'." *JEGP*, 61 (1962), 244–248.

1341 PRATT, Robert A. "A Geographical Problem in *Troilus and Criseyde.*" *MLN*, 61 (1946), 541–543.

1342 PROKOSCH, Frederic. "Geoffrey Chaucer." In *The English Novelists, A Survey of the Novel by Twenty Contemporary Novelists*, ed. Derek Verschoyle, pp. 3–15. London: Chatto & Windus, 1936.

1343 PROVOST, William. *The Structure of Chaucer's Troilus and Criseyde.* Copenhagen, 1974 (Anglistica, XX).

1344 RE, Arundell del. *The Secret of the Renaissance and other Essays and Studies.* Tokyo, 1930.

1345 REED, W. A. "On Chaucer's *Troilus and Criseyde* I, 228." *JEGP*, 20 (1921), 397–398.

1346 REISS, Edmund. "Troilus and the Failure of Understanding." *MLQ*, 29 (1968), 131–144.

1347 RENOIR, Alain. "Another Minor Analogue to Chaucer's Pandarus." *N&Q*, 203 (1958), 421–422.

1348 RENOIR, Alain. "Criseyde's Two Half Lovers." *Orbis Litterarum*, 16 (1961), 239–255.

1349 RENOIR, Alain. "Thebes, Troy, Criseyde and Pandarus: an Instance of Chaucerian Irony." *SN*, 32 (1960), 14–17.

1350 ROBBIE, May G. "Three-Faced Pandarus." *California English Jour.*, 3, No. 1 (1967), 47–54.

1351 ROBERTSON, D. W., Jr. "Chaucerian Tragedy." *ELH*, 19 (1952), 1–37. Reprinted in 593.

1352 ROLLINS, Hyder E. "The Troilus-Cressida Story from Chaucer to Shakespeare." *PMLA*, 32 (1917), 383–429.

1353 ROOT, Robert K. *The Manuscripts of Chaucer's Troilus, with Collotype Facsimiles of the Various Handwritings.* (Chaucer Soc., 98.) London: 1914.

1354 ROOT, Robert K. *The Textual Tradition of Chaucer's Troilus.* (Chaucer Soc., 99.) London: 1916.

1355 ROOT, Robert K., and H. N. RUSSELL. "A Planetary Date for Chaucer's *Troilus.*" *PMLA*, 39 (1924), 48–63.*

1356 ROSS, Thomas W. "*Troilus and Criseyde*, II. 582–587: A Note." *ChauR*, 5 (1970), 137–139.

1357 Rossetti, W. M. *A Detailed Comparison of the Troylus and Cryseyde with Boccaccio's Filostrato.* 2 vols. (Chaucer Soc., 44, 45.) London, 1873–83.

1358 Rowland, Beryl. "Pandarus and the Fate of Tantalus." *Orbis Litterarum,* 24 (1969), 3–15.

1359 Russell, Nicholas. "Characters and Crowds in Chaucer's *Troilus.*" *N&Q,* 211 (1966), 50–52.

1360 Rutherford, Charles S. "Pandarus as Lover: 'A Joly Wo' or 'Loves Shotes Keene'?" *AnM,* 13 (1972), 5–13.

1361 Saintonge, Constance. "In Defense of Criseyde." *MLQ,* 15 (1954), 312–320.

1362 Salter, Elizabeth. "*Troilus and Criseyde:* a Reconsideration." *Patterns of Love and Courtesy: Essays in Memory of C. S. Lewis,* ed. John Lawlor, pp. 86–106. London: Arnold, 1966.

1363 Sams, Henry W. "The Dual Time-Scheme in Chaucer's *Troilus.*" *MLN,* 56 (1941), 94–100. Reprinted in 593.

1364 Schaar, Claes. "Troilus' Elegy and Criseyde's." *SN* 29 (1952), 185–191.

1365 Scott, Forrest S. "The Seventh Sphere: A Note on *Troilus and Criseyde.*" *MLR,* 51 (1956), 2–5.

1366 Shanley, James L. "The *Troilus* and Christian Love." *ELH,* 6 (1939), 271–281. Reprinted in 593 and 628.

1367 Sharrock, Roger. "Second Thoughts: C. S. Lewis on Chaucer's *Troilus.*" *EIC,* 8 (1955), 123–137. Reprinted in 264.

1368 Shepherd, G. T. "*Troilus and Criseyde.*" 339, pp. 65–87. Reprinted in 211.

1369 Shimose, Michiro. "On the Rivalry between the Inflectional and the Periphrastic Subjunctive in Chaucer's *Troilus and Criseyde.*" *Maekawa Shunichi Kyoju Kanreki Kinenronbunshu* [Maekawa Festschrift], pp. 303–316. Tokyo: Eihosha, 1968.

1370 Sims, David. "An Essay at the Logic of *Troilus and Criseyde.*" *Cambridge Quar.,* 4 (1969), 125–149.

1371 Skeat, W. W. See 43.

1372 Slaughter, Eugene E. "Chaucer's Pandarus: Virtuous Uncle and Friend." *JEGP,* 48 (1949), 186–195.

1373 Slaughter, Eugene E. "Love and Grace in Chaucer's *Troilus.*" *Essays in Honor of Walter Clyde Curry,* pp. 61–76. Nashville: Vanderbilt Univ. Press, 1955.

1374 Smith, Fred M. "Chaucer's Prioress and Criseyde." *WVUPP,* 6 (1949), 1–11.

1375 Smithers, G. V. "Ten Cruces in Middle English Texts." *English and Germanic Stud.,* 3 (1949–50), 65–81. [*TC* IV. 207–10]

1376 Smyser, H. M. "The Domestic Background of *Troilus and Criseyde.*" *Speculum,* 31 (1956), 297–315.

1377 Somer, George J. "The Attitudes of the Narrator in Chaucer's *Troilus and Criseyde.*" *New York-Pa. MLA Newsl.,* 1, ii (1968), 1–5.

1378 Spargo, John W. "Chaucer's 'Kankedort'." *MLN,* 64 (1949), 264–266.

1379 Spearing, A. C. "Chaucer as Novelist." *Criticism and Medieval Poetry,* Chap. 5 (pp. 96–117). London: Edward Arnold, 1964; 2nd ed., 1972.

1380 Spitzer, Leo. "*Kanke(r)dort,* 'A State of Suspense, A Difficult Position'." *MLN,* 64 (1949), 502–504.

1381 STANLEY, E. G. "Stanza and Ictus: Chaucer's Emphasis in 'Troilus and Criseyde'." 54, pp. 123–148.

1382 STEADMAN, John M. "The Age of Troilus." *MLN*, 72 (1957), 89–90.

1383 STEADMAN, John M. *Disembodied Laughter: Troilus and the Apotheosis Tradition: A Reexamination of Narrative and Thematic Contexts.* Berkeley: Univ. of Calif. Press, 1972.

1384 STRAUSS, Jennifer. "Teaching *Troilus and Criseyde.*" *Southern Rev.* (Univ. of Adelaide), 5 (172), 13–20.

1385 STROUD, Theodore A. "Boethius' Influence on Chaucer's *Troilus,*" *MP*, 49 (1951–52), 1–9. Reprinted in 593.

1386 STURTEVANT, Peter A. "Chaucer's *Toilus and Criseyde*, III, 890." *Explicator,* 28 (1969), item 5.

1387 TAKANO, Hidekuni. "The Audience of *Troilus and Criseyde.*" *Bull. Faculty of Humanities, Seikei Univ.*, 8 (1972), 1–9.

1388 TATLOCK, John S. P. "Dante and Guinizelli in Chaucer's *Troilus.*" *MLN*, 35 (1920), 443.

1389 TATLOCK, John S. P. "The Date of the *Troilus*, and Minor Chauceriana." *MLN,* 50 (1935), 277–296.

1390 TATLOCK, John S. P. "The Dates of Chaucer's *Troilus and Criseyde* and *Legend of Good Women.*" *MP*, 1 (1903–04), 317–329.

1391 TATLOCK, John S. P. "The Epilog of Chaucer's *Troilus.*" *MP*, 18 (1920–21), 625–659.

1392 TATLOCK, John S. P. "The People in Chaucer's *Troilus.*" *PMLA*, 56 (1941), 85–104. Reprinted in 628.

1393 TATLOCK, John S. P. See 616.

1394 TAYLOR, Willene P. "Supposed Antifeminism in Chaucer's Troilus and Criseyde and Its Retraction in *The Legend of Good Women.*" *Xavier Univ. Stud.*, 9, ii (1970), 1–18.

1395 THOMPSON, Patricia. "The 'Canticus Troili': Chaucer and Petrarch." *CL,* 11 (1959), 313–328.

1396 UTLEY, Francis L. "Scene-division in Chaucer's Troilus and Criseyde." 48, pp. 109–138.

1397 UTLEY, Francis L. "Some Implications of Chaucer's Folktales." *IV. Intern. Congress for Folk-Narrative Research in Athens: Lectures and Reports,* ed. Georgias A. Megas, pp. 588–599. Athens, 1965.

1398 UTLEY, Francis L. "Stylistic Ambivalence in Chaucer, Yeats and Lucretius—The Cresting Wave and Its Undertow." *University Rev.,* 37 (1971), 174–198.

1399 UTLEY, Francis L. "Chaucer's Troilus and St. Paul's Charity." 53, pp. 272–287.

1400 VAN, Thomas A. "Imprisoning and Ensnarement in *Troilus* and *The Knight's Tale.*" *PLL,* 7 (1971), 3–12.

1401 VAN DOREN, Mark. "Troilus and Criseyde." In *The Noble Voice,* pp. 257–282. New York: Holt, 1946.

1402 WAGER, Willis. " 'Fleshly Love' in Chaucer's *Troilus.*" *MLR,* 34 (1939), 62–66.

1403 WALCUTT, Charles C. "The Pronoun of Address in *Troilus and Criseyde.*" *PQ* 14 (1935), 282–287.

1404 WALKER, Ian C. "Chaucer and 'Il Filostrato'." *ES,* 49 (1968), 318–326.

1405 WENZEL, Siegfried. "Chaucer's Troilus of Book IV." *PMLA,* 79 (1964), 542–547

1406 WHITING, B. J. "Troilus and Pilgrims in Wartime," *MLN,* 60 (1945), 47–49.

1407 WHITMAN, Fran H. *"Troilus and Criseyde* and Chaucer's Dedication to Gower." *TSL,* 18 (1973), 1–11

1408 WILKINS, Ernest H. "Cantus Troili." *ELH,* 16 (1949), 167–173.

1409 WILKINS, Ernest H. "Criseide." *MLN,* 24 (1909), 65–67.

1410 WILLIAMS, George. "The *Troilus and Criseyde* Frontispiece Again." *MLR,* 57 (1962), 173–178.

1411 WILLIAMS, George G. "Who Were Troilus, Criseyde, and Pandarus?" *Rice Institute Pamphlet,* 44, No. 1 (1957), 126–146. Incorporated in 307.

1412 WITLIEB, Bernard L. "Chaucer's Elysian Fields (*Troilus* IV, 789f.)." *N&Q,* 214 (1969), 250–251.

1413 WOOD, Chauncey. "On Translating Chaucer's *Troilus and Criseyde,* Book III, lines 12–14." *ELN,* 11 (1973) 9–14.

1414 YOUNG, Karl. "Aspects of the Story of Troilus and Criseyde." *Univ. of Wisconsin Stud. in Lang. and Lit.,* 2 (1919), 367–394.

1415 YOUNG, Karl. "Chaucer's Renunciation of Love in *Troilus."* *MLN,* 40 (1925), 270–276.

1416 YOUNG, Karl. "Chaucer's *Troilus and Criseyde* as Romance." *PMLA,* 53 (1938), 38–63.

1417 YOUNG, Karl. *The Origin and Development of the Story of Troilus and Criseyde.* (Chaucer Soc., 2nd Ser., No. 40.) London, 1908.

The Legend of Good Women

1418 AIKEN, Pauline. "Chaucer's *Legend of Cleopatra* and the *Speculum Historiale.*" *Speculum,* 13 (1938), 232–236.

1419 AMY, E. F. "The Manuscripts of the Legend of Good Women." *JEGP,* 21 (1922), 107–118.

1420 AMY, Ernest F. *The Text of Chaucer's Legend of Good Women.* Princeton Univ. Press, 1918. Reprinted New York: Haskell House, 1965.

1421 ATWOOD, E. Bagby. "Two Alterations of Virgil in Chaucer's *Dido."Speculum,* 13 (1938), 454–457.

1422 BAIRD, Joseph L. "Jason and His 'Sekte'." *AN&Q,* 8 (1970), 151–152.

1423 BAKER, Donald C. "Dreamer and Critic: The Poet in the *Legend of Good Women,"* *UCSLL,* No. 9 (1963), 4–18.

1424 BAUM, Paull F. "Chaucer's 'Glorious Legende'." *MLN,* 60 (1945), 377–381.

1425 BRADLEY, D. R. "Fals Eneas and Sely Dido." *PQ,* 39 (1960), 122–125

1426 BROWN, Carleton. "The Date of Prologue F to the *Legend of Good Women,"* *MLN,* 58 (1943), 274–278.

1427 BRYANT, Joseph A. "Another *appetite for form."* *MLN,* 58 (1943), 194–196.

1428 CALLAN, Norman. "Thyn Owne Book: A Note on Chaucer, Gower and Ovid." *RES,* 22 (1946), 269–281.

1429 CHAPMAN, Coolidge O. "Chaucer and Dante." *TLS,* Aug. 29, 1952, p. 565. [*LGW* 924-7]

1430 CLOGAN, Paul M. "Chaucer's Cybele and the *Liber Imaginum Deorum.*" *PQ,* 43 (1964), 272–274.

1431 CLOGAN, Paul M. "Chaucer's *The Legend of Good Women,* 2422." *Explicator,* 23 (1965), item 61.

1432 CONNELY, Willard. "Imprints of the Heroides of Ovid on Chaucer, The Legend of Good Women." *Classical Weekly,* 18 (1924), 9–13.

1433 CURRY, Walter C. See 2234.

1434 ESTRICH, Robert M. "Chaucer's Maturing Art in the Prologues to the *Legend of Good Women.*" *JEGP,* 36 (1937), 326–337.

1435 ESTRICH, Robert M. "Chaucer's Prologue to the *Legend of Good Women* and Machaut's *Le Judgement dou Roy de Navarre.*" *SP,* 36 (1939), 20–39.

1436 FRANK, Robert W., Jr. "The Legend of the *Legend of Good Women.*" *ChauR,* 1 (1966), 110–133.

1437 FRANK, Robert W., Jr. *Chaucer and The Legend of Good Women.* Cambridge, Mass.: Harvard Univ. Press, 1972.

1438 FRENCH, John C. *The Problem of the Two Prologues to Chaucer's Legend of Good Women.* Baltimore: Furst, 1905.

1439 FURNISS, W. Todd. "Gascoigne and Chaucer's *Pesen.*" *MLN,* 68 (1953), 115–118.

1440 GALWAY, Margaret. "Cancelled Tributes to Chaucer's Sovereign Lady." *N&Q* 193 (1948), 2–3.

1441 GALWAY, Margaret. "Chaucer's Sovereign Lady: A Study of the Prologue to the *Legend* and Related Poems." *MLR,* 33 (1938), 145–199. Cf. *TLS,* Oct. 10, 1942, p. 499.

1442 GALWAY, Margaret. "Joan of Kent and the Order of the Garter." *Univ. of Birmingham Hist. Jour.,* 1 (1947), 13–50.

1443 GALWAY, Margaret. " 'Lylye floures newe'." *TLS,* Sept. 29, 1945, p. 468.

1444 GARDNER, John. "The Two Prologues to the *Legend of Good Women.*" *JEGP,* 67 (1968), 594–611.

1445 GARRETT, Robert M. " 'Cleopatra the Martyr' and Her Sisters." *JEGP,* 22 (1923), 64–74.

1446 GHOSH, P. C. "Cleopatra's Death in Chaucer's *Legende of Gode Women.*" *MLR,* 26 (1931), 332–336.

1447 GODDARD, H. C. *Chaucer's Legend of Good Women.* Urbana, 1909. Reprinted from *JEGP,* 7, No. 4 (1908), 87–129; 8 (1909), 47–111.

1448 GRIFFITH, D. D. "An Interpretation of Chaucer's *Legend of Good Women.*" *Manly Anniversary Studies* (Chicago, 1923), pp. 32–41. Reprinted in 628.

1449 HALL, L. B. See 968.

1450 HAMILTON, Marie P. "Bernard the Monk: Postscript." *MLN,* 62 (1947), 191–192. Cf. *ibid.,* 432 (R. M. Smith).

1451 HAMILTON, Marie. "Chaucer's 'Marcia Catoun'." *MP,* 30 (1933), 361–364.

THE LEGEND OF GOOD WOMEN

1452 HAMMOND, Eleanor P. "Chaucer's 'Book of the Twenty-five Ladies'." *MLN*, 48 (1933), 514–516.

1453 HIBBARD, Laura A. "Chaucer's 'Shapen Was My Sherte'." *PQ* 1 (1922), 222–225. [*LGW* 2629]

1454 HOLTHAUSEN, F. "Die Ballade in Chaucers Legendenprolog." *Archiv*, 147 (1924), 251.

1455 HULBERT, James R. "A Note on the Prologues to the *Legend of Good Women*." *MLN*, 65 (1950), 534–536.

1456 HUPPÉ, Bernard F. "Historical Allegory in the Prologue to the *Legend of Good Women*." *MLR*, 43 (1948), 393–399. Cf. *ibid.*, 399–400 (Galway).

1457 JEFFERSON, Bernard L. "Queen Anne and Queen Alcestis." *JEGP*, 13 (1914), 434–443. Reprinted in 628.

1458 KAUT, Thelma. "Chaucer's Age and the Prologues to the Legend." *MLN*, 49 (1934), 87.

1459 KITTREDGE, George L. "Chaucer's Alceste." *MP*, 6 (1908–09), 435–439.

1460 KITTREDGE, George L. "Chaucer's *Medea* and the Date of the *Legend of Good Women*." *PMLA*, 24 (1909), 343–363.

1461 KNOPP, Sherron. "Chaucer and Jean de Meun as Self-Conscious Narrators: The Prologue to the *Legend of Good Women* and the *Roman de la Rose* 10307–680." *Comitatus*, 4 (1973), 25–39.

1462 KOCH, John. "Das Handscriftenverhältnis in Chaucers 'Legend of Good Women.' " *Anglia*, 43, (1919), 197–244; 44 (1920), 23–71.

1463 KOCH, John. "Nochmals zur Frage des Prologs in Chaucers 'Legend of Good Women.' " *Anglia*, 50 (1926), 62–69, 104–105.

1464 KOONGE, B. G. "Satan the Fowler." *MS*, 21 (1959), 176–184.

1465 LaHOOD, Marvin J. "Chaucer's The Legend of Lucrece." *PQ*, 43 (1964), 274–276.

1466 LANGE, Hugo. "Die Ähnlichkeitstheorie in Chaucers Legendenprolog F." *ESt*, 69 (1934–35), 32–34.

1467 LANGE, Hugo. "Die Legendenprologfrage: Zur Steuer der Wahrheit." *Anglia*, 44 (1920), 72–77.

1468 LANGE, Hugo. "Neue Beiträge zu einer endgültigen Lösung der Legendenprologfrage bei Chaucer." *Anglia*, 49 (1926), 173–180, 267–278.

1469 LANGE, Hugo. "Neue Wege zur Lösung der Legendenprologfrage bei Chaucer," *Anglia*, 52 (1928), 123–135.

1470 LANGE, Hugo. "Nochmals die Lengendprologfrage: Eine Entgegnung an V. Langhans." *Anglia*, 55 (1931), 106–113.

1471 LANGE, Hugo. "Die Paradiesvorstellung in Mandeville's Travels im Lichte mittelalterlicher Dichtung: Zur Lösung der Legendenprologfrage bei Chaucer." *ESt*, 72 (1937–38), 312–314.

1472 LANGE·, Hugo. "Die Sonnen- und die Lilienstelle in Chaucers Legendenprolog: Ein neuer Beweis für die Priorität der F.-Redaktion." *Anglia*, 44 (1920), 373–385.

1473 LANGE, Hugo. "Über die Farben König Richards II von England in Beziehung zur Chaucerdichtung: Eine heraldische Studie, zugleich ein weiterer Beitrag zur Legendenprologfrage." *Anglia*, 42 (1918), 142–144, 352–356.

1474 LANGE, Hugo. "Viktor Langhans und die Unechtheit des F-Prologs in Chaucers Legende von guten Frauen." *Anglia,* 51 (1927), 128–135.

1475 LANGHANS, Viktor. "Hugo Lange und die Lösung der Legendprologfrage bei Chaucer." *Anglia,* 50 (1926), 70–103.

1476 LANGHANS, Viktor. "Hugo Langes Artikel in Anglia, N.F. 32, S. 213." *Anglia,* 44 (1920), 337–345.

1477 LANGHANS, Viktor. "Nochmals Chaucers Legendenprolog und kein Ende?" *Anglia,* 54 (1930), 99–106.

1478 LANGHANS, Viktor. "Der Prolog zu Chaucers Legende von guten Frauen." *Anglia,* 41 (1917), 162–181.

1479 LANGHANS, Viktor. "Zu Chaucers Legendenprolog." *Anglia,* 43 (1919), 69–90.

1480 LANGHANS, Viktor. "Zur F-Fassung von Chaucers Legendenprolog." *ESt,* 56 (1922), 36–58

1481 LOOMIS, Roger S. See 891.

1482 LOSSING, Marian. "The Prologue to the Legend of Good Women and the *Lai de Franchise.*" *SP,* 39 (1942), 15–35.

1483 LOWES, John L. "Chaucer's 'Etik'." *MLN,* 25 (1910), 87–89.

1484 LOWES, John L. "Is Chaucer's *Legend of Good Women* a Travesty?" *JEGP,* 8 (1909), 513–569.

1485 LOWES, John L. "The Prologue to the *Legend of Good Women* as related to the French Marguerite Poems, and the *Filostrato.*" *PMLA,* 19 (1904), 593–683.*

1486 LOWES, John L. "The Prolgue to the *Legend of Good Women* Considered in Its Chronological Relations." *PMLA,* 20 (1905), 749–864.*

1487 LOWES, John L. "The Two Prologues to the *Legend of Good Women:* A New Test." 51, pp. 95–104. Cf. *Anglia Beiblatt,* 25 (1914), 335–337 (J. Koch).

1488 LUMIANSKY, Robert M. "Chaucer and the Idea of Unfaithful Men." *MLN,* 62 (1947), 560–562.

1489 MACDONALD, Charlotte. "Drayton's 'Tydy' and Chaucer's 'Tidif'." *RES,* 21 (1945), 127–133.

1490 MALONE, Kemp. "A Poet at Work: Chaucer Revising His Verses." *Proc. Amer. Philos. Soc.,* 94 (1950), 317–320.

1491 MATHER, Frank J., Jr. "Pesen at Actium—A Chaucer Crux." *JEGP,* 43 (1944), 375–379.

1492 McCALL, John P. "Chaucer and the Pseudo Origen *De Maria Magdalena:* A Preliminary Study." *Speculum,* 46 (1971), 491–509.

1493 McLAUGHLIN, John C. " 'The Honour and the Humble Obeysaunce': Prologue to *The Legend of Good Women,* 1. 135, G-text." *PQ* 38 (1959), 515–516.

1494 MEECH, Sanford B. See 800.

1495 MONTGOMERY, Marion. " 'For the Nones' Once More." *BUSE,* 3 (1957), 177–178. Cf. *ibid.,* 228–230 (C. S. Brown).

1496 MOORE, Samuel. "The Prologue to Chaucer's 'Legend of Good Women' in Relation to Queen Anne and Richard." *MLR,* 7 (1912), 488–493.

1497 MOSES, W. R. "An Appetite for Form." *MLN,* 49 (1934), 226–229. [*LGW* 1582–3]

1498 OVERBECK, Pat T. "Chaucer's Good Woman." *ChauR,* 2 (1967), 75–94.

1499 ROOT, Robert K. "Chaucer's Legend of Medea." *PMLA,* 24 (1909), 124–153.

1500 ROOT, Robert K. "The Date of Chaucer's *Medea.*" *PMLA,* 25 (1910), 228–240.

1501 ROWLAND, Beryl. "Chaucer's Daisy (Prol. *LGW,* F. 120–3, G. 109–11)." *N&Q,* 208 (1963), 210.

1502 RUGGIERS, Paul G. "Tyrants of Lombardy in Dante and Chaucer." *PQ,* 29 (1950), 445–448.

1503 SAMUEL, Irene. See 1101.

1504 SCHOFIELD, William H. "The Sea-Battle in Chaucer's *Legend of Cleopatra.*" 51, 139–152.

1505 SMITH, Roland M. "Action at Actium—An Alliterative Crux in Chaucer (He poureth pesen upon the haches slidere—LGW 648)." *JEGP,* 44 (1945), 56–61.

1506 SMITH, Roland M. "The Limited Vision of St. Bernard." *MLN,* 61 (1946), 38–44.

1507 SMITH, Roland M. See 601.

1508 TATLOCK, John S. P. "Chaucer and the *Legenda Aurea.*" *MLN,* 45 (1930), 296–298.

1509 TATLOCK, John S. P. "Chaucer's 'Bernard the Monk'." *MLN,* 46 (1931), 21–23.

1510 TATLOCK, John S. P. "The Source of the Legend, and Other Chauceriana." *SP,* 18 (1921), 419–428.

1511 TATLOCK, John S. P. See 1390 and 616.

1512 TUPPER, Frederick. "Chaucer's Lady of the Daisies." *JEGP,* 21 (1922), 293–317. Cf. *MP,* 24 (1927), 257–259 (Manly).

1513 WEBSTER, K. G. T. "Two Notes on Chaucer's Sea-Fight." *MP,* 25 (1927–28), 291–292.

1514 WEESE, Walter E. "Alceste and Joan of Kent." *MLN,* 63 (1948), 474–477.

1515 WIEN, C. E. "The Source of the Subtitle to Chaucer's *Tale of Philomela.*" *MLN,* 58 (1943), 605–607.

1516 WIMSATT, W. K., Jr. "Vincent of Beauvais and Chaucer's Cleopatra and Croesus." *Speculum,* 12 (1937), 375–381.

1517 YOUNG, Karl. "Chaucer's Appeal to the Platonic Deity." *Speculum,* 19 (1944), 1–13.

1518 YOUNG, Karl. "The *Dit de la Harpe* of Guillaume de Machaut." *Essays in Honor of Albert Feuillerat,* pp. 1–20. *Yale Romanic Stud.,* 22. New Haven, 1943.

The Canterbury Tales

Editions

1519 BAUGH, Albert C. See 248.

1520 CAWLEY, A. C., ed. *The Canterbury Tales.* London: Dent, 1958 (Everyman's Library).

1521 DONALDSON, E. T. See 250.

1522 *The Ellesmere Chaucer, Reproduced in Facsimile.* 2 vols., Manchester: Manchester Univ. Press, 1911.

1523 MANLY, John M., ed. *Canterbury Tales by Geoffrey Chaucer.* New York: Holt, 1928.

1524 MANLY, John M., and Edith RICKERT, eds. *The Text of the Canterbury Tales, Studied on the Basis of All Known Manuscripts:* with the Aid of Mabel Dean, Helen McIntosh, and Others; with a Chapter on Illuminations by Margaret Rickert. 8 vols., Chicago: Univ. of Chicago Press, 1940.*

1525 PRATT, Robert A., ed. *Selections from The Tales of Canterbury and Short Poems.* Boston: Houghton Mifflin, 1966. [Riverside Editions B 41]

1526 PRATT, Robert A., ed. *The Tales of Canterbury Complete.* Boston: Houghton Mifflin, 1974.

1527 ROBINSON, F. N. See 252.

1528 SKEAT, W. W. See 253.

Modernizations

1529 COGHILL, Nevill. *The Canterbury Tales, Translated into Modern English.* Harmondsworth: Penguin, 1951. [L 22-Pen]

1530 HILL, Frank E. *The Canterbury Tales, trans. into Modern English Verse.* London: Longmans, Green, 1935; New York: McKay, 1964. [15-Tartan]

1531 HOPPER, Vincent F. *Chaucer's Canterbury Tales: An Interlinear Translation.* Brooklyn: Barron, 1948.

1532 LUMIANSKY, Robert M. *The Canterbury Tales of Geoffrey Chaucer: A New Modern English Prose Translation.* New York: Simon and Schuster, 1948. [HRW]

1533 MORRISON, Theodore. See 254.

1534 NICHOLSON, J. U. *The Canterbury Tales, rendered into Modern English.* New York: Covici, Friede; London: Harrap, 1935.

1535 TATLOCK, John S. P., and Percy MACKAYE. See 255.

1536 WRIGHT, David. *The Canterbury Tales.* New York: Random House, 1965.

Criticism: Comprehensive Works

1537 BALDWIN, Ralph. *The Unity of the 'Canterbury Tales.'* Copenhagen, 1955 (*Anglistica,* V). Excerpts in 1548, 1700.

1538 BRYAN, W. F., and Germaine DEMPSTER, eds. *Sources and Analogues of Chaucer's Canterbury Tales.* Chicago: Univ. of Chicago Press, 1941.*

1539 CRAIK, T. W. *The Comic Tales of Chaucer.* London: Methuen; New York: Barnes and Noble, 1964.

1540 FURNIVALL, F. J., *et al.*, eds. *Originals and Analogues of (Some of) Chaucer's Canterbury Tales.* (Chaucer Soc., 2nd Scr., Nos. 7, 10, 15, 20, 22). London, 1872–88.

1541 HOFFMAN, Richard L. "The Canterbury Tales." *Critical Approaches to Six Major English Works,* ed. R. M. Lumiansky and Herschel Baker, pp. 41–80. Philadelphia: Univ. of Pennsylvania Press, 1971.

1542 Huppé, Bernard F. *A Reading of the Canterbury Tales.* [New York]: State Univ. of New York, 1964.

1543 Lawrence, William W. *Chaucer and the Canterbury Tales.* New York: Columbia Univ. Press, 1950.

1544 Lumiansky, Robert M. *Of Sondry Folk: The Dramatic Principle in the Canterbury Tales.* Austin: Univ. of Texas Press, 1955.

1545 MacLaine, Allan H. *The Student's Comprehensive Guide to the Canterbury Tales.* Great Neck, N.Y.: Barron's Educ. Ser., 1964.

1546 Manly, John M. *Some New Light on Chaucer.* New York: Holt, 1926.*

1547 McCormick, Sir William, with the assistance of Janet E. Heseltine. *The Manuscripts of Chaucer's Canterbury Tales: A Critical Description of Their Contents.* Oxford: Clarendon Press, 1933.

1548 Owen, Charles A., Jr., ed. *Discussions of the Canterbury Tales.* Boston: Heath, [1962].

1549 Pearsall, D. A. "The Canterbury Tales." 161, pp. 163–194.

1550 Ruggiers, Paul G. *The Art of the Canterbury Tales.* Madison and Milwaukee: Univ. of Wisconsin Press, 1965. [W-65]

1551 Skeat, W. W. *The Evolution of the Canterbury Tales.* London, 1907 (Chaucer Soc., 2nd Ser., No. 38). Also in *Trans. Philol. Soc., 1907–1910,* Part I, appendix, pp. 5–37.

1552 Whittock, Trevor. *A Reading of the* Canterbury Tales. London: Cambridge Univ. Press, 1968.

Criticism: Special Topics

1553 Anderson, Jons K. "An Analysis of the Framework Structure of Chaucer's *Canterbury Tales." Orbis Litterarum,* 27 (1972), 179–201.

1554 Baker, Donald C. "The Bradshaw Order of *The Canterbury Tales:* A Dissent." *NM,* 63 (1962), 245–261.

1555 Bartholomew, Barbara. *Fortuna and Natura: A Reading of Three Chaucer Narratives.* The Hague: Mouton, 1966.

1556 Beck, Richard J. "Educational Expectation and Rhetorical Result in *The Canterbury Tales." ES,* 44 (1963), 241–253.

1557 Berger, Harry, Jr. "The F-Fragment of the Canterbury Tales: Part I." *ChauR,* 1 (1966), 88–102, 135–156.

1558 Biggins, D. "More Chaucerian Ambiguities: A 652, 664, D 1346." *N&Q,* 207 (1962), 165–167.

1559 Braddy, Haldeen. "Two Chaucer Notes." *MLN,* 62 (1947), 173–179. [1, Chaucer on Murder: *De Petro Rege de Cipro;* 2. Chaucer's 'bretheren two' and 'thilke wikke ensample of Canace.']

1560 Bradshaw, Henry. "The Skeleton of Chaucer's Canterbury Tales." *Collected Papers of Henry Bradshaw,* pp. 102–148. Cambridge: Cambridge Univ. Press, 1889.

1561 Brookhouse, Christopher. "The Confessions of Three Pilgrims." *Laurel Rev.,* 8, No. 2 (1968), 49–56.

1562 BROWN, Beatrice D. "A Thirteenth-Century Chaucerian Analogue." *MLN*, 52 (1937), 28–31.

1563 BROWN, Carleton. "Author's Revisions in the *Canterbury Tales.*" *PMLA*, 57 (1942), 29–50.

1564 BROWN, Carleton. "The Evolution of the Canterbury 'Marriage Group'." *PMLA*, 48 (1933), 1041–1059.

1565 BROWN, Carleton. "The Text of the Canterbury Tales." *MLN*, 55 (1940), 606–621. [Review article on 1534.]

1566 BROWN, Carleton. "Three Notes on the Text of the *Canterbury Tales.*" *MLN*, 56 (1941), 163–175.

1567 BÜHLER, Curt F. " 'Wirk alle thyng by conseil'." *Speculum*, 24 (1949), 410–412.

1568 CLAWSON, W. H. "The Framework of *The Canterbury Tales.*" *UTQ*, 20 (1951), 137–154. Reprinted in 628.

1569 CLINE, Ruth H. "Four Chaucer Saints." *MLN*, 60 (1945), 480–482.

1570 COFFMAN, George R. "Chaucer's Library and Literary Heritage for the *Canterbury Tales.*" *SP*, 38 (1941), 571–583. [Review article.]

1571 COGHILL, Nevill. "Chaucer's Narrative Art in *The Canterbury Tales.*" 339, pp. 114–139.

1572 COX, Lee S. "A Question of Order in the *Canterbury Tales.*" *ChauR*, 1 (1967), 228–252.

1573 CROMIE, Henry. See 34.

1574 CROW, Martin M. "Corrections in the Paris Manuscript of Chaucer's *Canterbury Tales:* A Study in Scribal Collaboration." *Stud. in English* (Univ. of Texas), No. 15 (1935), pp. 5–18.

1575 CROW, Martin M. "John of Angoulême and His Chaucer Manuscript." *Speculum*, 17 (1942), 86–99.

1576 CROW, Martin M. "Unique Variants in the Paris Manuscript of Chaucer's Canterbury Tales." *Stud. in English* (Univ. of Texas), No. 16 (1936), pp. 17–41.

1577 CROW, Martin M. "John of Angoulême and His Chaucer Manuscript." *Stud. in Medieval, Renaissance, American Lit.: A Festschrift,* ed. Betsey F. Colquitt, pp. 33–44. Fort Worth: Texas Christian Univ. Press, 1971. (Revision of 1575).

1578 CURRY, Walter C. "Two Notes on Chaucer." *MLN*, 36 (1921), 272–276.

1579 DEAN, Christopher. "Imagery in the *Knight's Tale* and the *Miller's Tale.*" *MS*, 31 (1969), 149–163.

1580 DELASANTA, Rodney. "The Horsemen of the *Canterbury Tales.*" *ChauR*, 3 (1969) 29–36.

1581 DELASANTA, Rodney. "The Theme of Judgement in *The Canterbury Tales.*" *MLQ*, 31 (1970), 298–307.

1582 DEMPSTER, Germaine. "A Chapter of the Manuscript History of the *Canterbury Tales:* The Ancester of Group *d:* the Origin of Its Texts, Tale-order, and Spurious Links." *PMLA*, 63 (1948), 456–484. See 1584.*

1583 DEMPSTER, Germaine. "The Fifteenth-Century Editors of the *Canterbury Tales* and the Problem of Tale Order." *PMLA*, 64 (1949), 1123–1142.

1584 DEMPSTER, Germaine. "Manly's Conception of the Early History of the *Canterbury Tales.*" *PMLA*, 61 (1946), 379–415.*

1585 DEMPSTER, Germaine. "On the Significance of Hengwrt's Change of Ink in the *Merchant's Tale.*" *MLN,* 63 (1948), 325–330.

1586 DEMPSTER, Germaine. "A Period in the Development of the *Canterbury Tales* Marriage Group and of Block B² and C." *PMLA,* 68 (1953), 1142–1159.*

1587 DONALDSON, E. Talbot. "Chaucer the Pilgrim." *PMLA,* 69 (1954), 928–936. Reprinted in 273, 1548, 1700.

1588 DONALDSON, E. T. "The Ordering of the *Canterbury Tales.*" 56, pp. 193–204.

1589 DUNN, Thomas F. *The Manuscript Source of Caxton's Second Edition of the Canterbury Tales.* Chicago, 1940 (part of Univ. of Chicago diss.).

1590 ELIASON, Norman E. "Personal Names in the *Canterbury Tales.*" *Names,* 21 (1973), 137–152.

1591 ENGEL, Hildegard. *Structure and Plot in Chaucer's Canterbury Tales.* Bonn, 1931 (diss.).

1592 EVERETT, Dorothy. "Another Collation of the Ellesmere Manuscript of the *Canterbury Tales.*" *MÆ,* 1 (1932), 42–55.

1593 EWALD, Wilhelm. *Der Humor in Chaucers Canterbury Tales.* (*Studien zur engl. Phil.,* 45.) Halle, 1911.

1594 FARINA, Peter M. "The Twenty-nine Again: Another Count of Chaucer's Pilgrims." *USF Lang. Quar.* (Univ. of South Florida), 9 (1971), 29–32.

1595 FARINA, Peter M. "Two Notes on Chaucer: (1) The keepere of the celle [Gen. Prol. 172]; (2) The Storm Motif in *Troilus and Criseyde* [III, 512 ff.]." *USF Lang. Quar.* (Univ. of South Florida), 10 (1972), 23–26.

1596 FARNHAM, Willard. "England's Discovery of the *Decameron.*" *PMLA,* 39 (1924), 123–139.

1597 FISHER, John H. "Chaucer's Last Revision of the *Canterbury Tales.*" *MLR,* 67 (1972), 241–251.

1598 FISHER, John H. "The Three Styles of Fragment I of the *Canterbury Tales.*" *ChauR,* 8 (1973), 119–127.

1599 FLÜGEL, Ewald. "A New Collation of the Ellesmere MS." *Anglia,* 30 (1907), 401–412.

1600 FROST, William. "What Is a Canterbury Tale?" *WHR,* 27 (1973), 39–59.

1601 FURNIVALL, F. J., and R. E. G. KIRK, Eds. *Analogues of Chaucer's Canterbury Pilgrimage.* (Chaucer Soc., 2nd Ser., No. 36). London, 1903.

1602 FURNIVALL, F. J. *A Temporary Preface to the Chaucer Society's Six-Text Edition of Chaucer's Canterbury Tales.* (Chaucer Soc., 2nd Ser., No. 3.)* London, 1868.*

1603 GALEWSKI, Barbro. *Simplicity and Directness in Chaucer's Canterbury Tales.* Uppsala: Univ. of Uppsala, 1970.

1604 GARBÁTY, Thomas J. "The Monk and the *Merchant's Tale:* An Aspect of Chaucer's Building Process in the *Canterbury Tales.*" *MP,* 67 (1969), 18–24.

1605 GARDNER, John. "The Case against the 'Bradshaw Shift'; or, the Mystery of the Manuscript in the Trunk." *PLL,* Summer Suppl. (1967), 80–106.

1606 GAYLORD, Alan T. "*Sentence* and *Solaas* in Fragment VII of the *Canterbury Tales:* Harry Bailly as Horseback Editor." *PMLA,* 82 (1967), 226–235.

1607 GOFFIN, R. C. "Notes on Chaucer." *MLR,* 18 (1923), 335–337. [B 1189, A 323]

1608 GRAULS, Jan, and J. F. VANDERHEIJDEN. "Two Flemish Proverbs in Chaucer's Canterbury Tales." *Revue belge de phil. et d'histoire,* 13 (1934), 745–749.

1609 GREEN, A. Wigfall. "Chaucer's Clerks and the Mediaeval Scholarly Tradition as Represented by Richard de Bury's *Philobiblon.*" *ELH,* 18 (1951), 1–6.

1610 GREG, W. W. "The Early Printed Editions of the *Canterbury Tales.*" *PMLA,* 39 (1924), 737–761.

1611 HALES, J. W. "The Date of the Canterbury Tales." *Folia Literaria,* pp. 99–102. New York: Macmillan, 1893. Originally published in *Athenaeum,* April 8, 1893.

1612 HALL, D. J. *English Mediaeval Pilgrimage.* London: Routledge & Kegan Paul, 1966.

1613 HAMMOND, Eleanor P. "On the Order of the Canterbury Tales." *MP,* 3 (1905–06), 159–178.

1614 HARTUNG, Albert E. "The Clerk's Endlink in the *d* Manuscripts." *PMLA,* 67 (1952), 1173–1177. Cf. *ibid.,* 1177–1181 (Dempster), 1181 (Hartung).

1615 HASELMAYER, Louis A. "The Portraits in Chaucer's Fabliaux." *RES,* 14 (1938), 310–314.

1616 HASKELL, Ann S. "The Golden Ambiguity of the *Canterbury Tales.*" *Erasmus Rev.,* 1 (1971), 1–9.

1617 HEIST, William W. "Folklore Study and Chaucer's Fabliau-like Tales." *PMASAL,* 36 (1950), 251–258.

1618 HEMINGWAY, S. B. "Chaucer's Monk and Nun's Priest." *MLN,* 31 (1916), 479–483.

1619 HENCH, Atcheson L. "Printer's Copy for Tyrwhitt's Chaucer." *SP,* 3 (1950), 265–266.

1620 HINCKLEY, Henry B. "The Debate on Marriage in the Canterbury Tales." *PMLA,* 32 (1917), 292–305. Reprinted in 628.

1621 HINCKLEY, Henry B. "The Framing-Tale." *MLN,* 48 (1934), 69–80.

1622 HINCKLEY, Henry B. *Notes on Chaucer: A Commentary on the Prologue and Six Canterbury Tales.* Northampton, Mass.: Nonotuck Press, 1907.

1623 HIRA, Toshinori. "Chaucer's Gentry in the Historical Background." *Essays in English and American Literature: In Commemoration of Professor Takejiro Nakayama's Sixty-first Birthday,* pp. 31–44. Tokyo: Shohakusha, 1961.

1624 HODGE, James L. "The Marriage Group: Precarious Equilibrium." *ES,* 46 (1965), 289–300.

1625 HOFFMAN, Richard L. See 780.

1626 HOLBROOK, David. "Chaucer's Debate on Marriage." *The Quest for Love,* pp. 91–126. London: Methuen, 1964.

1627 HOWARD, Donald R. "The Conclusion of the Marriage Group: Chaucer and the Human Condition." *MP,* 57 (1960), 213–232.

1628 HOWARD, Donald R. "*Canterbury Tales:* Memory and Form." *ELH,* 38 (1971), 319–328.

1629 HOY, Michael, and Michael STEVENS. *Chaucer's Major Tales.* (Essays on *Gen Prol, Knt, PrT, ClT, CYT, FranklT, PardT, NPT.*) London: Norton Bailey, 1969.

1630 HULBERT, J. R. "*The Canterbury Tales* and Their Narrators," *SP,* 45 (1948), 565–577.

1631 IMMACULATE, Sister Mary. " 'Sixty' as a Conventional Number and Other Chauceriana." *MLQ,* 2 (1941), 59–66.

1632 JONES, H. S. V. "The Plan of the *Canterbury Tales.*" *MP,* 13 (1915–16), 45–48.

1633 JORDAN, Robert M. "Chaucer's Sense of Illusion: Roadside Drama Reconsidered." *ELH,* 29 (1962), 19–33.

1634 JOSEPH, Gerhard. "Chaucerian 'game'—'earnest' and the 'argument of herbergage' in *The Canterbury Tales.*" *ChauR,* 5 (1970), 83–96.

1635 JOSIPOVICI, G. D. "Fiction and Game in *The Canterbury Tales.*" *CritQ,* 7 (1965), 185–197.

1636 KASE, C. Robert. *Observations on the Shifting Positions of Groups G and DE in the Manuscripts of the Canterbury Tales.* See 621.

1637 KASKE, R. E. "Chaucer's Marriage Group." 528, pp. 45–65.

1638 KENYON, John S. "Further Notes on the Marriage Group in the *Canterbury Tales.*" *JEGP,* 15 (1916), 282–288.

1639 KILGOUR, Margaret. "The Manuscript Source of Caxton's Second Edition of the *Canterbury Tales.*" *PMLA,* 44 (1929), 186–201. Cf. *ibid.,* pp. 1251–1253 (W. W. Greg), 1253 (Kilgour).

1640 KIMPEL, Ben. "The Narrator of the *Canterbury Tales.*" *ELH,* 20 (1953), 77–86.

1641 KITTREDGE, George L. "Chaucer's Discussion of Marriage." *MP,* 9 (1912), 435–467. Reprinted in 1700 and 628.

1642 KNAPP, Daniel. "The Relyk of a Seint: A gloss on Chaucer's Pilgrimage." *ELH,* 39 (1972), 1–26.

1643 KNOX, Norman. "The Satiric Pattern of the *Canterbury Tales.*" In *Six Satirists,* by A. F. Sochatoff *et al.,* pp. 17–34. Pittsburgh: Carnegie Inst. of Tech., 1965 (*Carnegie Ser. in Eng.* 9).

1644 KOLINSKY, Muriel. "Pronouns of Address and the Status of Pilgrims in the *Canterbury Tales.*" *PLL,* 3, Summer Suppl. (1967), 40–48.

1645 LAWRENCE, William W. "The Marriage Group in the Canterbury Tales." *MP,* 11 (1913), 247–258.

1646 LEVY, Bernard S. "The Spiritual Direction of the Canterbury Pilgrimage." *Historical and Literary Perspectives: Essays and Studies in Honor of Albert D. Menut,* ed. Sandro Sticca, pp. 47–64. Binghampton, 1973.

1647 LINDNER, Felix. "The Alliteration in Chaucer's Canterbury Tales." In *Essays on Chaucer, Part III,* pp. 197–226 (Chaucer Soc., 2nd Ser., No. 16).

1648 LINKE, Hansjürgen. "Szenischer Bildwechsel in Chaucers *Canterbury Tales.*" *NS,* n.s. 11 (1962), 485–496.

1649 LOSSING, M. L. S. "The Order of the Canterbury Tales: A Fresh Relation between A and B Types of MSS." *JEGP,* 37 (1938), 153–163.

1650 LOWES, John L. "Chaucer and the Seven Deadly Sins." *PMLA,* 30 (1915), 237–371.

1651 LUMIANSKY, Robert M. "Two Notes on the Canterbury Tales." 55, pp. 227–232.

1652 LYONS, Clifford P. "The Marriage Debate in the *Canterbury Tales.*" *ELH,* 2 (1935), 252–262.

1653 MACDONALD, Donald. "Proverbs, *Sententiae,* and *Exempla* in Chaucer's Comic Tales: The Function of Comic Misapplication." *Speculum,* 41 (1966), 453–465.

1654 MAJOR, John M. "The Personality of Chaucer the Pilgrim." *PMLA*, 75 (1960), 160–162.

1655 MANLY, John M. "Tales of the Homeward Journey." *SP*, 28 (1931), 613–617 (*Royster Memorial Studies*, pp. 81–85).

1656 MARBURG, Clara. "Notes on the Cardigan Chaucer Manuscript." *PMLA*, 41 (1926), 229–251.

1657 McCANN, Garth A. "Chaucer's First Three Tales: Unity in Trinity." *Bull. Rocky Mtn. M.L.A.*, 27 (1973), 10–16.

1658 MEHL, Dieter. "Erscheinungsformen des Erzählers in Chaucers 'Canterbury Tales'." 54, pp. 189–206.

1659 MILLER, Robert P. "Allegory in the Canterbury Tales." 296, pp. 268–290.

1660 MOGAN, Joseph J., Jr. "Chaucer and the *Bona Matrimonii*." *ChauR*, 4 (1970), 123–141.

1661 MONTGOMERY, Franz. "The Musical Instruments in 'The Canterbury Tales'." *Musical Quar.*, 17 (1931), 439–448.

1662 MOORE, Samuel. "The Date of Chaucer's Marriage Group." *MLN*, 26 (1911), 172–174.

1663 MOORE, Samuel. "The Position of Group C in the Canterbury Tales." *PMLA*, 30 (1915), 116–123.

1664 MOORMAN, Charles. "The Philosophical Knights of the *Canterbury Tales*." *SAQ*, 64 (1965), 87–99.

1665 MORSBACH, L. "Chaucers Canterbury Tales und das Decameron." *Nachrichten aus der Neueren Philologie und Literaturgeschichte*, Bd. I, 1934–37 (1937), 49–70 (Gesellschaft der Wissenschaften zu Göttingen).

1666 MORSBACH, L. "Chaucers Plan der *Canterbury Tales* und Boccaccios Decamerone." *ESt*, 42 (1910), 43–52. Cf. *ibid.*, 44 (1912), 1–7 (Root).

1667 MROCZKOWSKI, P. "Mediaeval Art and Aesthetics in *The Canterbury Tales*." *Speculum*, 33 (1958), 204–221.

1668 MUSCATINE, Charles. "*The Canterbury Tales:* Style of the Man and Style of the Work." In 339, pp. 88–113.

1669 NATHAN, Norman. "Pronouns of Address in the *Canterbury Tales*." *MS*, 21 (1959), 193–201.

1670 NIST, John. "Chaucer's Apostrophic Mode in the *Canterbury Tales*." *TSL*, 15 (1970), 85–98.

1671 OLSON, Clair C. "The Interludes of the Marriage Group in the *Canterbury Tales*." 53, pp. 164–172.

1672 OWEN, Charles A., Jr. "The *Canterbury Tales:* Early Manuscripts and Relative Popularity." *JEGP*, 54 (1955), 104–110.

1673 OWEN, Charles A., Jr. "Chaucer's *Canterbury Tales:* Aesthetic Design in Stories of the First Day." *ES*, 35 (1954), 49–56.

1674 OWEN, Charles A., Jr. "The Crucial Passages in Five of the Canterbury Tales: A Study in Irony and Symbol." *JEGP*, 52 (1953), 294–311. Reprinted in 628 and 1548.

1675 OWEN, Charles A., Jr. "The Development of the *Canterbury Tales*." *JEGP*, 57 (1958), 449–476.

THE CANTERBURY TALES

1676 OWEN, Charles A., Jr. "The Earliest Plan of the *Canterbury Tales.*" *MS,* 21 (1959), 202–210.

1677 OWEN, Charles A., Jr. "Morality as a Comic Motif in the *Canterbury Tales.*" *CE,* 16 (1956), 226–232.

1678 OWEN, Charles A., Jr. "The Plan of the Canterbury Pilgrimage." *PMLA,* 66 (1950), 820–826.

1679 OWEN, Charles A., Jr. "The Design of The Canterbury Tales." 296, pp. 192–207.

1680 PIPER, Edwin F. "The Miniatures of the Ellesmere Chaucer." *PQ,* 3 (1924), 241–256.

1681 PIPER, Edwin F. "The Royal Boar and the Ellesmere Chaucer." *PQ,* 5 (1926), 330–340.

1682 PRATT, Robert A. "Giovanni Sercambi, Speziale." *Italica,* 25 (1948), 12–14.

1683 PRATT, Robert A. "The Order of the *Canterbury Tales.*" *PMLA,* 66 (1951), 1141–1167.

1684 PRINS, A. A. "Further Notes on the Canterbury Tales." *ES,* 32 (1951), 250–251.

1685 PRINS, A. A. "The Dating in the *Canterbury Tales.*" 53, pp. 342–347.

1686 RAMSEY, Vance. "Modes of Irony in The Canterbury Tales." 296, pp. 291–312.

1687 REISS, Edmund. "The Pilgrimage Narrative and the *Canterbury Tales.*" *SP,* 67 (1970), 295–305.

1687a RICHARDSON, Cynthia C. "The Function of the Host in *The Canterbury Tales.*" *TSLL,* 12 (1970), 325–344.

1688 RICHARDSON, Janette. *'Blameth Nat Me': A Study of Imagery in Chaucer's Fabliaux.* The Hague: Mouton, 1970.

1689 ROBINSON, Ian. "Chaucer's Religious Tales." *CR,* 10 (1967), 18–32.

1690 ROCKWELL, K. A. "Canterbury Tales: General Prologue, 526, The Wife of Bath's Prologue, 435, 'spiced conscience'." *N&Q,* 202 (1957), 84.

1691 ROGERS, Franklin R. "The *Tale of Gamelyn* and the Editing of the *Canterbury Tales.*" *JEGP,* 58 (1959), 49–59.

1692 ROGERS, P. Burwell. "The Names of the Canterbury Pilgrims." *Names,* 16 (1968), 339–346.

1693 ROOT, Robert K. "The Text of the Canterbury Tales." *SP,* 38 (1941), 1–13. [Review article on 1524.]

1694 ROSENFELD, Mary-Virginia. "Chaucer and the Liturgy." *MLN,* 55 (1940), 357–360.

1695 ROUCAUTE, Danielle. "Champ sémantique de l'erotique dans les *Contes de Canterbury* de Chaucer." *Cahiers Elizabethains,* 1 (1972), 3–24.

1696 RUGGIERS, Paul G. "The Form of *The Canterbury Tales:* Respice Fines." *CE,* 17 (1956), 439–444.

1697 RUTLEDGE, Sheryl P. "Chaucer's Zodiac of Tales." *Costerus,* 9 (1973), 117–143.

1698 RYDLAND, Kurt. "The Meaning of 'Variant Readings' in the Manly-Rickert 'Canterbury Tales'." *NM,* 73 (1972), 805–814.

1699 SAVAGE, James E. "The Marriage Problem in *The Canterbury Tales.*" *Mississippi Quar.,* 9 (1955), 27–29.

1700 SCHOECK, Richard J., and Jerome TAYLOR, eds. *Chaucer Criticism, The Canterbury Tales: An Anthology.* Notre Dame: Univ. of Notre Dame Press, 1960. [NDP-1]

1701 SCHULZ, Herbert C. *The Ellesmere Manuscript of Chaucer's Canterbury Tales* (with five color plates). San Marino, Calif.: Huntington Library, 1966.

1702 SEVERS, J. Burke. "Author's Revision in Block C of the *Canterbury Tales.*" *Speculum,* 29 (1954), 512–530.

1703 SEVERS, J. Burke. "The Tales of Romance." 296, pp. 229–246.

1704 SHAIN, Charles E., "Pulpit Rhetoric in Three Canterbury Tales." *MLN,* 70 (1955), 235–245.

1705 SILVIA, Daniel S. "Some Fifteenth-Century Manuscripts of the Canterbury Tales." 53, pp. 153–163.

1706 SPENCER, William. "Are Chaucer's Pilgrims Keyed to the Zodiac?" *ChauR,* 4 (1970), 147–170.

1707 STOKOE, W. C. "Structure and Intention in the First Fragment of the *Canterbury Tales.*" *UTQ,* 21 (1952), 120–127.

1708 STROHM, Paul. "Some Generic Distinctions in the *Canterbury Tales.*" *MP,* 68 (1971), 321–328.

1709 STROUD, Theodore A. The MS Fitzwilliam: An Examination of Miss Rickert's Hypothesis." *MP,* 46 (1948), 7–17.

1710 STROUD, Theodore A. "Scribal Errors in Manly and Rickert's Text." *MLN,* 68 (1953), 234–237.

1711 SUDO, Jun. "The Order of the *Canterbury Tales* Reconsidered." *HSELL,* 10, i (1963), 77–89.

1712 TATLOCK, John S. P. "Boccaccio and the Plan of Chaucer's *Canterbury Tales.*" *Anglia.* 37 (1913), 69–117.

1713 TATLOCK, John S. P. "The Canterbury Tales in 1400." *PMLA,* 50 (1935), 100–139.

1714 TATLOCK, John S. P. "The Duration of the Canterbury Pilgrimage." *PMLA,* 21 (1906), 478–485.

1715 TATLOCK, John S. P. *The Harleian MS 7334 and Revision of the Canterbury Tales.* (Chaucer Soc., 2nd Ser., No. 41.) London, 1909.

1716 TATLOCK, John S. P. "Notes on Chaucer: The Canterbury Tales," *MLN,* 29 (1914), 140–144.

1717 TUPPER, Frederick. "The Bearings of the Shipman's Prologue." *JEGP,* 33 (1934), 352–371.

1718 TUPPER, Frederick. "Chaucer and the Cambridge Edition." *JEGP,* 39 (1940), 503–526.

1719 TUPPER, Frederick. "Chaucer and the Seven Deadly Sins." *PMLA,* 29 (1914), 93–128.

1720 TUPPER, Frederick. "Chaucer's Sinners and Sins." *JEGP,* 15 (1916), 56–106.

1721 TUPPER, Frederick. "The Envy Theme in Prologues and Epilogues [in M. E. lit.]." *JEGP,* 16 (1917), 551–572.

1722 TUPPER, Frederick. "The Quarrels of the Canterbury Pilgrims." *JEGP,* 14 (1915), 256–270.

1723 TUPPER, Frederick. "Saint Venus and the Canterbury Pilgims." *Nation,* 97 (Oct. 16, 1913), 354–356.

1724 UHLIG, Claus. *Chaucer und die Armut: Zum Prinzip der kontextuellen Wahrheit in den Canterbury Tales.* Mainz: Akad. der Wissenschaften, 1974.

1725 UTLEY, Francis L. "Some Implications of Chaucer's Folktales." In IV. *Intern. Congress for Folk-Narrative Research in Athens: Lectures and Reports,* pp. 588–599. (Athens, 1965).

1726 WHITE Beatrice. "Two Chaucer Notes: 1. Proper Names in the *Canterbury Tales;* 2. A 'Minced' Oath in *Sir Thopas." NM,* 64 (1963), 170–175.

1727 WHITING, B. J. "A Colt's Tooth." In *Mediaeval Studies in Honor of Jeremiah Denis Matthias Ford,* pp. 319–331. Cambridge, Mass.: Harvard Univ. Press. 1948.

1728 WHITTOCK, Trevor. "The Marriage Debate." *Theoria* (Univ. of Natal), 14 (1960), 55–66; 15 (1960), 43–53.

1729 WILLIAMS, Arnold. "Chaucer and the Friars." *Speculum,* 28 (1953), 499-513. Reprinted in 1700.

1730 WILSON, James H. "The Pardoner and the Second Nun: A Defense of the Bradshaw Order." *NM,* 74 (1973), 292–296.

1731 WIMSATT, James I. "Chaucer and the Canticle of Canticles." 524, pp. 66–90.

1732 WOO, Constance, and William MATTHEWS. "The Spiritual Purpose of the Canterbury Tales." *Comitatus,* 1 (1970), 85–109.

1733 WOOD, Chauncey. "The April Date as a Structural Device in the *Canterbury Tales." MLQ,* 25 (1964), 259–271.

1734 WORK, James A. "The Position of the Tales of the Maniciple and the Parson on Chaucer's Canterbury Pilgrimage." *JEGP,* 31 (1932), 62–65.

1735 YOUNG, Karl. "The Plan of the *Canterbury Tales." 51,* pp. 405–417.

Criticism: The General Prologue

1736 BAUM, Paull F. "Canterbury Tales A 24." *MLN,* 69 (1954), 551–552.

1737 BAUM, Paull F. "Chaucer's 'Faste by the Belle', *C.T.* A. 719." *MLN,* 36 (1921), 307–309.

1738 BOWDEN, Muriel. *A Commentary on the General Prologue to the Canterbury Tales.* New York: Macmillan, 1948; 2nd ed., 1967.

1739 BRADDY, Haldeen. "Chaucerian Minutiae." *MLN,* 58 (1943), 18–23. In 258.

1740 BROOKS, Harold F. *Chaucer's Pilgrims: The Artistic Order of the Portraits in the Prologue,* London: Methuen, 1962.

1741 BROWN, Carleton. "The Squire and the Number of Canterbury Pilgrims." *MLN,* (1934), 216–222.

1742 BURGESS, Anthony. " 'Whan that Aprille'." *Horizon,* 13, No. 2 (1971), 45–59.

1743 CAMDEN, Carroll, Jr. "Chauceriana." *MLN,* 47 (1932), 360–362. [A 43, 307, 333, 417–18]

1744 CONRAD, Bernard R. "The Date of Chaucer's 'Prologue' ." *N&Q,* 152 (1927), 385.

1745 COPLAND, R. A. "A Line from Chaucer's Prologue to the Canterbury Tales." *N&Q,* 215 (1970), 45–46.

1746 COURTNEY, Neil. "Chaucer's Poetic Vision." *CR*, No. 8 (1965), pp. 129–140.

1747 CUMMINGS, Hubertis. "Chaucer's *Prologue*, 1–7." *MLN*, 37 (1922), 86–90.

1748 CUNNINGHAM, J. V. "The Literary Form of the Prologue to the *Canterbury Tales.*" *MP*, 49 (1952), 172–81.

1749 CUNNINGHAM, J. V. "Convention as Structure: The Prologue to the Canterbury Tales." *Tradition and Poetic Structure*, pp. 59–75. Denver: Alan Swallow, 1960.

1750 DALEY, A. Stuart. "Chaucer's 'droghte of March' in Medieval Farm Lore." *ChauR*, 4 (1970), 171–179.

1751 DANBY, John F. "Eighteen Lines of Chaucer's 'Prologue.'" *CritQ*, 2 (1960), 28–32.

1752 DUNCAN, Edgar H. "Narrator's Points of View in the Portrait-sketches, Prologue to the *Canterbury Tales.*" *Essays in Honor of Walter Clyde Curry*, pp. 77–101. Nashville: Vanderbilt Univ. Press. 1955.

1753 ELLIOTT, Ralph W. V. *Chaucer's Prologue to the Canterbury Tales.* New York: Barnes and Noble. 1960; Oxford: Blackwell, [1960].

1755 EVANS, Robert O. "Whan That Aprill(e)?" *N&Q*, 202 (1957), 234–237.

1756 EVERETT, Dorothy. "If Euen-song and Morwe-song Accorde' (*Canterbury Tales, Prologue*, 830)." *RES*, 8 (1932), 446–447.

1757 FARINA, Peter M. "The Twenty-nine Again: Another Count of Chaucer's Pilgrims." *Lang. Quar.* (Univ. of South Fla.), 9, iii–iv (1971), 29–32.

1758 FARINA, Peter M. "Two Notes on Chaucer." *Lang. Quar.*, (Univ. of South Fla.), 10, iii–iv (1972), 23–26.

1759 FLÜGEL, Ewald. "Some Notes on Chaucer's Prologue." *Jour. of Germanic Phil.*, 1 (1897–98), 118–135.

1760 FOSTER, Brian. "Chaucer's 'Sëynt Loy': An Anglo-French Pun." *N&Q*, 213 (1968), 244–245.

1761 GALWAY, Margaret. " 'Whan that Aprille. . . .' " *TLS*, Oct. 6, 1950, p. 629.

1762 GILLMEISTER, Heiner. "Chaucers Mönch und die 'Reule of Seint Maure or of Seint Beneit." *NM*, 69 (1968), 222–232.

1763 GÖRLACH, Manfred. " 'Canterbury Tales' Prologue, 60: The Knight's Army." *N&Q*, 218 (1973), 363–365.

1764 GREENFIELD, Stanley B. "Sittingbourne and the Order of *The Canterbury Tales.*" *MLR*, 48 (1953), 51–52.

1765 HANKINS, John E. "Chaucer and the *Pervigilium Veneris.*" *MLN*, 49 (1934), 80–83.

1766 HART, James A. " 'The Droghte of March': A Common Misunderstanding." *TSLL*, 4 (1962), 525–529.

1767 HIGDON, David L. "Diverse Melodies in Chaucer's 'General Prologue'." *Criticism*, 14 (1972), 97–108.

1768 HOFFMAN, Arthur W. "Chaucer's Prologue to Pilgrimage: The Two Voices." *ELH*, 21 (1954), 1–16. Reprinted in 628 and 1548.

1769 HULBERT, J. R. "Chaucer's Pilgrims." *PMLA*, 64 (1949), 823–828. Reprinted in 628.

1770 KEEN, William. " 'To Doon Yow Ese': A Study of the Host in the *General Prologue* of the *Canterbury Tales." Topic,* 9, Topic 17 (1969), 5–18.

1771 KIRBY, Thomas A. "The General Prologue." 296, pp. 208–228.

1772 LENAGHAN, R. T. "Chaucer's *General Prologue* as History and Literature." *Compar. Stud. in Soc. and Hist.,* 12 (1970), 73–82.

1773 LITTLEHALES, H., ed. *Some Notes on the Road from London to Canterbury in the Middle Ages.* (Chaucer Soc., 2nd Ser., No. 30.) London, 1898.

1774 LUMIANSKY, Robert M. "Benoit's Portraits and Chaucer's General Prologue." *JEGP,* 55 (1956), 431–438.

1775 LUMIANSKY, Robert M. "Chaucer's *Canterbury Tales,* Prologue, 784–787." *Explicator,* 5 (1946), item 20. Cf. *ibid.,* item 38 (T. M. Pearce).

1776 MAGOUN, F. P., Jr. "Canterbury Tales A 11." *MLN,* 70 (1955), 399.

1777 MALONE, Kemp. "Style and Structure in the Prologue to the *Canterbury Tales." ELH,* 13 (1946), 38–45.

1778 MANLY, John M. See 509.

1779 MANN, Jill. *Chaucer and Medieval Estates Satire: The Literature of Social Classes and the General Prologue to the Canterbury Tales.* Cambridge: Cambridge Univ. Press, 1973.

1780 McKEE, John. "Chaucer's *Canterbury Tales,* General Prologue." *Explicator,* 32 (1974), item 54.

1781 MILLER, B. D. H. "Chaucer's General Prologue, A 673: Further Evidence." *N&Q* 205 (1960), 404–406.

1782 NATHAN, Norman. "The Number of the Canterbury Pilgrims." *MLN,* 67 (1952), 533–534.

1783 NEVO, Ruth. "Chaucer: Motive and Mask in the *General Prologue." MLR,* 58 (1963), 1–9.

1784 OWEN, Charles A., Jr. "The Twenty-Nine Pilgrims and the Three Priests." *MLN,* 76 (1961), 392–397.

1785 PRESSON, Robert K. "The Aesthetic of Chaucer's Art of Contrast." *EM,* 15 (1964), 9–23.

1786 REA, John A. "An Old French Analogue to General Prologue 1–18." *PQ,* 46 (1967), 128–130.

1787 REIDY, John. "Grouping of Pilgrims in the General Prologue to *The Canterbury Tales." PMASAL,* 47 (1962), 595–603.

1788 STEADMAN, John M. "Chaucer's Thirty Pilgrims and Activa Vita." *Neophil,* 45 (1961), 224–230.

1789 SWART, J. "The Construction of Chaucer's *General Prologue." Neophil,* 38 (1954), 127–136.

1790 TUPPER, Frederick. "Chaucer's Bed's Head." *MLN,* 30 (1915), 5–12.

1791 TUVE, Rosemond. "Spring in Chaucer and before Him." *MLN,* 52 (1937), 9–16.

1792 VANHERK, A. "Chauceriana." *Neophil,* 2 (1917), 292–294.

1793 WILLARD, Rudolph. "Chaucer's 'holt and heeth'. " *AS,* 22 (1947), 196–198.

1794 WOOLF, Rosemary. "Chaucer as a Satirist in the General Prologue to the Canterbury Tales." *CritQ* 1 (1959), 150–157.

Criticism: The Pilgrims
(in order of appearance)

The Knight

1795 BRYANT, Frank E. "Did Boccaccio Suggest the Character of Chaucer's Knight?" *MLN*, 17 (1902), 470–471.

1796 COOK, Albert S. "Beginning the Board in Prussia." *JEGP*, 14 (1915), 375–388.

1797 COOK, Albert S. *The Historical Background of Chaucer's Knight.* New Haven, 1916 (*Trans. Conn. Acad.*, XX, 161–240.) Reprinted New York: Haskell House, 1966.

1798 EBNER, Dean. "Chaucer's Precarious Knight." *Imagination and the Spirit: Essays in Literature and Christian Faith Presented to Clyde S. Kilby*, ed. Charles A. Huttar, pp. 87–100. Grand Rapids, Mich.: Eerdmans, 1971.

1799 ENGEL, Clair-Elaine. "Les croisades du chevalier." *Revue de sciences humaines* No. 120 (1965), 577–585.

1800 ETHEL, Garland. "Horse or Horses: A Chaucerian Textual Problem." *MLN*, 75 (1960), 97–101. Cf. *ibid.*, 76 (1961), 293–295 (W. H. French).

1801 FINK, Z. S. "Another Knight Ther Was." *PQ* 17 (1938), 321–330.

1802 GORSKI, Karol. "The Teutonic Order in Prussia." *M&H*, 17 (1966), 20–37.

1803 HATTON, Thomas J. "Chaucer's Crusading Knight: A Slanted Ideal." *ChauR*, 3 (1968), 77–87.

1804 LINTHICUM, M. Channing. " 'Faldyng' and 'Medlee'. " *JEGP*, 34 (1935), 39–41.

1805 MANLY, John M. "A Knight ther was." *Trans. Amer. Philol. Assoc.*, 38 (1907), 89–107. Reprinted in 628.

1806 MITCHELL, Charles. "The Worthiness of Chaucer's Knight." *MLQ*, 25 (1964), 66–75.

1807 MOORMAN, Charles. *A Knight There Was: The Evolution of the Knight in Literature.* Lexington: Univ. of Kentucky Press, 1967.

1808 SEDGWICK, W. B. "Satalye (Chaucer, *C.T. Prol.* 58)." *RES*, 2 (1926), 346.

1809 STILLWELL, Gardiner, and Henry J. WEBB. "Chaucer's Knight and the Hundred Years' War." *MLN*, 59 (1944), 45–47.

The Squire

1810 FLEMING, John V. "Chaucer's Squire, the *Roman de la Rose*, and the *Romaunt*," *N&Q*, 212 (1967), 48–49.

1811 GAYLORD, Alan. "A 85–88: Chaucer's Squire and the Glorious Campaign." *PMASAL*, 45 (1960), 341–360.

1812 KUHL, Ernest P., and Henry J. WEBB. "Chaucer's Squire." *ELH*, 6 (1939), 282–284.

1813 WOOD, Chauncey. "The Significance of Jousting and Dancing as Attributes of Chaucer's Squire." *ES*, 52 (1971), 116–118.

The Yeoman

1814 BIRNEY, Earle. "The Squire's Yeoman." *REL,* 1, No. 3 (1960), 9–18.

1815 KRAPPE, Edith S. "A Note on Chaucer's Yeoman." *MLN,* 43 (1928), 176–177.

1816 MALARKEY, Stoddard. "Chaucer's Yeoman Again." *CE,* 24 (1963), 289–295.

1817 MROCZKOWSKI, P. "Chaucer's Green 'Yeoman' and *Le Roman de Renart.*" *N&Q,* 207 (1962), 325–326.

1818 TEST, George A. "Archer's Feathers in Chaucer and Ascham." *AN&Q,* 2 (1964), 67–68.

The Prioress

1819 BOYD, Beverly. "Chaucer's Prioress: Her Green Gauds." *MLQ,* 11 (1950), 404–416.

1820 BRENNAN, Maynard J. "Speaking of the Prioress." *MLQ,* 10 (1949), 451–457.

1821 CLARK, Thomas B. "Forehead of Chaucer's Prioress." *PQ,* 9 (1930), 312–314.

1822 DAVIES, R. T. "Chaucer's Madame Eglantine." *MLN,* 67 (1952), 400–402.

1823 ELIASON, Norman E. "Chaucer's Second Nun?" *MLQ,* 3 (1942), 9–16.

1824 FISCHER, Walther. "Die französischen Sprachkenntnisse von Chaucers Priorin." *Probleme der engl. Sprache und Kultur: Festschrift Johannes Hoops,* pp. 149–151 (*Germanische Bibl.,* Abt. II: Untersuchungen und Texte, 20). Heidelberg: Winter, 1925.

1825 FOSTER, Brian. "Chaucer's 'Sëynt Loy': An Anglo-French Pun?" *N&Q,* 213 (1968), 244–245.

1826 FRIEDMAN, John B. "The Prioress's Beads 'of smal corel'." *MÆ,* 39 (1970), 301–305.

1827 FURNIVALL, F. J. "Chaucer's Prioress, Her Chaplain and Three Priests, Illustrated by the Survey of the Abbey . . . of St. Mary, Winchester, 11 May, 1537 A.D." *Essays on Chaucer,* Part III, pp. 181–196 (Chaucer Soc., 2nd Ser., No. 16).

1828 HAMILTON, Marie P. "The Convent of Chaucer's Prioress and Her Priests." In *Philologica: The Malone Anniversary Studies,* pp. 179–190. Baltimore: Johns Hopkins Press, 1949.

1829 HARPER, Gordon H. "Chaucer's Big Prioress." *PQ,* 12 (1933), 308–310.

1830 KIRBY, Thomas A. "The French of Chaucer's Prioress." In *Studies for William A. Read,* pp. 29–34. University, La.: Louisiana State Univ. Press, 1940.

1831 KNIGHT, S. T. "'Almoost a spanne brood'." *Neophil,* 52 (1968), 178–180.

1832 KNOEPFLMACHER, U. C. "Irony through Scriptural Allusion: A Note on Chaucer's Prioresse." *ChauR,* 4 (1970), 180–183.

1833 KUHL, E. P. "Chaucer's Madame Eglantine." *MLN,* 60 (1945), 325–326. Reprinted in 475.

1834 KUHL, E. P. "Notes on Chaucer's Prioress." *PQ,* 2 (1923), 302–309. Reprinted in 475.

1835 LOWES, John L. "The Prioress's Oath." *RR,* 5 (1914), 368–385.

1836 LOWES, John L. "Simple and Coy: A Note on Fourteenth Century Poetic Diction." *Anglia,* 33 (1910), 440–451.

1837 LYNCH, James J. "The Prioress's Greatest Oath, Once More." *MLN,* 72 (1957), 242–249.

1838 MADELEVA, Sister Mary. See 505.

1839 MANLY, John M. "The Prioress of Stratford." *TLS,* Nov. 10, 1927, p. 817.

1840 McCARTHY, Sister Brigetta. "Chaucer's Pilgrim-Prioress." *Benedictine Rev.,* 6 (1951), 38–40.

1841 MOORE, Arthur K. "The Eyen Greye of Chaucer's Prioress." *PQ,* 26 (1947), 307–312.

1842 POWER, Eileen. "Madame Eglentyne, Chaucer's Prioress in Real Life." In *Medieval People,* Chap. III. [Chap. IV in 10th ed., 1963.] London: Methuen, 1924.

1843 REID, T. B. W. "Chaucer's 'Ferthing of Grece'. " *N&Q,* 209 (1964), 373–374.

1844 SIMONS, Rita D. "The Prioress's Disobedience of the Benedictine Rule." *CLAJ,* 12 (1968), 77–83.

1845 SMITH, Fred M. See 1374.

1846 STEADMAN, John M. " 'Hir Gretteste Ooth': The Prioress, St. Eligius, and St. Godebertha." *Neophil,* 43 (1959), 49–57.

1847 STEADMAN, John M. "The Prioress' Brooch and St. Leonard." *ES,* 44 (1963), 350–353.

1848 STEADMAN, John M. "The Prioress' Dogs and Benedictine Discipline." *MP,* 54 (1956–57), 1–6.

1849 WAINWRIGHT, Benjamin B. "Chaucer's Prioress Again: An Interpretive Note." *MLN,* 48 (1933), 34–37.

1850 WENTWORTH, Clarence L. "The Prioress' Oath." *RR,* 27 (1936), 268–269.

The Prioress's Companions

1851 EMERSON, O. F. See 395, 396. [Preestes thre.]

1852 FÖRSTER, Max. "Chauceriana I: Die Nonnen-Kaplanin' (me. chapeleine)." *Archiv,* 132 (1914), 399–401.

1853 KASTNER, V. "Chaucer: Prestes thre' or 'prest estré"?" *Athenaeum,* Feb. 24, 1906, pp. 231–232. Cf. *ibid.,* March 3, p. 265 (A. L. Mayhew), March 10, p. 299 (Kastner), March 17, p. 329 (Mayhew).

1854 LEHMANN, W. P. "A Rare Use of Numerals in Chaucer." *MLN,* 67 (1952), 317–321. Cf. *ibid.,* 502–504 (Spitzer).

1855 SHERBO, Arthur. "Chaucer's Nun's Priest Again." *PMLA,* 64 (1949), 236–246.

The Monk

1856 BEICHNER, Paul E. "Daun Piers, Monk and Business Administrator." *Speculum,* 34 (1959), 611–619. Reprinted in 1700.

1857 BERNDT, David E. "Monastic *Acedia* and Chaucer's Characterization of Daun Piers." *SP,* 68 (1971), 435–450.

1858 BRESSIE, Ramona. See 2399.

1859 CRAWFORD, S. J. "Chaucer and St. Augustine." *TLS,* Nov. 13, 1930, p. 942.

1860 EICHLER, Albert. "Zu Chaucer, *Canterbury Tales, General Prologue,* 1. 207." *ESt,* 70 (1935), 102–105.

1861 EMERSON, O. F. "Some of Chaucer's Lines on the Monk." *MP*, 1 (1903–04), 105–15. Reprinted in 395.

1862 GILLMEISTER, Heiner. "Chaucers Mönch und die 'Reule of Seint Maure or of Seint Beneit." *NM*, 69 (1968), 222–232.

1863 GRENNEN, Joseph E. "Chaucerian Portraiture: Medicine and the Monk." *NM*, 69 (1968), 569–574.

1864 GRENNEN, Joseph E. "Chaucer's Monk: Baldness, Venery and Embonpoint." *AN&Q*, 6 (1968), 83–85.

1865 PRINS, A. A. "Two Notes to the Prologue of Chaucer's Canterbury Tales." *ES*, 30 (1949), 83–86. Cf. *ibid.*, p. 133 (F. T. Visser), 133–134 (Prins).

1866 REISS, Edmund. "The Symbolic Surface of the *Canterbury Tales:* The Monk's Portrait'" *ChauR*, 2 (1968), 254–272; 3 (1968), 12–28.

1867 TATLOCK, John S. P. See 2429.

1868 USSERY, Huling E. "The Status of Chaucer's Monk: Clerical, Official, Social, and Moral." *TSE*, 17 (1969), 1–30.

1869 WHITE, Robert B., Jr. "Chaucer's Daun Piers and the Rule of St. Benedict: The Failure of an Ideal." *JEGP*, 70 (1971), 13–30.

1870 WILLARD, Rudolph. "Chaucer's 'text that seith that hunters ben nat hooly men'. " *Stud. in English* (Univ. of Texas), 1947, pp. 209–251.

The Friar

1871 BLOOMFIELD, Morton W. "The Magic of *In Principio.* " *MLN*, 70 (1955), 559–565.

1872 BRUCE, J. Douglas. "Prologue to the Canterbury Tales: His purchas was wel bettre than his rente." *MLN*, 34 (1919), 118–119.

1873 FRANK, Robert W., Jr. "Chaucer and the London Bell-Founders." *MLN*, 68 (1953), 524–528.

1874 GREENLAW, Edwin. "A Note on Chaucer's *Prologue.* " *MLN*, 23 (1908), 142–144. [Purchas—rente.]

1875 HORTON, Oze E. "The Neck of Chaucer's Friar." *MLN*, 48 (1933), 31–34.

1876 JEFFREY, David L. "The Friar's Rent." *JEGP*, 70 (1971), 600–606.

1877 LAW, Robert A. " 'In Principio'. " *PMLA*, 37 (1922), 208–215.

1878 MUSCATINE, Charles. "The Name of Chaucer's Friar." *MLN*, 70 (1955), 169–172.

1879 PEARCY, Roy J. "The Marriage Costs of Chaucer's Friar." *N&Q*, 17 (1970), 124–125.

1880 REISS, Edmund. "Chaucer's Friar and the Man in the Moon." *JEGP*, 62 (1963), 481–485.

1881 SPARGO, John W. "Chaucer's Love-Days." *Speculum*, 15 (1940), 36–56.

1882 SZÖVERFFY, Joseph. "Chaucer's Friar and St. Nicholas (Prologue 212)." *N&Q*, 16 (1969), 166–167.

1883 TILLOTSON, Kathleen. "The Friar's Lisp." *TLS*, April 25, 1936, p. 356.

1884 WHITESELL, J. Edwin. "Chaucer's Lisping Friar." *MLN*, 71 (1956), 160–161.

1885 WILLIAMS, Arnold. "The 'Limitour' of Chaucer's Time and His 'Limitacioun'. " *SP*, 57 (1960), 463–478.

1886 WILLIAMS, Arnold. "Two Notes on Chaucer's Friars." *MP,* 54 (1956–57), 117–120.

1887 YOUNG, Karl. "A Note on Chaucer's Friar." *MLN,* 50 (1935), 83–85.

The Merchant

1888 CRANE, John K. "An Honest Debtor?: A Note on Chaucer's Merchant, line A 276." *ELN,* 4 (1966), 81–85.

1889 JOHNSON, Oscar E. "Was Chaucer's Merchant in Debt? A Study in Chaucerian Syntax and Rhetoric." *JEGP,* 52 (1953), 50–57.

1890 KNOTT, T. A. "Chaucer's Anonymous Merchant." *PQ,* 1 (1922), 1–16.

1891 MILLER, F. "The Middleburgh Staple, 1383–88." *Cambridge Hist. Jour.,* 2 (1926), 63–65.

1892 PARK, B. A. "The Character of Chaucer's Merchant." *ELN,* 1 (1964), 167–175.

1893 STILLWELL, Gardiner. "Chaucer's Merchant: No Debts?" *JEGP,* 57 (1958), 192–196.

1894 WALKER, A. S. "Note on Chaucer's Prologue." *MLN,* 38 (1923). 314. [A 276–7]

The Clerk

1895 FLEMING, John. "Chaucer's Clerk and John of Salisbury." *ELN,* 2 (1964), 5–6.

1896 JONES, H. S. V. "The Clerk of Oxenford." *PMLA,* 27 (1912), 106–115.

1897 MORSE, J. Mitchell. "Chaucer: A Meaning of 'philosophye'. " *N&Q,* 200 (1955), 11.

1898 RICHARDSON, M. E. "The Clerk of Oxenford." *TLS,* May 5, 1932, p. 331. Cf. *ibid.,* May 19, p. 368 (R. B. Turton), May 26, p. 390 (Richardson).

1899 USSERY, Huling E. "How Old is Chaucer's Clerk?" *TSE,* 15 (1967), 1–18.

1900 USSERY, Huling E. "Fourteenth-Century English Logicians: Possible Models for Chaucer's Clerk." *TSE,* 18 (1970), 1–15.

1901 WOOD, Chauncey. "Chaucer's Clerk and Chalcidius." *ELN,* 4 (1967). 166–172.

The Sergeant of the Law

1902 BAUGH, Albert C. "Chaucer's Serjeant of the Law and the Year Books." *"Mélanges de langue et de littérature du moyen âge et de la renaissance offerts à Jean Frappier,* Vol. I, pp. 65–76. 2 vols., Geneva: Droz, 1970.

1903 DELASANTA, Rodney. "And of Great Reverence: Chaucer's Man of Law." *ChauR,* 5 (1971), 288–310.

1904 FROST, George L. "Chaucer's Man of Law at the Parvis." *MLN,* 44 (1929), 496–501.

1905 GOFFIN, R. C. "Notes on Chaucer." *MLR,* 18 (1923), 335–337. [A 323, B 1189]

1906 KNOWLTON, E. C. See 2247.

1907 LAMBKIN, Martha D. "Chaucer's Man of Law as a Purchasour." *Comitatus,* 1 (1970), 81–84.

1908 WYATT, A. J. "Chaucer's 'In Termës.' " *RES,* 4 (1928), 439.

The Franklin

1909 BIRNEY, Earle. "The Franklin's 'Sop in wyn'. " *N&Q,* 204 (1959), 345–347.

1910 BRYANT, Joseph A., Jr. "The Diet of Chaucer's Franklin." *MLN,* 63 (1948), 318–325.

1911 FRANKIS, P. J. "Chaucer's 'vavasour' and Chrétien de Troyes." *N&Q,* 213 (1968), 46–47.

1912 GEROULD, G. H. "The Social Status of Chaucer's Franklin." *PMLA,* 41 (1926), 262–279. Reprinted in 410.

1913 SAVAGE, Henry. " 'Seint Julian He Was'. " *MLN,* 58 (1943), 47–48.

1914 WOOD-LEIGH, K. L. "The Franklin." *RES,* 4 (1923), 145–151.

The Five Gildsmen

1915 CAMDEN, Carroll, Jr. "Query on Chaucer's Burgesses." *PQ,* 7 (1928), 314–317.

1916 FULLERTON, Ann B. "The Five Craftsmen." *MLN,* 61 (1946), 515–523.

1917 GARBÁTY, Thomas J. "Chaucer's Guildsmen and Their Fraternity." *JEGP,* 59 (1960), 691–709.

1918 HERNDON, Sarah. "Chaucer's Five Gildsmen." *Florida State Univ. Stud.,* V (1952), 33–44.

1919 KIRBY, Thomas A. "The Haberdasher and His Companions." *MLN,* 53 (1938), 504–505.

1920 KUHL, Ernest P. "Chaucer's Burgesses." *TWA* 18, Part 2 (1916), 652–675. Reprinted in 475.

1921 LISCA, Peter. "Chaucer's Gildsmen and Their Cook." *MLN,* 70 (1955), 321–324.

1922 McCUTCHAN, J. Wilson. " 'A Solempne and a Greet Fraternitee'. " *PMLA,* 74 (1959), 313–317.

The Cook

1923 BRADDY, Haldeen. "The Cook's Mormal and Its Cure." *MLQ,* 7 (1946), 265–267.

1924 LUMIANSKY, Robert M. "Chaucer's Cook-Host Relationship." *MS,* 17 (1955), 208–209.

1925 LYON, Earl D. See 2223.

The Shipman

1926 DONOVAN, Mortimer J. "Chaucer's Shipman and the Integrity of His Cargo." *MLR,* 50 (1955), 489–490.

1927 GALWAY, Margaret. "Chaucer's Shipman in Real Life." *MLR,* 34 (1939), 497–514.

1928 KARKEEK, P. O. "Chaucer's Shipman and His Barge 'The Maudelayne', with Notes on Chaucer's Horses." *Essays on Chaucer,* Part V, pp. 453–500 (Chaucer Soc., 2nd Ser., No. 19).

1929 MALONE, Kemp. "From Hulle to Cartage." *MLN,* 45 (1930), 229–230.

1930 STILLWELL, Gardiner. "Chaucer's Shipman and the 'Shipman's Gild' ." *N&Q,* 192 (1947), 203–205. Cf. *ibid.,* p. 372 (T. A. Mabbott).

1931 STOBIE, Margaret R. "Chaucer's Shipman and the Wine." *PMLA,* 64 (1949), 565–569.

1932 WHITE, Florence E. "Chaucer's Shipman." *MP,* 26 (1928–29), 249–255, 379–384; 27 (1929–30), 123–128.

The Physician

1933 AIKEN, Pauline. "Vincent of Beauvais and the 'houres' of Chaucer's Physician." *SP,* 53 (1956), 22–24.

1934 BASHFORD, H. H. "Chaucer's Physician and his Forbears." *Nineteenth Cent.,* 104 (1929), 237–248.

1935 CURRY, W. C. "Chaucer's Doctor of Phisyk." *PQ,* 4 (1925), 1–24.

1936 GRENNEN, Joseph E. "*Double Entendre* and the Doctour of Phisik." *AN&Q,* 1 (1963), 131–132.

1937 MORRIS, E. E. "The Physician in Chaucer." 50, pp. 338–346.

1938 ROBBINS, Rossell H. "The Physician's Authorities." 55, pp. 335–341.

1939 SULLIVAN, Frank. "Chaucer's Physician and *Genesis* XXXI, 20." *Los Angeles Tidings,* Dec. 31, 1948, p. 9.

1940 TUPPER, Frederick. "Chaucer's 'Doctour of Phisik'. " *Nation,* 96 (1913), 640–641.

1941 USSERY, Huling E. *Chaucer's Physician: Medicine and Literature in Fourteenth-Century England.* New Orleans: Tulane Univ. Dept. of English, 1971 (*TSE,* 19).

The Wife of Bath

1942 BIGGINS, D. "Chaucer's General Prologue, A 467." *N&Q,* 205 (1960), 129–130.

1943 FLEISSNER, R. F. "The Wife of Bath's Five." *ChauR,* 8 (1973), 128–132.

1944 HOFFMAN, Richard L. "The Wife of Bath as Student of Ovid." *N&Q,* 209 (1964), 287–288.

1945 HOFFMAN, Richard L. "The Wife of Bath's Uncharitable Offerings." *ELN,* 11 (1974), 165–167.

1946 REISNER, Thomas A. "The Wife of Bath's Dower: A Legal Interpretation." *MP,* 71 (1974), 301–302.

1947 SILVIA, D. S. "The Wife of Bath's Marital State." *N&Q,* 212 (1967), 8–10.

1948 WRETLIND, Dale E. "The Wife of Bath's Hat." *MLN,* 63 (1948), 381–382.

The Parson

1949 BODE, Edward L. "The Source of Chaucer's 'Rusted Gold'. " *MS,* 24 (1962), 369–370.

1950 FLEMING, John. "The 'figure' of Chaucer's Good Parson and a Reprimand by Grosseteste." *N&Q,* 209 (1964), 167.

1951 IVES, Doris V. "A Man of Religion." *MLR,* 27 (1932), 144–148.

1952 ROCKWELL, K. A. "Canterbury Tales: General Prologue, 526, The Wife of Bath's Prologue, 435; 'Spiced Conscience'. " *N&Q,* 202 (1957), 84.

The Plowman

1953 HORRELL, Joe. "Chaucer's Symbolic Plowman." *Speculum,* 14 (1939), 82–92. Reprinted in 1700.

1954 STILLWELL, Gardiner. "Chaucer's Plowman and the Contemporary English Peasant." *ELH,* 6 (1939), 285–290.

The Miller

1955 BLOCK, Edward A. "Chaucer's Millers and Their Bagpipes." *Speculum,* 29 (1954), 239–243.

1956 GALWAY, Margaret. "The History of Chaucer's Miller." *N&Q,* 195 (1950), 486–488.

1957 JONES, George F. "Chaucer and the Medieval Miller." *MLQ,* 16 (1955), 3–15.

1958 McCRACKEN, Samuel. "Chaucer's Canterbury Tales, A 565–566." *Explicator,* 23 (1965), item 55.

1959 PRATT, Robert A. "The Beard of Chaucer's Miller." *N&Q,* 195 (1950), 568.

1960 REISS, Edmund. "Chaucer's Miller, Pilate, and the Devil." *AnM,* 5 (1964), 21–25.

1961 SCOTT, Kathleen L. "Sow-and-Bagpipe Imagery in the Miller's Portrait." *RES.* 18 (1967), 287–290.

1962 WHITING, B. J. "The Miller's Head." *MLN,* 52 (1937), 417–419. Cf. *ibid.,* 53 (1938), 505–507 (A. N. Wiley), 56 (1941), 534–536 (Utley), 69 (1954), 309–310 (Whiting).

The Manciple

See under *The Manciple's Prologue and Tale.*

The Reeve

1964 BENNETT, H. S. "The Reeve and the Manor in the Fourteenth Century." *EHR,* 41 (1926), 358–365.

1965 FOREHAND, Brooks. "Old Age and Chaucer's Reeve." *PMLA,* 69 (1954), 984–989.

1966 MOFFETT, H. Y. "Oswald the Reeve." *PQ,* 4 (1925), 208–223.

1967 POWLEY, Edward B. "Chaucer's Reeve." *TLS,* July 14, 1932, p. 516.

The Summoner

1968 AIKEN, Pauline. "The Summoner's Malady." *SP,* 33 (1936), 40–44.

1969 BIGGINS, D. "Chaucer's Summoner: 'Wel Loved He Garleek, Oynons, and eek Lekes', *C.T.* I, 634." *N&Q,* 209 (1964), 48.

1970 BIGGINS, D. "More Chaucerian Ambiguities: A 652, 664, D 1346." *N&Q,* 207 (1962), 165–167.

1971 BLOOMFIELD, Morton W. "Chaucer's Summoner and the Girls of the Diocese." *PQ,* 28 (1949), 503–507.

1972 CAWLEY, A. C. See 2610.

1973 CURRY, Walter C. "The Malady of Chaucer's Summoner." *MP,* 19 (1921–22), 395–404.

1974 ERICSON, Eston E. "Pulling Finches and Woodcocks." *ES,* 42 (1961), 306. Cf. *ibid.,* 44 (1963), 278 (D. Biggins).

1975 GARBÁTY, Thomas J. "Chaucer's Summoner: An Example of the Assimilation Lag in Scholarship." *PMASAL,* 47 (1962), 605–611.

1976 GARBÁTY, Thomas J. "The Summoner's Occupational Disease." *Medical Hist.,* 7 (1963), 348–358.

1977 HASELMAYER, L. A. "The Apparitor and Chaucer's Summoner." *Speculum,* 12 (1937), 43–57.

1978 KASKE, Robert E. "The Summoner's Garleek, Oynons, and eek Lekes." *MLN,* 74 (1959), 481–484.

1979 PACE, George B. "Physiognomy and Chaucer's Summoner and Alisoun." *Traditio,* 18 (1962), 417–420.

1980 PELTOLA, Niilo. "Chaucer's Summoner: Fyr-reed Cherubynnes Face." *NM,* 69 (1968), 560–568.

1981 SLEETH, Charles R. "The Friendship of Chaucer's Summoner and Pardoner." *MLN,* 56 (1941), 138.

1982 SPARGO, John W. " 'Questio quid iuris'. " *MLN,* 62 (1947), 119–122.

1983 WOOD, Chauncey. "The Sources of Chaucer's Summoner's 'garleek, onyons, and eke lekes'. " *ChauR,* 5 (1971) 240–244.

1984 WOOLF, Henry B. "The Summoner and His Concubine." *MLN,* 68 (1953), 118–121.

The Pardoner

1985 BIGGINS, D. "Chaucer's General Prologue, A 163 [*sc.* A 673]." *N&Q,* 204 (1959), 435–436 Cf. *ibid.,* 205 (1960), 404–406 (B. D. H. Miller).

1986 BIGGINS, D. "Chaucer's General Prologue, A. 696–698." *N&Q,* 205 (1960), 93–95.

1987 BLOOMFIELD, Morton W. "The Pardons of Pamplona and the Pardoner of Rounceval: *Piers Plowman B* XVII 252." *PQ,* 35 (1956), 60–68.

1988 CURRIE, Felicity. "Chaucer's Pardoner Again." *LeedsSE,* 4 (1970), 11–22.

1989 CURRY, Walter C. See 2911.

1990 EVANOFF, Alexander. "The Pardoner as Huckster: A Dissent from Kittredge." *BYUS,* 4 (1962), 209–217.

1991 HENDRICKSON, D. W. "The Pardoner's Hair—Abundant or Sparse?" *MLN,* 66 (1951), 328–329.

1992 JUSSERAND, J. J. "Chaucer's Pardoner and the Pope's Pardoner." *Essays on Chaucer,* Part V, pp. 421–436 (Chaucer Soc., 2nd Ser., No. 19).

1993 KELLOGG, Alfred L., and Louis A. HASELMAYER. "Chaucer's Satire of the Pardoner." *PMLA,* 66 (1951), 251–277. Reprinted in 456.

1994 KIEHL, James M. "Dryden's Zimri and Chaucer's Pardoner: A Comparative Study of Verse Portraiture." *Thoth,* 6 (1965), 3–12.

1995 MOORE, Samuel. "Chaucer's Pardoner of Rouncival." *MP,* 25 (1927–28), 59–66.

1996 ROWLAND, Beryl. "Animal Imagery and the Pardoner's Abnormality." *Neophil,* 48 (1964), 56–60.

1997 SCHAUT, Quentin L. "Chaucer's Pardoner and Indulgences." *Greyfriar*, 1961, pp. 25–39.

1998 SCHWEITZER, Edward C., Jr. "Chaucer's Pardoner and the Hare." *ELN*, 4 (1967), 247–250.

1999 TATLOCK, John S. P. "*Bretherhed* in Chaucer's *Prolog.*" *MLN*, 31 (1961), 139–142.

2000 THURSTON, Herbert. "The Medieval Pardoner." *Month*, 142 (1923), 522–532.

2001 WILLIAMS, Arnold. "Some Documents on English Pardoners, 1350–1400." *Mediaeval Studies in Honor of Urban Tigner Holmes, Jr.*, pp. 197–207; *Univ. of No. Carolina Stud. in Romance Lang. and Lit.*, 56, Chapel Hill 1966.

2002 YOUNG, Karl. "Chaucer and the Liturgy." *MLN*, 30 (1915), 97–99.

The Host

2003 KEEN, William. " 'To Doon Yow Ese': A Study of the Host in the *General Prologue* of the *Canterbury Tales.*" *Topic*, 9 Topic 17 (1969), 5–18.

2004 MALONE, Kemp. "Harry Bailey and Godelief." *ES*, 31 (1950), 209–215.

2004a PAGE, Barbara. "Concerning the Host." *ChauR*, 4 (1970), 1–13.

Criticism: Individual Tales

The Knight's Tale

2005 ACKERMAN, Robert W. "Tester: *Knight's Tale*, 2499." *MLN*, 49 (1934), 397–400.

2006 AIKEN, Pauline. "Arcite's Illness and Vincent of Beauvais." *PMLA*, 51 (1936), 361–369.

2007 BAKER, Courtland D. "A Note on Chaucer's *Knight's Tale.*" *MLN*, 45 (1930), 460–462.

2008 BAUM, Paull F. "Characterization in the 'Knight's Tale'. " *MLN*, 46 (1931), 302–304.

2009 BEIDLER, Peter G. "Chaucer's *Knight's Tale* and Its Teller." *English Record*, 18 (1968), 54–60.

2010 BENNETT, J. A. W. "Chaucer, Dante, and Boccaccio." *MÆ*, 22 (1953), 114–115.

2011 BENSON, C. David. "The *Knight's Tale* as History." *ChauR*, 3 (1968), 107–123.

2012 BLAKE, Kathleen A. "Order and the Noble Life in Chaucer's *Knight's Tale.*" *MLQ*, 34 (1973), 3–19.

2013 BOLTON, W. F. "The Topic of the *Knight's Tale.*" *ChauR*, 1 (1967), 217–227.

2014 BROOKS, Cleanth. "Chaucer: Saturn's Daughter." *MLN*, 49 (1934), 459–461. [A 2453]

2015 BROOKS, Douglas, and Alastair FOWLER. "The Meaning of Chaucer's *Knight's Tale.*" *MÆ*, 39 (1970), 123–146.

2016 CAMERON, Allen B. "The Heroine in The Knight's Tale." *SSF*, 5 (1968), 119–127.

2017 CAPONE, Gino. *La* Novella del Cavalier—*Knight's Tale*—di Geoffrey Chaucer e la Teseide di Giovanni Boccaccio. Assaggi di critica comparata. 2 vols., Sussari: Capone, 1907-9.

2018 Cozart, William R. "Chaucer's *Knight's Tale:* A Philosophical Re-appraisal of a Medieval Romance." *Medieval Epic to the 'Epic Theater' of Brecht,* ed. Rosario P. Armato and John M. Spalek. *Univ. of So. California Stud. in Compar. Lit.,* 1, pp. 25–34. Los Angeles, 1968.

2019 Curry, Walter C. "Arcite's Intellect." *JEGP,* 29 (1930), 83–99.

2020 Curry, Walter C. "Astrologising the Gods." *Anglia,* 47 (1923), 213–243.

2021 Dean, Christopher. "The 'place' in *The Knight's Tale.*" *N&Q,* 211 (1966), 90–92.

2022 Delasanta, Rodney. "Uncommon Commonplaces in *The Knight's Tale.*" *NM,* 70 (1969), 683–690.

2023 Delasanta, Rodney. "James Smith and Chaucer." *EIC,* 22 (1972), 221–225. A reply to 2088.

2024 Dustoor, P. E. "Chaucer's Astrology in "The Knight's Tale'. " *TLS,* May 5, 1927, p. 318.

2025 Dustoor, P. E. "Notes on 'The Knight's Tale'. " *MLR,* 22 (1927), 438–441.

2026 Elbow, Peter H. "How Chaucer Transcends Oppositions in the *Knight's Tale.*" *ChauR,* 7 (1972), 97–112.

2027 Emerson, O. F. "Chaucer's 'Opie of Thebes Fyn'. " *MP,* 17 (1919–20), 287–291. Reprinted in 395.

2028 Emerson, O. F. "A New Note on the Date of Chaucer's Knight's Tale." *Stud. in Lang. and Lit. [presented to] James Morgan Hart,* pp. 203–254, New York: Holt, 1910. Reprinted in 395.

2029 Emerson, O. F. See 395, 396.

2030 Fairchild, Hoxie N. "Active Arcite, Contemplative Palamon." *JEGP,* 26 (1927), 285–293.

2031 Fifield, Merle. "The *Knight's Tale:* Incident, Idea, Incorporation." *ChauR,* 3 (1968), 95–106.

2032 Foster, Edward E. "Humor in the *Knight's Tale.*" *ChauR,* 3 (1968), 88–94.

2033 French, W. H. "The Lovers in the *Knight's Tale.*" *JEGP,* 48 (1949), 320–328.

2034 Frost, William. "An Interpretation of Chaucer's Knight's Tale." *RES,* 25 (1949), 289–304. Reprinted in 1700.

2035 Garvin, Katharine. "Note on the Tournament in the *Knight's Tale.*" *MLN,* 46 (1931), 453–454.

2036 Gaylord, Alan T. "The Role of Saturn in the *Knight's Tale.*" *ChauR,* 8 (1974), 171–190.

2037 Gibbs, Lincoln R. "The Meaning of feeldes in Chaucer's *Knight's Tale,* vv. 975–977." *MLN,* 24 (1909), 197–198. Cf. *ibid.,* 25 (1910), 28 (Kittredge).

2038 Gunn, Alan M. F. See 1237.

2039 Haller, Robert S. "The *Knight's Tale* and the Epic Tradition." *ChauR,* 1 (1966), 67–84.

2040 Halverson, John. "Aspects of Order in the Knight's Tale." *SP,* 57 (1960), 606–621.

2041 Ham, Edward B. "Knight's Tale 38." *ELH,* 17 (1950), 252–261.

2042 Harrington, David V. "Rhetoric and Meaning in Chaucer's *Knight's Tale.*" *PLL,* 3, Summer Suppl. (1967), 71–79.

2043 HELTERMAN, Jeffery. "The Dehumanizing Metamorphoses of the *Knight's Tale.*" *ELH,* 38 (1971), 493–511.

2044 HERBEN, Stephen J. "Knight's Tale, A 1881 ff." *MLN,* 53 (1938), 595.

2045 HERZ, Judith S. "Chaucer's Elegiac Knight." *Criticism,* 6 (1964), 212–224.

2046 HINCKLEY, Henry B. "The Grete Emetreus the King of Inde." *MLN,* 48 (1933), 148–149.

2047 HOFFMAN, Richard L. "The *felaweshipe* of Chaucer's *love* and *lordshipe.*" *C&M,* 25 (1964), 263–273.

2048 HOFFMAN, Richard L. "Mercury, Argus, and Chaucer's Arcite: *Canterbury Tales* I (A) 1384–90." *N&Q,* 210 (1965), 128–129.

2049 HOFFMAN, Richard L. "Ovid and Chaucer's Myth of Theseus and Pirithoüs." *ELN,* 2 (1965), 252–257.

2050 HOFFMAN, Richard L. "Two Notes on Chaucer's Arcite." *ELN,* 4 (1967), 172–175.

2051 HULBERT, J. R. "What Was Chaucer's Aim in the *Knight's Tale?*" *SP,* 26 (1929), 375–385.

2052 KELLOGG, Alfred L., and Robert C. Cox. See 458.

2053 KOCH, John. "Ein Beitrag zur Kritik Chaucer's." *ESt,* 1 (1877), 249–293. Reprinted (enlarged) in English in 398, Part IV.

2054 KOVETZ, Gene H. "Canterbury Tales, A 2349–52." *N&Q,* 203 (1958), 236–237.

2055 LLOYD, Michael. "A Defence of Arcite." *EM,* 10 (1959), 11–25.

2056 LOOMIS, Dorothy B. "Saturn in Chaucer's 'Knight's Tale'." 54, pp. 149–161.

2057 LOWES, John L. "Hereos Again." *MLN,* 31 (1916), 185–187.

2058 LOWES, John L. "The Loveres Maladye of Hereos." *MP,* 11 (1913–14), 491–546. Cf. *Nation,* 97 (1913), 233.

2059 LOWES, John L. "The Tempest at hir Hoom-cominge." *MLN,* 19 (1904), 240–243.

2060 LUMIANSKY, Robert M. "Chaucer's Philosophical Knight." *TSE,* 3 (1952), 47–68.

2061 MARCKWARDT, Albert H. *Characterization in Chaucer's Knight's Tale.* (*Univ. of Michigan Contrib. in Mod. Phil.,* No. 5.) Ann Arbor, Mich., 1947.

2062 MATHER, Frank J., Jr. "On the Date of the *Knight's Tale.*" 50, pp. 300–313.

2063 McKENZIE, James J. "A Chaucerian Emendation." *N&Q,* 199 (1954), 463.

2064 McKENZIE, James. "Chaucer's *The Knight's Tale,* 1053." *Explicator,* 20 (1962), item 69.

2065 MEIER, T. K. "Chaucer's Knight as 'Persona': Narration as Control." *EM,* 20 (1969), 11–21.

2066 MIDDLETON, Anne. "The Modern Art of Fortifying: *Palamon and Arcite* as Epicurean Epic." *ChauR,* 3 (1968), 124–143.

2067 MITCHELL, Edward R. "The Two Mayings in Chaucer's *Knight's Tale.*" *MLN,* 71 (1956), 560–564.

2068 MUSCATINE, Charles. "Form, Texture, and Meaning in Chaucer's *Knight's Tale.*" *PMLA,* 65 (1950), 911–929. Reprinted in 628.

2069 NAKATANI, Kiichiro. "A Perpetual Prison: The Design of Chaucer's *The Knight's Tale.*" *HSELL,* 9, i–ii (1963), 75–89.

2070 NEUSE, Richard. "The Knight: The First Mover in Chaucer's Human Comedy." *UTQ,* 31 (1962), 299–315.

2071 PARR, Johnstone. "Chaucer's 'Cherles Rebellyng'," *MLN,* 69 (1954), 393–394.

2072 PARR, Johnstone. "The Date and Revision of Chaucer's *Knight's Tale.*" *PMLA,* 60 (1945), 307–324.

2073 PARR, Johnstone. " 'Life Is a Pilgrimage' in Chaucer's *Knight's Tale* 2847–49." *MLN,* 67 (1952), 340–341.

2074 PENNINGER, F. Elaine. "Chaucer's *Knight's Tale* and the Theme of Appearance and Reality in *The Canterbury Tales.*" *SAQ,* 63 (1964), 398–405.

2075 PRATT, Robert A. " 'Joye after Wo' in the *Knight's Tale.*" *JEGP,* 57 (1958), 416–423.

2076 PRATT, Robert A. "Was Chaucer's *Knight's Tale* Extensively Revised after the Middle of 1390?" *PMLA,* 63 (1948), 726–736. Cf. *ibid.,* 736–739 (J. Parr).

2077 PRATT, Robert A. See 560.

2078 QUINN, Betty N. See 997.

2079 ROBERTSON, Stuart. "Elements of Realism in the *Knight's Tale.*" *JEGP,* 14 (1915), 226–255.

2080 RODEFFER, J. D. "Chaucer and the *Roman de Thèbes.*" *MLN,* 17 (1902), 471–473.

2081 ROWLAND, Beryl. "Chaucer's The Knight's Tale, A. 1810." *Explicator,* 21 (1963), item 73.

2082 RUGGIERS, Paul G. "Some Philosophical Aspects of *The Knight's Tale.*" *CE,* 19 (1958), 296–302. Cf. *ibid.,* 20 (1959), 193–194 (W. A. Madden).

2083 RUMBLE, T. C. "Chaucer's *Knight's Tale,* 2680–82." *PQ,* 43 (1964), 130–133.

2084 SALTER, Elizabeth. *Chaucer: The Knight's Tale and The Clerk's Tale.* London: Arnold, 1962.

2085 SAVAGE, Henry. "Arcite's Maying." *MLN,* 55 (1940), 207–209.

2086 SCHMIDT, A. V. C. "The Tragedy of Arcite: A Reconsideration of the *Knight's Tale.*" *EIC,* 19 (1969), 107–117.

2087 SMITH, C. Alphonso. "Under the sonne he loketh." *MLN,* 37 (1922), 120–121. Cf. *ibid.,* 376–377 (Klaeber), 377 (Tatlock); 38 (1923), 59 (G. L. van Roosbroeck), 60 (Patch); 44 (1929), 182 (S. B. Hustvedt); *TLS,* June 14, 1934, p. 424 (H. Savage).

2088 SMITH, James. "Chaucer, Boethius, and Recent Trends in Criticism." *EIC,* 22 (1972), 4–32.

2089 SMITH, Roland M. See 611.

2090 STEADMAN, John M. "Venus' *citole* in Chaucer's *Knight's Tale* and Berchorius." *Speculum,* 34 (1959), 620–624.

2091 TATELBAUM, Linda. "Venus' *Citole* and the Restoration of Harmony in Chaucer's *Knight's Tale.*" *NM,* 74 (1973), 649–664.

2092 THURSTON, Paul T. *Artistic Ambivalence in Chaucer's Knight's Tale.* Gainesville: Univ. of Florida Press, 1968.

2093 TORRACA, Francesco. "The Knightes Tale e la Teseide." *Società Reale di Napoli. Atti della reale Accademia di Archeologia, Lettere e Belle Arti,* n.s. 10 (1928), 199–217.

2094 TRIPP, A. Raymond, Jr. "The Knight's Tale and the Limitations of Language." *Rendezvous,* 6 (1971), 23–28.

2095 TURNER, Frederick. "A Structuralist Analysis of the *Knight's Tale.*" ChauR, 8 (1974), 279–296.

2096 UNDERWOOD, Dale. "The First of *The Canterbury Tales.*" ELH, 26 (1959), 455–469. Reprinted in 1548.

2097 VAN, Thomas A. "Second Meanings in Chaucer's *Knight's Tale.*" ChauR, 3 (1968), 69–76.

2098 VAN, Thomas A. "Theseus and the 'Right Way' of the *Knight's Tale.*" *Stud. in the Literary Imagination,* 4, ii (1971), 83–100.

2099 VAN, Thomas A. See 1400.

2100 VANN, J. Don. "A Character Reversal in Chaucer's *Knight's Tale.*" AN&Q, 3 (1965), 131–132.

2101 WAGER, Willis J. "The So-Called Prologue to the *Knight's Tale.*" MLN, 50 (1935) 296–307.

2102 WALDRON, R. A. "*Knight's Tale* A 1037: 'fressher than the May'." ES, 46 (1965), 402–406.

2103 WEBB, Henry J. "A Reinterpretation of Chaucer's Theseus." RES, 23 (1947), 289–296.

2104 WEESE, Walter E. " 'Vengeance and Pleyn Correccioun', KnT 2461." MLN, 63 (1948), 331–333.

2105 WESTLUND, Joseph. "The *Knight's Tale* as an Impetus for Pilgrimage." PQ, 43 (1964), 526–537.

2106 WHITTOCK, T. G. "Chaucer's *Knight's Tale.*" Theoria (Univ. of Natal), 13 (1959), 27–38.

2107 WILKINS, Ernest H. See 1027.

2108 WILSON, H. S. "*The Knight's Tale* and the *Teseida* Again." UTQ, 18 (1949), 131–146.

2109 WITLIEB, Bernard L. "Chaucer and a French Story of Thebes." ELN, 11 (1973), 5–9.

The Miller's Prologue and Tale

2110 ALBRECHT, W. P. "Chaucer's Miller's Tale." *Explicator,* 9 (1951), item 25.

2111 BARNOUW, A. J. "Chaucer's *Miller's Tale.*" MLR, 7 (1912), 145–148.

2112 BEICHNER, Paul E. "Absolon's Hair." MS, 12 (1951), 222–233.

2113 BEICHNER, Paul E. "Characterization in *The Miller's Tale.*" 1700, pp. 117–129.

2114 BEICHNER, Paul E. "Chaucer's Hende Nicholas." MS, 14 (1952), 151–153.

2115 BENTLEY, Joseph. "Chaucer's Fatalistic Miller." SAQ, 64 (1965), 247–253.

2116 BIRNEY, Earle. "The Inhibited and the Uninhibited: Ironic Structure in the *Miller's Tale.*" Neophil, 44 (1960), 333–338.

2117 BLOOMFIELD, Morton W. "The Miller's Tale—An UnBoethian Interpretation." 56, pp. 205–211.

2118 BOLTON, W. F. "The *Miller's Tale:* An Interpretation." *MS,* 24, (1962), 83–94.

2119 BOOTHMAN, Janet. " 'Who Hath No Wyf, He Is No Cokewold': A Study of John and January in Chaucer's Miller's and Merchant's Tales." *Thoth,* 4 (1963), 3–14.

2120 BRATCHER, James T., and Nicolai VON KREISLER. "The Popularity of the *Miller's Tale.*" *SFQ,* 35 (1971), 325–335.

2121 BROWN, William J. "Chaucer's Double Apology for the *Miller's Tale.*" *Univ. of Colorado Stud.: Ser. in Lang. and Lit.,* No. 10 (1966), 15–22.

2122 BRUSENDORFF, Aage. "He Knew Nat Catoun for His Wit Was Rude'." *Studies in English Philology: A Miscellany in Honor of Frederick Klaeber,* pp. 320–339. Minneapolis: Univ. of Minnesota Press, 1929.

2123 BURKHART, Robert E. "Chaucer's Absolon: A Sinful Parody of the Miller." *Cithara,* 8, ii (1969), 47–54.

2124 CARRINGTON, Evelyn. "A Note on the 'White paternoster'." *Folk-lore Record,* 2 (1879), 127–134.

2125 CLINE, Ruth H. "Three Notes on *The Miller's Tale.*" *HLQ,* 26 (1963), 131–145.

2126 COFFMAN, George R. "*The Miller's Tale:* 3187–3215: Chaucer and the Seven Liberal Arts in Burlesque Vein." *MLN,* 67 (1952), 329–331.

2127 COFFMAN, George R. "A Note on the Miller's Prologue." *MLN,* 50 (1935), 311–312.

2128 COLLINS, Fletcher, Jr. "The Kinges Note: *The Miller's Tale,* line 31." *Speculum,* 8 (1933), 195–197.

2129 COLLINS, Fletcher, Jr. "*Solas* in the Miller's Tale." *MLN,* 47 (1932), 363–364. Cf. *ibid.,* 48 (1933), 369–370 (David Brown).

2130 CURRY, Walter C. See 2188.

2131 DONALDSON, E. T. "Chaucer's *Miller's Tale,* A 3483–6." *MLN,* 69 (1954), 310–313. Reprinted in 273.

2132 DONALDSON, E. T. "Idiom of Popular Poetry in the *Miller's Tale.*" *English Inst. Essays, 1950,* pp. 116–140. Reprinted in *Explication as Criticism: Selected Papers from the English Institute 1941–1952,* ed. W. K. Wimsatt, Jr., pp. 27–51. New York: Columbia Univ. Press, 1963. Reprinted in 211 and 273.

2133 DONALDSON, E. Talbot. "Medieval Poetry and Medieval Sin." 273, pp. 164–174.

2134 ELLINWOOD, LEONARD. "A Further Note on 'Pilates Voys'." *Speculum,* 26 (1951), 482.

2135 FROST, George L. "The Music of *The Kinges Note.*" *Speculum,* 8 (1933), 526–528.

2136 GARRETT, R. M. "Chaucer in Minnesota." *Dialect Notes,* 5 (1923), 245. [Pig's eye.]

2137 GELLRICH, Jesse M. "Nicholas' 'Kynges Note' and 'Melodye'." *ELN,* 8 (1971), 249–252.

2138 GELLRICH, Jesse M. "The Parody of Medieval Music in the *Miller's Tale.*" *JEGP,* 73 (1974), 176–188.

2139 HANSON, Thomas B. "Physiognomy and Characterization in the *Miller's Tale.*" *NM,* 72 (1971), 477–482.

2140   HARDER, Kelsie B. "Chaucer's Use of the Mystery Plays in the *Miller's Tale.*" *MLQ,* 17 (1956), 193–198.

2141   HATTON, Thomas J. "Absolon, Taste, and Odor in *The Miller's Tale.*" *PLL,* 7 (1971), 72–75.

2142   HENCH, Atcheson L. "Chaucer's *Miller's Tale,* 1. 3226." *ELN,* 3 (1965), 88–92.

2143   HILL, Betty. "Chaucer: *The Miller's* and *Reeve's Tales.*" *NM,* 74 (1973), 665–675.

2144   HOFFMAN, Richard L. " 'Ovid's' *Ictibus agrestis* and the *Miller's Tale.*" *N&Q,* 209 (1964), 49–50.

2145   KASKE, Robert E. "The *Canticum Canticorum* in the *Miller's Tale.*" *SP,* 59 (1962), 479–500.

2146   KREUZER, James R. "The Swallow in Chaucer's *Miller's Tale.*" *MLN,* 73 (1958), 81.

2147   KUHL, E. P. "Daun Gerveys." *MLN,* 29 (1914), 156. Reprinted in 475.

2148   LEWIS, Robert E. "Alisoun's 'Coler': Chaucer's *Miller's Tale* ll. 3239, 3242, 3265." *MS,* 32 (1970), 337–339.

2149   LEYLAND, A. "Miller's Tale [I(A) 3449]." *N&Q,* 219 (1974), 126–127.

2150   MacDONALD, Angus. "Absolon and St. Neot." *Neophil,* 48 (1964), 235–237.

2151   McCRACKEN, Samuel. " 'Miller's Tale' [I(A) 3384]." *N&Q,* 218 (1973), 283.

2152   MILLER, Robert P. "The *Miller's Tale* as Complaint." *ChauR,* 5 (1970), 147–160.

2153   MOGAN, Joseph J., Jr. "The Mutability Motif in *The Miller's Tale.*" *AN&Q,* 8 (1969), 19.

2154   MULLANY, Peter F. "Chaucer's Miller and *Pilates Voys.*" *AN&Q,* 3 (1964), 54–55.

2155   NOVELLI, Cornelius. "Absolon's 'Freend so deere': A Pivotal Point in The Miller's Tale." *Neophil,* 52 (1968), 65–69.

2156   O'CONNOR, John J. "The Astrological Background of the *Miller's Tale.*" *Speculum,* 31 (1956), 120–125.

2157   OLSON, Paul A. "Poetic Justice in the *Miller's Tale.*" *MLQ,* 24 (1963), 227–236.

2158   OWEN, Charles A., Jr. "One Robyn or Two." *MLN,* 67 (1952), 336–338.

2159   PACE, George B. See 1979.

2160   PARKER, Roscoe E. " 'Pilates Voys'." *Speculum,* 25 (1950), 237–244.

2161   PEARCY, Roy J. "A Minor Analogue to the Branding in *The Miller's Tale.*" *N&Q,* 214 (1969), 333–335.

2162   POTEET, Daniel P., II. "Avoiding Women in Times of Affliction: An Analogue for the *Miller's Tale,* A 3589–91." *N&Q,* 217 (1972), 89–90.

2163   PRATT, Robert A. "Was Robyn the Miller's Youth Misspent?" *MLN,* 59 (1944), 47–49.

2164   REED, Mary B. "Chaucer's Sely Carpenter." *PQ,* 41 (1962), 768–769.

2165   REISS, Edmund. "Daun Gerveys in the *Miller's Tale.*" *PLL,* 6 (1970), 115–124.

2166   ROWLAND, Beryl, "Alison Identified (*The Miller's Tale,* 3234)." *AN&Q,* 3 (1964), 3–4, 20–21, 39.

2167   ROWLAND, Beryl. "The Play of the *Miller's Tale:* A Game within a Game." *ChauR,* 5 (1970), 140–146.

2168 ROWLAND, Beryl. "Chaucer's Blasphemous Churl: A New Interpretation of the *Miller's Tale.*" 53, pp. 43–55.

2169 SIEGEL, Paul N. "Comic Irony in *The Miller's Tale.*" *BUSE,* 4 (1960), 114–120.

2170 SIMMONDS, James D. " 'Hende Nicholas' and the Clerk." *N&Q,* 207 (1962), 446.

2171 SPITZER, Leo. "A Chaucerian Hapax Legomenon: *upon the viritoot.*" *LangQ.,* 26 (1950), 389–393. [A 3770]

2172 STILLWELL, Gardiner. "The Language of Love in Chaucer's Miller's and Reeve's Tales and in the Old French Fabliaux." *JEGP,* 54 (1955), 693–699.

2173 THOMS, William J. "Chaucer's Night-Spell." *Folk-lore Record,* 1 (1878), 145–154.

2174 THRO, A. Booker. "Chaucer's Creative Comedy: A Study of the *Miller's Tale* and the *Shipman's Tale.*" *ChauR,* 5 (1970), 97–111.

2175 VINE, Guthrie. "The Miller's Tale: A Study of an Unrecorded Fragment of a Manuscript in the John Rylands Library in Relation to the First Printed Text." *BJRL,* 17 (1933), 333–347.

2176 WENZEL, Siegfried. "Two Notes on Chaucer and Grosseteste." *N&Q,* 215 (1970), 449–451. [A 3455, D 1825 ff.]

2177 WORDSWORTH, Jonathan. "A Link between the Knight's Tale and the Miller's." *MÆ,* 27 (1958), 21.

2178 YOFFIE, Leah R. C. "Chaucer's 'White Paternoster', Milton's Angels, and a Hebrew Night Prayer." *SFQ,* 15 (1951), 203–210.

The Reeve's Prologue and Tale

2179 BAIRD, Joseph L. "Law and the *Reeve's Tale.*" *NM,* 70 (1969), 679–683.

2180 BAUM, Paull F. "The Mare and the Wolf." *MLN,* 37 (1922), 350–353.

2181 BIGGINS, Dennis. "Sym(e)kyn/*simia:* The Ape in Chaucer's Millers." *SP,* 65 (1968), 44–50.

2182 BLOCK, Edward A. " . . . and it is half-way pryme." *Speculum,* 32 (1957), 826–833.

2183 BREWER, Derek S. "The *Reeve's Tale* and the King's Hall, Cambridge." *ChauR,* 5 (1971), 311–317.

2184 BURBRIDGE, Roger T. "Chaucer's *Reeve's Tale* and the Fabliau 'Le meunier et les .II. clers." *AnM,* 12 (1971), 30–36.

2185 COPLAND, M. "*The Reeve's Tale:* Harlotrie or Sermonyng?" *MÆ,* 31 (1962), 14–32.

2186 CORREALE, Robert M. "Chaucer's Parody of Compline in the *Reeve's Tale.*" *ChauR,* 1 (1966), 161–166.

2187 CROW, Martin M. "*The Reeve's Tale* in the Hands of a North Midland Scribe." *Stud. in English* (Univ. of Texas), 1938, pp. 14–24.

2188 CURRY, Walter C. "Chaucer's Reeve and Miller." *PMLA,* 35 (1920), 189–209.

2189 DELANY, Sheila. "Clerks and Quiting in the *Reeve's Tale.*" *MS,* 29 (1967), 351–356.

2190 DEMPSTER, Germaine. "On the Source of the *Reeve's Tale.*" *JEGP,* 29 (1930), 473–488.

2191 Eliason, Norman E. "Some Word-Play in Chaucer's Reeve's Tale." *MLN,* 71 (1956), 162–164.

2192 Elliott, Charles. "*The Reeve's Prologue and Tale* in the Ellesmere and Hengwrt Manuscripts." *N&Q,* 209 (1964), 167–170.

2193 Emerson, Katherine T. "The Question of 'Lusty Malyne'." *N&Q,* 202 (1957), 277–278.

2194 Frank, Robert W., Jr. "The *Reeve's Tale* and the Comedy of Limitation." *Directions in Literary Criticism: Contemporary Approaches to Literature,* ed. Stanley Weintraub and Philip Young, pp. 53–69. University Park: Penn. State Univ. Press, 1973.

2195 Friedman, John B. "A Reading of Chaucer's *Reeve's Tale.*" *ChauR,* 2 (1967), 8–19.

2196 Garbáty, Thomas J. "Satire and Regionalism: The Reeve and His Tale." *ChauR,* 8 (1973), 1–8.

2197 Hart, Walter M. "The Reeve's Tale: A Comparative Study of Chaucer's Narrative Art." *PMLA,* 23 (1908), 1–44.

2198 Harvey, R. W. "The Reeve's Polemic." *Wascana Rev.,* 2, No. 1 (1967), 62–73.

2199 Hinton, Norman D. "Two Names in The *Reeve's Tale.*" *Names,* 9 (1961), 117–120. [Malyne, Aleyn.]

2200 Holthausen, F. "Zu Chaucers 'Reeves Tale'." *Anglia Beiblatt,* 33 (1922), 103–104.

2201 Kaske, Robert E. "An Aube in the *Reeve's Tale.*" *ELH,* 26 (1959), 295–310.

2202 Kirby, Thomas A. "An Analogue (?) to the *Reeve's Tale.*" 53, pp. 381–383.

2203 Lancashire, Ian. "Sexual Innuendo in the *Reeve's Tale.*" *ChauR,* 6 (1972), 159–170.

2204 Lange, Marius. *Vom Fabliau zu Boccaccio und Chaucer: Ein Vergleich zweier Fabliaux mit Boccaccios Decamerone (IX. 6) und mit Chaucers Reeves Tale.* Hamburg, 1934 (*Britannica,* No. 8).

2205 MacLaine, A. H. "Chaucer's Wine-cask Image: Word Play in The *Reeve's Prologue.*" *MÆ,* 31 (1962), 129–131.

2206 Montgomery, Franz. "A Note on the Reeve's Prologue." *PQ,* 10 (1931), 404–405.

2207 Myers, Louis M. "A Line in the Reeve's Prologue." *MLN,* 49 (1934), 222–226. [Comment on 2206.]

2208 O'Keefe, Timothy J. "Meanings of 'Malyne' in The *Reeve's Tale.*" *AN&Q,* 12 (1973), 5–7.

2209 Olson, Glending. " 'The Reeve's Tale' and 'Gombert'." *MLR,* 64 (1969), 721–725.

2210 Olson, Glending. "The *Reeve's Tale* as a Fabliau." *MLQ,* 35 (1974), 219–230.

2211 Olson, Paul A. "The *Reeve's Tale:* Chaucer's *Measure for Measure.*" *SP,* 59 (1962), 1–17.

2212 Pratt, Robert A. "Chaucer and the Holy Cross of Bromholm." *MLN,* 70 (1955), 324–325.

2213 Pratt, Robert A. "Symkyn koude 'turne coppes': The *Reeve's Tale* 3928." *JEGP,* 59 (1960), 208–211.

2214 STEADMAN, John M. "Simkin's Camus Nose: A Latin Pun in the *Reeve's Tale?*" *MLN,* 75 (1960), 4–8.

2215 STILLWELL, Gardiner. See 2172.

2216 TOLKIEN, J. R. R. "Chaucer as a Philologist: *The Reeve's Tale.*" *Trans. Phil. Soc.* 1934, pp. 1–70.

2217 TURNER, W. A. "Chaucer's 'Lusty Malyne'." *N&Q,* 199 (1954), 232.

2218 WILSON, Robert C. "Chaucer's *Reeve's Tale.*" *Explicator,* 24 (1965), item 32.

The Cook's Prologue and Tale

2219 BIGGINS, Dennis. "Erroneous Punctuation in Chaucer, CT I (A) 4394–96." *PQ,* 44 (1965), 117–120.

2220 BLENNER-HASSETT, R. "When he his 'papir soghte', CT A-4404." *MLN,* 57 (1942), 34–35.

2221 CALL, Reginald. " 'Whan He His Papir Soghte' (Chaucer's *Cook's Tale,* A 4404)." *MLQ,* 4 (1943), 167–176.

2222 EMERSON, Katherine T. "Chaucer's *Canterbury Tales,* A. 4353." *Explicator,* 16, (1958), item 51.

2223 LYON, Earl D. "Roger de Ware, Cook." *MLN,* 52 (1937), 491–494.

2224 RICKERT, Edith. " 'Chaucer's Hodge of Ware'." *TLS,* Oct. 20, 1932, p. 761.

The Man of Law: Introduction and Tale

2225 BAUM, Paull F. "*The Man of Law's Tale.*" *MLN,* 64 (1949), 12–14.

2226 BEICHNER, Paul E. "Chaucer's Man of Law and *Disparitas Cultus.*" *Speculum,* 23 (1948), 70–75.

2227 BLOCK, Edward A. "Originality, Controlling Purpose, and Craftsmanship in Chaucer's *Man of Law's Tale.*" *PMLA,* 68 (1953), 572–616.

2228 BLOOMFIELD, Morton W. "The Man of Law's Tale: A Tragedy of Victimization and a Christian Comedy." *PMLA,* 87 (1972), 384–390; also (in Italian) *Strumenti Critici* (Torino), 8 (1969), 195–207.

2229 BOWEN, R. O. "Chaucer, The Man of Law's Introduction and Tale." *MLN,* 71 (1956), 165.

2230 BROWN, Carleton. "The Man of Law's Head-link and the Prologue of the Canterbury Tales." *SP,* 34 (1937), 8–35.

2231 BRUNT, Andrew. "Constance's Covering Her Child's Eyes in Chaucer's *Man of Law's Tale* 837f." *N&Q,* 214 (1969), 87–88.

2232 BURROW, J. " 'A maner Latyn corrupt.' " *MÆ,* 30 (1961), 33–37.

2233 CULVER, T. D. "The Imposition of Order: A Measure of Art in the Man of Law's Tale." *YES,* 2 (1972), 13–20.

2234 CURRY, Walter C. "O Mars, O Atazir." *JEGP,* 22 (1923), 347–368.

2235 CURTISS, Joseph T. "The Horoscope in Chaucer's *Man of Law's Tale.*" *JEGP,* 26 (1927), 24–32.

2236 DAVID, Alfred. "The Man of Law vs. Chaucer: A Case of Poetics." *PMLA,* 82 (1967), 217–225.

THE MAN OF LAW'S TALE

2237 Duffey, Bernard I. "The Intention and Art of *The Man of Law's Tale.*" *ELH,* 14 (1947), 181–193.

2238 Edwards, A. C. "Knaresborough Castle and 'The Kynges Modres Court'." *PQ,* 19 (1940), 306–309. Reprinted in 628.

2239 Farrell, Robert T. "Chaucer's Use of the Theme of the Help of God in the *Man of Law's Tale.*" *NM,* 71 (1970), 239–243.

2240 Giffin, Mary. " 'Allas Custaunce Thow Nast No Champioun'." 413, pp. 67–88.

2241 Gough, Alfred B. *The Constance Saga.* (*Palaestra,* 23.) Berlin, 1902.

2242 Hamilton, Marie P. "The Dramatic Suitability of the *Man of Law's Tale.*" 55, pp. 153–163.

2243 Harrington, David V. "Chaucer's Man of Law's Tale: Rhetoric and Emotion." *Moderna Språk,* 61 (1967), 353–362.

2244 Hornstein, Lilliam H. "Trivet's Constance and the *King of Tars.*" *MLN,* 55 (1940), 354–357.

2245 Isaacs, Neil D. "Constance in Fourteenth-Century England." *NM,* 59 (1958), 260–277.

2246 Jones, Claude E. "Chaucer's Custance." *NM,* 64 (1963), 175–180.

2247 Knowlton, E. C. "Chaucer's Man of Law." *JEGP,* 23 (1924), 83–93.

2248 Labriola, Albert C. "The Doctrine of Charity and the Use of Homiletic 'Figures' in the *Man of Law's Tale.*" *TSLL,* 12 (1970), 5–14.

2249 Leffingwell, William. "Saints' Lives and the Sultaness: A Note on a Perplexing Episode in Chaucer's *Man of Law's Tale.*" *Thoth,* 12 (1971), 29–32.

2250 Lewis, Robert E. "Chaucer's Artistic Use of Pope Innocent III's *De Miseria Humane Conditionis* in the Man of Law's Prologue and Tale." *PMLA,* 81 (1966), 485–492.

2251 Lewis, Robert E. "Glosses to the *Man of Law's Tale* from Pope Innocent III's *De Miseria Humane Conditionis.*" *SP,* 64 (1967), 1–16.

2252 Loganbill, Dean. See 2695.

2253 McNeal, Thomas H. "Chaucer and *The Decameron.*" *MLN,* 53 (1938), 257–258.

2254 Norman, Arthur. "The Man of Law's Tale." *Stud. in Lang., Lit., and Culture of the Middle Ages and Later,* ed. E. Bagby Atwood and Archibald A. Hill, pp. 312–323. Austin: Univ. of Texas, 1969.

2255 Parr, Johnstone. "Chaucer's Semiramis." *ChauR,* 5 (1970), 57–61.

2256 Paull, Michael R. "The Influence of the Saint's Legend Genre in the *Man of Law's Tale.*" *ChauR,* 5 (1971), 179–194.

2257 Peed, Michael R. "An Analogue of the 'Man of Law's Tale'." *AN&Q,* 12 (1974), 94–95.

2258 Pratt, Robert A. See 807.

2259 Rosenfeld, Mary-Virginia. "Chaucer and the Liturgy." *MLN,* 55 (1940), 357–360.

2260 Scheps, Walter. "Chaucer's Man of Law and the Tale of Constance." *PMLA,* 89 (1974), 285–295.

2261 Schlauch, Margaret. *Chaucer's Constance and Accused Queens.* New York: New York Univ. Press, 1927.

2262 SCHLAUGH, Margaret. "Historical Precursors of Chaucer's Constance." *PQ,* 29 (1950), 402–412.

2263 SCHLAUGH, Margaret. "A Polish Analogue of the *Man of Law's Tale.*" 53, pp. 372–380.

2264 SCHLAUGH, Margaret. "Chaucer's Constance, Jonah, and the *Gesta Romanorum.*" *Kwartalnik Neofilologiczny,* 20 (1973), 305–306.

2265 SEVERS, J. Burke. "A Lost Chaucerian Stanza?" *MLN,* 74 (1959), 193–198.

2266 SHANNON, Edgar F. "Chaucer's *Metamorphoseos.*" *MLN,* 35 (1920), 288–291.

2267 SMITH, Roland M. "Chaucer's *Man of Law's Tale* and Constance of Castile." *JEGP,* 47 (1948), 343–351.

2268 STEVENS, Martin. "Malkyn in the Man of Law's Headlink." *LeedsSE,* 1 (1967), 1–5.

2269 SULLIVAN, William L. "Chaucer's Man of Law as a Literary Critic." *MLN,* 68 (1953), 1–8.

2270 TUPPER, Frederick. "Wilful and Impatient Poverty." *Nation,* 99 (1914), 41.

2271 WICKERT, Maria. "Chaucers Konstanze und die Legende der guten Frauen." *Anglia,* 69 (1950), 89–104.

2272 WOOD, Chauncey. "Chaucer's Man of Law as Interpreter." *Traditio,* 23 (1967), 149–190.

2273 YUNCK, John A. "Religious Elements in Chaucer's *Man of Law's Tale.*" *ELH,* 27 (1960), 249–261.

The Man of Law's Endlink and The Shipman's Tale

2274 ADAMS, George R. "Chaucer's *The Shipman's Tale,* 173–177." *Explicator,* 24 (1966), item 41.

2275 CALDWELL, Robert A. "Chaucer's *taillynge ynough, Canterbury Tales,* B² 1624." *MLN,* 55 (1940), 262–265.

2276 CHAPMAN, Robert L. "The *Shipman's Tale* was Meant for the Shipman." *MLN,* 71 (1956), 4–5. Cf. *ibid.,* 72 (1957), 87–88 (W. W. Lawrence), *N&Q,* 201 (1956), 372–373 (Appleman).

2277 COPLAND, Murray. "*The Shipman's Tale:* Chaucer and Boccaccio." *MÆ,* 35 (1966), 11–28.

2278 DELIGIORGIS, S. See 372.

2279 FISHER, Ruth M. " 'Cosyn' and 'Cosynage': Complicated Punning in Chaucer's *Shipman's Tale.*" *N&Q,* 210 (1965), 168–170.

2280 FRIES, Maureen. "An Historical Analogue to the 'Shipman's Tale'?" *Comitatus,* 3 (1972), 19–32.

2281 GALWAY, Margaret. "A Basque Word [*phislyas*] in Chaucer." *TLS,* Oct. 3, 1942, p. 492. Cf. *ibid.,* Oct. 24, p. 525 (K. Sisam), Nov. 14, p. 564 (R. Gallop), Jan. 23, 1943, p. 43 (Root), April 10, p. 180 (Galway).

2282 GUERIN, Richard. "The *Shipman's Tale:* The Italian Analogues." *ES,* 52 (1971), 412–419.

2283 HOGAN, Moreland H., Jr. "A New Analogue of the *Shipman's Tale.*" *ChauR,* 5 (1971), 245–246.

2284 JONES, Claude. "Chaucer's *taillynge ynough.*" *MLN,* 52 (1937), 570.

2285 LAWRENCE, William W. "Chaucer's *Shipman's Tale.*" *Speculum,* 33 (1958), 56–68. Reprinted in 211.

2286 LEVY, Bernard S. "The Quaint World of *The Shipman's Tale.*" *SSF,* 4 (1967), 112–118.

2288 McCLINTOCK, Michael W. "Games and the Players of Games: Old French Fabliaux and the *Shipman's Tale.*" *ChauR,* 5 (1970), 112–136.

2289 PRATT, Robert A. "Chaucer's Shipman's Tale and Sercambi." *MLN,* 55 (1940), 142–145.

2290 RICHARDSON, Janette. "The Façade of Bawdry: Image Patterns in Chaucer's *Shipman's Tale.*" *ELH,* 32 (1965), 303–313.

2291 SILVERMAN, Albert H. "Sex and Money in Chaucer's *Shipman's Tale.*" *PQ,* 32 (1953), 329–336.

2292 SINGER, Armand E. "Chaucer and Don Juan." *WVUPP,* 13 (1961), 25–30.

2293 SKEAT, W. W. "Chaucer: The Shipman's Prologue." *MLR,* 5 (1910), 430–434.

2294 SMITH, Roland M. "The Six Gifts." *Jour. of Celtic Stud.,* 1 (1949), 98–104.

2295 SPARGO, John W. *Chaucer's Shipman's Tale: The Lover's Gift Regained.* (*FF Communications,* No. 91). Helsinki, 1930.

2296 STILLWELL, Gardiner. "Chaucer's 'Sad' Merchant." *RES,* 20 (1944), 1–18.

2297 SULLIVAN, Hazel. "A Chaucerian Puzzle." In *A Chaucerian Puzzle and Other Medieval Essays,* ed. N. G. Lawrence and J. A. Reynolds, pp. 1–46. Coral Gables: Univ. of Miami Press, 1961.

2298 THRO, A. Booker. See 2174.

2299 TUPPER, Frederick. "The Bearings of the Shipman's Prologue." *JEGP,* 33 (1934), 352–372.

2300 WHITING, B. J. " 'By My Fader Soule' (*CT,* II [*B*], 1178)." *JEGP,* 44 (1945), 1–8; 46 (1947), 297.

The Prioress's Prologue and Tale

2301 BEICHNER, Paul E. "The Grain of Paradise." *Speculum,* 36 (1961), 302–307.

2302 BOYD, Beverly. "The Little Clergeon's *Alma Redemptoris Mater.*" *N&Q,* 202 (1957), 277.

2303 BOYD, Beverly. "Young Hugh of Lincoln and Chaucer's *The Prioress's Tale.*" *Radford Rev.,* 14 (1960), 1–5.

2304 BRATCHER, James T. "The 'Greyn' in the *Prioress's Tale.*" *N&Q,* 208 (1963), 444–445.

2305 BRENNAN, John P. "Reflections on a Gloss to the *Prioress's Tale* from Jerome's *Adversus Jovinianum.*" *SP,* 70 (1973), 243–251.

2306 BROWN, C. F. "Chaucer's 'Litel Clergeon'." *MP,* 3 (1905–06), 467–491.

2307 BROWN, Carleton F. "Chaucer's *Prioresses Tale* and Its Analogues." *PMLA,* 21 (1906), 486–518.

2308 BROWN, Carleton. *A Study of the Miracle of Our Lady Told by Chaucer's Prioress.* (Chaucer Soc., 2nd Ser., No. 45.) London, 1910.

2309 BROWN, Carleton. "William Herebert and Chaucer's *Prioresses Tale.*" *MLN,* 38 (1923), 92–94.

2310 COHEN, Maurice. "Chaucer's Prioress and Her Tale: A Study of Anal Character and Anti-Semitism." *Psychoanalytic Quar.,* 31 (1962), 232–249.

2311 DEROCQUIGNY, J. "Note sur Chaucer (Canterbury Tales, B, 1687, an heep)." *Revue anglo-amer.,* 5 (1927), 160–161.

2312 DRAPER, J. W. "Chaucer's 'Wardrobe'." *ESt,* 60 (1926), 238–251.

2313 FRIEND, Albert C. "Chaucer's Prioress' Tale: An Early Analogue." *PMLA,* 51 (1936), 621–625.

2314 GAGE, Phyllis C. "Syntax and Poetry in Chaucer's *Prioress's Tale.*" *Neophil,* 50 (1966), 252–261.

2315 GAYLORD, Alan T. "The Unconquered Tale of the Prioress." *PMASAL,* 47 (1962), 613–636.

2316 GEROULD, G. H. "An Early Analogue of Chaucer's *Prioresses Tale,*" *MLN,* 24 (1909), 132–133.

2317 HAMILTON, Marie P. "Echoes of Childermas in the Tale of the Prioress." *MLR,* 34 (1939), 1–8. Reprinted in 628.

2318 HART, M. H. "Some Old French Miracles of Our Lady and Chaucer's *Prioresses Tale.*" *The Charles Mills Gayley Anniversary Papers* (Univ. of Calif. Pub. in Mod. Phil., XI), pp. 31–53. Berkeley, 1922.

2319 HAWKINS, Sherman. "Chaucer's Prioress and the Sacrifice of Praise." *JEGP,* 63 (1964), 599–624.

2320 KELLY, Edward H. "By Mouth of Innocents: The Prioress Vindicated." *PLL,* 5 (1969), 362–374.

2321 LANGMUIR, Gavin L. "The Knight's Tale of Young Hugh of Lincoln." *Speculum,* 47 (1972), 459–482. [The knight is Sir John de Lexinton.]

2322 LYNCH, James J. "The Prioress's Gems." *MLN,* 57 (1942), 440–441.

2323 MAGOUN, Francis P., Jr. "Canterbury Tales B 1761–63, 1839." *MLN,* 71 (1956), 165–166.

2324 MASUI, Michio. "*The Prioress's Prologue* and *Tale:* A Structural and Semantic Approach." *Studies Presented to Professor Chiaki Higashida* ... pp. 9–18. Osaka, 1974.

2325 PITTOCK, Malcolm. *"The Prioress's Tale" and "The Wife of Bath's Tale."* Oxford: Blackwell, 1973.

2326 PRATT, Robert A. See 559.

2327 PRESTON, Raymond. "Chaucer, His Prioress, the Jews, and Professor Robinson." *N&Q,* 206 (1961), 7–8.

2328 RIDLEY, Florence H. *The Prioress and the Critics.* Univ. of Calif. Pub., English Stud., 30. Berkeley and Los Angeles, 1965.

2329 ROSS, Woodburn O. "Another Analogue to *The Prioresses Tale.*" *MLN,* 50 (1935), 307–310.

2330 ROSS, Woodburn O. "A *B* Version of the Legend Told by Chaucer's Prioress," *MLN,* 52 (1937), 23–25.

2331 RUSSELL, G. H. "Chaucer: The Prioress's Tale." *Medieval Literature and Civilization: Studies in Memory of G. N. Garmonsway,* ed. D. A. Pearsall and R. A. Waldron, pp. 211–227. London: Athlone, 1969.

2332 SCHOECK, Richard J. "Chaucer's Prioress: Mercy and Tender Heart." *The Bridge: Yearbook of Judaeo-Christian Stud.,* 2 (1956), 239–255. Reprinted in 1700.

2333 STATLER, Margaret H. "The Analogues of Chaucer's *Prioress' Tale:* the Relation of Group C to Group A." *PMLA,* 65 (1950), 896–910.

2334 STEADMAN, John M. "The *Prioress's Tale* and 'Granella' of *Paradiso.*" *MS,* 24 (1962), 388–391.

2335 TAYLOR, Gary. "*Greyn* and the Resuscitation of the Little Clergeon." *SFQ,* 34 (1970), 82–89.

2336 WENK, J. C. "On the Sources of *The Prioress's Tale.*" *MS,* 17 (1955), 214–219.

2337 YUNCK, John A. " 'Lucre of Vileyne': Chaucer's Prioress and the Canonists." *N&Q,* 205 (1960), 165–167.

Sir Thopas: Prologue and Tale

2338 BLAU, E. "Zu Chaucers *Tale of Sir Topas.*" *Anglia Beiblatt,* 31 (1920), 237. [Payndemayn.]

2339 BROOKHOUSE, Christopher. "Sir Thopas, 11. 901–2." *N&Q,* 210 (1965), 293–294.

2340 BURROW, J. A. " 'Listeth Lordes': *Sir Thopas,* 712 and 833." *N&Q,* 213 (1968), 326–327.

2341 BURROW, John. " 'Worly under wede' in *Sir Thopas.*" *ChauR,* 3 (1969), 170–173.

2342 BURROW, J. A. " 'Sir Thopas': An Agony in Three Fits." *RES,* 22 (1971), 54–58.

2343 CAMDEN, Carroll, Jr. "The Physiognomy of Thopas." *RES,* 11 (1935), 326–330.

2344 CULLEN, Dolores L. "Chaucer's *The Tale of Sir Thopas.*" *Explicator,* 32 (1974), item 35.

2345 DONOVAN, Mortimer J. "*Sir Thopas,* 772–774." *NM,* 57 (1956), 237–246.

2346 EDDY, Elizabeth R. "Sir Thopas and Sir Thomas Norny: Romance Parody in Chaucer and Dunbar." *RES,* 22 (1971), 401–409.

2347 EVERETT, Dorothy. "A Note on 'Ypotis'." *RES,* 6 (1930), 446–448.

2348 FICKE, H. S. "Iewes Werk." *PQ,* 7 (1928), 82–85.

2349 GREEN, A. Wigfall. "Chaucer's *Sir Thopas:* Meter, Rhyme, and Contrast." *UMSE,* 1 (1960), 1–11.

2350 GREENE, Richard L. "The Hunt Is Up, Sir Thopas: Irony, Pun, and Ritual." *N&Q,* 211 (1966), 169–171.

2351 HANLEY, Katherine. "Chaucer's Horseman: Word Play in the *Tale of Sir Thopas.*" *Northeast MLA Newsl,* 2 (1970), 112–121.

2352 KNOTT, Thomas A. "A Bit of Chaucer Mythology." *MP,* 8 (1910–11), 135–139.

2353 LANGE, Hugo. "Chaucers Sir Thopas, 'Ritter Honiggold': Ein Beitrag zur Kenntnis Chaucers und Froissarts." *Deutsche Literaturzeitung,* 37 (1916), 1299–1303, 1669–1672, 1827–1832.

2354 LAWRENCE, William W. "Satire in *Sir Thopas.*" *PMLA,* 50 (1935), 81–91.

2355 LINN, Irving. "The Arming of Sir Thopas." *MLN,* 51 (1936), 300–311.

2356 LOOMIS, Laura H. "Chaucer and the Auchinleck MS: 'Thopas' and 'Guy of Warwick'." 49, pp. 111–128. Reprinted in 194.

2357 LOOMIS, Laura H. "Chaucer's 'Jewes Werk' and *Guy of Warwick.*" *PQ,* 14 (1935), 371–373.

2358 LOOMIS, Laura H. "Sir Thopas and David and Goliath." *MLN,* 51 (1936), 311–313.

2359 LUMIANSKY, Robert M. "The Meaning of Chaucer's Prologue to 'Sir Thopas'." *PQ,* 26 (1947), 313–320.

2360 MAGOUN, Francis P., Jr. "The Source of Chaucer's *Rime of Sir Thopas.*" *PMLA,* 42 (1927), 833–844.

2361 MANLY, John M. "Sir Thopas: A Satire." *E&S,* 13 (1928), 52–73.

2362 MANLY, John M. "The Stanza-Forms of *Sir Thopas.*" *MP,* 8 (1910–11), 141–144.

2363 MCCRACKEN, Sam. "Chaucer's *Sir Thopas,* B, 1914–1915." *Explicator,* 17 (1959), item 57.

2364 MELTON, John L. "Sir Thopas' 'charbocle'." *PQ,* 35 (1956), 215–217.

2365 MOORE, Arthur K. "*Sir Thopas* as Criticism of Fourteenth-Century Minstrelsy." *JEGP,* 53 (1954), 532–545.

2366 MOORE, George F. "Ciclatoun Scarlet." 51, pp. 25–36.

2367 PATTERSON, R. F. "Paindemaine." *MLR,* 7 (1912), 376.

2368 ROPPOLO, J. P. "The Meaning of 'at erst': Prologue to *Sir Thopas* B², 1884." *MLN,* 63 (1948), 365–371.

2369 ROSS, Woodburn O. "A Possible Significance of the Name *Thopas.*" *MLN,* 45 (1930), 172–174.

2370 ROWLAND, Beryl. "'Bihoold the Murye Wordes of the Hoost to Chaucer'." *NM,* 64 (1963), 48–52.

2371 ROWLAND, Beryl. "Chaucer's 'Bukke and Hare' (*Thop,* VII, 756)." *ELN,* 2 (1964), 6–8.

2372 SCHEPS, Walter. "Sir Thopas: The Bourgeois Knight, the Minstrel and the Critics." *TSL,* 11 (1966), 35–43.

2373 SNYDER, Franklin B. "A Note on *Sir Thopas.*" *MP,* 6 (1908–09), 133–135.

2374 STANLEY, E. G. "The Use of Bob-lines in *Sir Thopas.*" 52, pp. 417–426.

2375 STRONG, Caroline. "Sir Thopas and Sir Guy." *MLN,* 23 (1908), 73–77, 102–106.

2376 TUCKER, S. I. "Sir Thopas and the Wild Beasts." *RES,* n.s. 10 (1959), 54–56.

2377 WHITE, Beatrice. See 1726.

2378 WOOD, Chauncey. "Chaucer and 'Sir Thopas': Irony and Concupiscence." *TSLL,* 14 (1972), 389–403.

The Tale of Melibee

2379 BAUM, Paull F. "Chaucer's Metrical Prose." *JEGP,* 45 (1946), 38–42.

2380 BRERETON, Georgine E. "Viper into Weasel (A note on a line in Chaucer's *Melibee*)." *MÆ,* 27 (1958), 173–174.

2381 BÜHLER, Curt F. "The Morgan Manuscript (M 39) of *Le Livre de Melibee et de Prudence.*" 55, pp. 49–54.

2382 CLARK, John W. " 'This litel tretys' Again." *ChauR*, 6 (1971), 152–156.

2383 HOTSON, J. Leslie. "The *Tale of Melibeus* and John of Gaunt." *SP*, 18 (1921), 429–452.

2384 KONAGAYA, Yataka. "*The Tale of Melibeus* and Chaucer." *SELit*, 42 (1965), 13–18.

2385 KREUZER, James R. "A Note on Chaucer's *Tale of Melibee.*" *MLN*, 63 (1948), 53–54.

2386 LAWRENCE, William W. "The Tale of Melibeus." 49, pp. 100–110, Reprinted in 211.

2387 OIZUMI, Akio. "On Colloquial Words in Chaucer's Translation of *Le livre de Mellibee et Prudence:* A Stylistic Comparison of the English Translation with the French Version." *SELit*, 48 (1971), 95–108.

2388 OWEN, Charles A., Jr. "The *Tale of Melibee.*" *ChauR*, 7 (1973), 267–280.

2389 PALOMO, Dolores. "What Chaucer Really Did to *Le Livre de Mellibee.*" *PQ*, 53 (1974), 304–320.

2390 SEVERS, J. Burke. "The Source of Chaucer's *Melibeus.*" *PMLA*, 50 (1935), 92–99.

2391 STILLWELL, Gardiner. "The Political Meaning of Chaucer's *Tale of Melibee.*" *Speculum*, 19 (1944), 433–444.

2392 STROHM, Paul. "The Allegory of the *Tale of Melibee.*" *ChauR*, 2 (1967), 32–42.

2393 TURNER, W. Arthur. See 2783.

The Monk's Prologue and Tale

2394 AIKEN, Pauline. "Vincent of Beauvais and Chaucer's *Monk's Tale.*" *Speculum*, 17 (1942), 56–68.

2395 BABCOCK, R. W. "The Mediæval Setting of Chaucer's *Monk's Tale.*" *PMLA*, 46 (1931), 205–213.

2396 BRADDY, Haldeen. "Chaucer's Don Pedro and the Purpose of the Monk's Tale." *MLQ*, 13 (1952), 3–5. Reprinted in 258.

2397 BRADDY, Haldeen. "The Two Petros in the *Monk's Tale.*" *PMLA*, 50 (1935), 69–80. Reprinted in 258.

2398 BRADDY, Haldeen. See 1559.

2399 BRESSIE, Ramona. " 'A Governour Wily and Wys'." *MLN*, 54 (1939), 477–490.

2400 BROWN, Joella O. "Chaucer's Daun Piers: One Monk or Two?" *Criticism*, 6 (1964), 44–52.

2401 BYERS, John R., Jr. "Harry Bailey's St. Madrian." *ELN*, 4 (1966), 6–9.

2402 EMERSON, O. F. "Seith Trophee." *MLN*, 31 (1916), 142–146. Reprinted in 395.

2403 FROST, George L. "That Precious Corpus Madrian." *MLN*, 57 (1942), 177–179.

2404 FRY, Donald K. "The Ending of the *Monk's Tale.*" *JEGP*, 71 (1972), 355–368.

2405 GELBACH, Marie. "On Chaucer's Version of the Death of Croesus." *JEGP*, 6 (1907), 657–660.

2406 GRENNEN, Joseph E. " 'Sampsoun' in the *Canterbury Tales:* Chaucer Adapting a Source." *NM*, 67 (1966), 117–122.

2407 HASKELL, Ann S. "The Host's *precious corpus Madrian.*" *JEGP*, 67 (1968), 430–440.

2408 HATTON, Thomas J. See 2463.

2409 HOFFMAN, Richard L. "Ovid and the Monk's Tale of Hercules." *N&Q*, 210 (1965), 406–409.

2410 JENKINS, T. Atkinson. "*Vitremyte:* Mot latin-fraçais employé par Chaucer." *Mélanges de linguistique et de littérature offerts à M. Alfred Jeanroy,* pp. 141–147. Paris: Droz, 1928.

2411 JOHNSON, Dudley R. "The Biblical Characters of Chaucer's Monk." *PMLA*, 66 (1951), 827–843.

2412 JONES, Claude. "The Monk's Tale, a Mediaeval Sermon." *MLN*, 52 (1937), 570–572.

2413 KASKE, R. E. "The Knight's Interruption of the *Monk's Tale.*" *ELH*, 24 (1957), 249–268.

2414 KITTREDGE, George L. "The Pillars of Hercules and Chaucer's 'Trophee'." *Putnam Anniversary Volume,* pp. 545–566. New York: Stechert, 1909.

2415 LÜDEKE, Henry. "Chaucers persische Zenobia." *Festschrift. . . Theodor Spira,* pp. 98–99. Heidelberg: Winter, 1961.

2416 MALONE, Kemp. "Harry Bailly and Godelief." *ES*, 31 (1950), 209–215.

2417 McDERMOTT, William C. "Chaucer and Virgil." *C&M*, 23 (1962), 216–217. [B 3295]

2418 NORRIS, Dorothy M. "Harry Bailey's 'Corpus Madrian'." *MLN*, 48 (1933), 146–148.

2419 ORUCH, Jack B. "Chaucer's Worldly Monk." *Criticism*, 8 (1966), 280–288.

2420 PACE, George B. "Adam's Hell." *PMLA*, 78 (1963), 25–35. Cf. 604.

2421 PRATT, Robert A. "Chaucer and the Pillars of Hercules." *Studies in Honor of Berthold L. Ullman,* pp. 118–125. St. Louis: The Classical Bull., 1960.

2422 RICKERT, Edith. "Goode Lief, My Wyf." *MP*, 25 (1927), 79–82. Cf. *TLS,* Dec. 16, 1926, p. 935; Jan. 20, 1927, p. 44 (H. G. Richardson).

2423 SAVAGE, Henry. "Chaucer and the 'Pitous Deeth' of 'Petro, Glorie of Spayne.' " *Speculum,* 24 (1949), 357–375.

2424 SEATON, Ethel. " 'Goode lief my wife.' " *MLR*, 41 (1946), 196–202.

2425 SILVERSTEIN, H. Theodore. "Chaucer's 'Brutus Cassius'." *MLN*, 47 (1932), 148–150.

2426 SOCOLA, Edward M. "Chaucer's Development of Fortune in the *Monk's Tale.*" *JEGP*, 49 (1950), 159–171.

2427 SPENCER, Theodore. "The Story of Ugolino in Dante and Chaucer." *Speculum,* 9 (1934), 295–301.

2428 STRANGE, William C. "The *Monk's Tale:* A Generous View." *ChauR,* 1 (1966), 167–180.

2429 TATLOCK, John S. P. "Chaucer's Monk." *MLN*, 55 (1940), 350–354. Cf. *ibid.,* 480 (Kuhl), 56 (1941), 80 (Tatlock), 161–162 (Bressie).

2430 TATLOCK, John S. P. "Chaucer's *Vitremyte.*" *MLN*, 21 (1906), 62. See *ibid.,* 192 (J. M. Hart).

2431 TAYLOR, Estelle W. "Chaucer's 'Monk's Tale': An Apology." *CLAJ*, 13 (1969), 172–182.

2432 TUPPER, Frederick. "Chaucer and Trophee." *MLN*, 31 (1916), 11–14.

2433 WATSON, Charles S. See 2503.

2434 YOUNG, Karl. "Chaucer's 'Vitremyte'." *SP*, 40 (1943), 494–501.

The Nun's Priest's Prologue and Tale

2435 AIKEN, Pauline. "Vincent of Beauvais and Dame Pertelote's Knowledge of Medicine." *Speculum*, 10 (1935), 281–287.

2436 ALLEN, Judson B. "The Ironic Fruyt: Chauntecleer as Figura." *SP*, 66 (1969), 25–35.

2437 ANDERSON, Judith H. " 'Nat worth a boterflye': *Muipotmos* and *The Nun's Priest's Tale.*" *Jour. of Medieval and Renaissance Stud.*, 1 (1971), 89–106.

2438 BERGNER, Heinz. "*The Fox and the Wolf* und die Gattung des Tierepos in der mittelenglischen Literatur." *GRM*, 54 (1973), 268–285.

2439 BOONE, Lalia P. "Chauntecleer and Partlet Identified." *MLN*, 64 (1949), 78–81.

2440 BRINDLEY, D. J. "The Mixed Style of the *Nun's Priest's Tale.*" *ESA*, 7 (1964), 148–156.

2441 BROES, Arthur T. "Chaucer's Disgruntled Cleric: *The Nun's Priest's Tale.*" *PMLA*, 78 (1963), 156–162.

2442 BROSNAHAN, Leger. "Does the Nun's Priest's Epilogue Contain a Link?" *SP*, 58 (1961), 468–482.

2443 BROWN, Carleton. "Mulier est Hominis Confusio." *MLN*, 35 (1920), 479–482.

2444 CHAMBERLAIN, David S. "The Nun's Priest's Tale and Boethius's *De Musica.*" *MP*, 68 (1970), 188–191.

2445 CLARK, George. "Chauntecleer and Deduit." *ELN*, 2 (1965), 168–171.

2446 COOK, James W. "The Nun's Priest and the Hebrew Pointer." *AN&Q*, 7 (1968), 53–54.

2447 CURRY, W. C. "Chauntecleer and Pertelote on Dreams." *ESt*, 58 (1924), 24–60.

2448 DAHLBERG, Charles. "Chaucer's Cock and Fox." *JEGP*, 53 (1954), 277–290.

2449 DANIELS, Edgar F. "Chaucer's *The Nun's Priest's Tale*, B², 4054." *Explicator*, 23 (1964), item 23.

2450 DARGAN, E. P. "Cock and Fox: A Critical Study of the History and Sources of the Mediæval Fable." *MP*, 4 (1906–07), 39–65.

2451 DELASANTA, Rodney K. " 'Namoore of this': Chaucer's Priest and Monk." *TSL*, 13 (1968), 117–132.

2452 D[ICKENS], B. "Seynd bacoun." *Leeds Studies in English and Kindred Langs.*, No. 4 (1935), 76–77.

2453 DIECKMANN, Emma M. " '. . . Moore feelynge than had Boece . . . '." *MLN*, 53 (1938), 177–180.

2454 DONOVAN, Mortimer J. "The *moralite* of the Nun's Priest's Sermon." *JEGP*, 52 (1953), 493–508.

2455 DRONKE, Peter. "Chaucer and Boethius' *De Musica.*" *N&Q*, 211 (1966), 92.

2456 FISH, Stanley E. "*The Nun's Priest's Tale* and Its Analogues." *CLAJ,* 5 (1962), 223–228.

2457 FRIEDMAN, John B. "The *Nun's Priest's Tale:* The Preacher and the Mermaid's Song." *ChauR,* 7 (1973), 250–266.

2458 GIBBONS, Robert F. "Does the Nun's Priest's Epilogue Contain a Link?" *SP,* 51 (1954), 21–33.

2459 GRENNEN, Joseph E. "Chauntecleer's 'Venymous' Cathartics." *N&Q,* 208 (1963), 286–287.

2460 GUERIN, Richard. "The Nun's Priest and Canto V of the *Inferno.*" *ES,* 54 (1973), 313–315.

2461 HAMM, Victor M. "Chaucer: 'Heigh Ymaginacioun'." *MLN,* 69 (1954), 394–395.

2462 HARRINGTON, David V. "The Undramatic Character of Chaucer's Nun's Priest." *Discourse,* 8 (1965), 80–89.

2463 HATTON, Thomas J. "Chauntecleer and the Monk, Two False Knights." *PLL,* 3 Summer Suppl. (1967), 31–39.

2464 HEMINGWAY, Samuel B. "Chaucer's Monk and Nun's Priest." *MLN,* 31 (1916), 479–483.

2465 HENNING, Standish. "Chauntecleer and Taurus." *ELN,* 3 (1965), 1–4.

2466 HIEATT, Constance B. "The Moral of *The Nun's Priest's Tale.*" *SN,* 42 (1970), 3–8.

2467 HOTSON, J. Leslie. "Colfax *vs.* Chauntecleer." *PMLA,* 39 (1924), 762–781. Reprinted in 628.

2468 JOHNSTON, Everett C. "The Medieval Versions of the Reynard-Chanticleer Episode." *LangQ,* 4 (1966), 7–10.

2469 JOSELYN, Sister M. "Aspects of Form in the Nun's Priest's Tale." *CE,* 25 (1964), 566–571.

2470 KAUFFMAN, Corinne E. "Dame Pertelote's Parlous Parle." *ChauR,* 4 (1970), 41–48.

2471 KEALY, J. Kieran. "Chaucer's *Nun's Priest's Tale,* VII. 3160–71." Explicator, 33 (1974), item 12.

2472 KELLOGG, Alfred L., and Robert C. Cox. See 458.

2473 KLINEFELTER, Ralph A. "Chaucer's *Nun's Priest's Tale,* 2843." *Explicator,* 10 (1952), item 32.

2474 LECOMPTE, I. C. "Chaucer's *Nonne Prestes Tale* and the *Roman de Renard.*" *MP,* 14 (1916–17), 737–749.

2475 LENAGHAN, R. T. "The Nun's Priest's Fable." *PMLA,* 78 (1963), 300–307.

2476 LEVY, Bernard S., and George R. ADAMS. "Chauntecleer's Paradise Lost and Regained." *MS,* 29 (1967), 178–192.

2477 LUMIANSKY, Robert M. "The Nun's Priest in *The Canterbury Tales.*" *PMLA,* 68 (1953), 896–906.

2478 MACDONALD, Donald. "Henryson and Chaucer: Cock and Fox." *TSLL,* 8 (1967), 451–461.

2479 MANNING, Stephen. "The Nun's Priest's Morality and the Medieval Attitude toward Fables." *JEGP,* 59 (1960), 403–416.

2480 MAVEETY, Stanley R. "An Approach to *The Nun's Priest's Tale.*" *CLAJ* (Baltimore), 4 (1960), 132–137.

2481 MEREDITH, Peter. "Chauntecleer and the Mermaids." *Neophil,* 54 (1970), 81–83.

2482 MYERS, D. E. "Focus and 'Moralite' in the *Nun's Priest's Tale.*" *ChauR,* 7 (1973), 210–220.

2483 PEARCY, Roy J. "The Epilogue to *The Nun's Priest's Tale.*" *N&Q,* 213 (1968), 43–45.

2484 PÉREZ MARTÍN, Jesus. "El tono de voz en *The Nun's Priest Tale,* de Chaucer." *FMod,* 6 (1966), 323–327.

2485 PETERSEN, Kate O. *On the Sources of the Nonne Prestes Tale.* Boston, 1898 (*Radcliffe College Monograph,* No. 10). Reprinted New York: Haskell House, 1966.

2486 PRATT, Robert A. "The Classical Lamentations in the *Nun's Priest's Tale.*" *MLN,* 64 (1949), 77–78.

2487 PRATT, Robert A. "Three Old French Sources of the Nonnes Preestes Tale." *Speculum,* 47 (1972), 422–444, 646–668.

2488 RAND, George I. "The Date of 'Nun's Priest's Tale'." *AN&Q,* 7 (1969), 149–150.

2489 ROBBINS, Rossell H. " 'Lawriol': *CT,* B 4153." *ChauR,* 3 (1968), 68.

2490 ROWLAND, Beryl. " 'Owles and Apes' in Chaucer's *Nun's Priest's Tale,* 3092." *MS,* 27 (1965), 322–325.

2491 ROWLAND, Beryl. " 'A Sheep That Highte Malle' (NPT, VII, 2831)." *ELN,* 6 (1968), 84–87.

2492 SAKANISHI, Shio. "A Note on the Nonne Preestes Tale." *MLN,* 47 (1932), 150–151.

2493 SCHEPS, Walter. "Chaucer's Anti-Fable: *Reductio ad Absurdum* in the *Nun's Priest's Tale.*" *LeedsSE,* 4 (1971), 1–10.

2494 SCHRADER, Richard J. "Chauntecleer, the Mermaid, and Daun Burnel." *ChauR,* 4 (1970), 284–290.

2495 SEVERS, J. Burke. "Chaucer's Originality in the *Nun's Priest's Tale.*" *SP,* 43 (1946), 22–41.

2496 SHAVER, Chester L. "Chaucer's 'owles and apes'." *MLN,* 58 (1943), 105–107.

2497 STANDOP, Ewald. "Zur allegorischen Deutung der *Nonnes Preestes Tale.*" *Festschrift . . . Theodor Spira,* pp. 88–97. Heidelberg: Winter, 1961.

2498 STEADMAN, John M. "Champier and the *Altercatio Hadriani:* Another Chaucer Analogue." *N&Q,* 210 (1965), 170. [Mulier est hominis confusio.]

2499 STEADMAN, John M. "Chauntecleer and Medieval Natural History." *Isis,* 50 (1959), 236–244.

2500 STEADMAN, John M. "Flattery and the *Moralitas* of The Nonne Preestes Tale." *MÆ,* 28 (1959), 172–179.

2501 SZÖVÉRFFY, Joseph. " 'Roma' and 'Anglia': Survival of a Poetic Image." *N&Q,* 205 (1960), 248–250.

2502 WATKINS, Charles A. "Chaucer's *Sweete Preest.*" *ELH,* 36 (1969), 455–469.

2503 WATSON, Charles S. "The Relationship of the *Monk's Tale* and the *Nun's Priest's Tale.*" *SSF,* 1 (1964), 277–288.

2504 YOUNG, Karl. "Chaucer and Geoffrey of Vinsauf." *MP,* 41 (1943–44), 172–182.

2505 ZACHARIAS, Richard. "Chaucer's *Nun's Priest's Tale,* B².4552–63." *Explicator,* 32 (1974), item 60.

The Wife of Bath's Prologue and Tale

2506 ALBERTINI, Virgil R. "Chaucer's Artistic Accomplishment in Molding the *Wife of Bath's Tale.*" *Northwest Missouri State College Stud.,* 28, iv (1964), 3–16.

2507 ALLEN, Judson B., and Patrick GALLACHER. "Alisoun through the Looking Glass: or Every Man His Own Midas." *ChauR,* 4 (1970), 99–105.

2508 BAKER, Donald C. "Chaucer's Clerk and the Wife of Bath on the Subject of 'Gentilesse'." *SP,* 59 (1962), 631–640.

2509 BIGGINS, Dennis. "Chaucer's *Wife of Bath's Prologue,* D. 608." *Explicator,* 32 (1974), item 44.

2510 BIGGINS, Dennis. "O Jankyn, Be Ye There?" 53, pp. 249–254.

2511 BOYD, Beverly. "The Wife of Bath's Gay *Lente.*" *AN&Q,* 1 (1963), 85–86.

2512 BRADLEY, Sister Ritamary. "The *Wife of Bath's Tale* and the Mirror Tradition." *JEGP,* 55 (1956), 624–630.

2513 CARY, Meredith. "Sovereignty and Old Wife." *PLL,* 5 (1969), 375–388.

2514 COFFMAN, George R. "Another Analogue for the Violation of the Maiden in the 'Wife of Bath's Tale'." *MLN,* 59 (1944), 271–274.

2515 COFFMAN, George R. "Chaucer and Courtly Love Once More—'The Wife of Bath's Tale'." *Speculum,* 20 (1945), 43–50.

2516 COLMER, Dorothy. "Character and Class in *The Wife of Bath's Tale.*" *JEGP,* 72 (1973), 329–339.

2517 COOMARASWAMY, Ananda K. "On the Loathly Bride." *Speculum,* 20 (1945), 391–404.

2518 COTTER, James F. "The Wife of Bath and the Conjugal Debt." *ELN,* 6 (1969), 169–172.

2519 COTTER, James F. "The Wife of Bath's Lenten Observance." *PLL,* 7 (1971), 293–297.

2520 CURRY, W. C. "More about Chaucer's Wife of Bath." *PMLA,* 37 (1922), 30–51.

2521 CURTIS, Penelope. "Chaucer's Wyf of Bath." *CR,* 10 (1967), 33–45.

2522 DELASANTA, Rodney. "*Quoniam* and the Wife of Bath." *PLL,* 8 (1972), 202–206.

2523 DELEHAYE, Philippe. "Le Dossier Anti-Matrimonial de *l'Adversus Jovinianum* et Son Influence sur Quelques Écrits Latins du XIIe Siècle." *MS,* 13 (1951), 65–86.

2524 DEMPSTER, Germaine. "'Thy Gentillesse' in *Wife of Bath's Tale,* D 1159–62." *MLN,* 57 (1942), 173–176.

2525 DONALDSON, E. T. "Chaucer, *Canterbury Tales,* D 117: A Critical Edition." *Speculum,* 40 (1965), 626–622. Reprinted in 273.

2526 DUNCAN, Edgar H. "'Bear on Hand' in *The Wife of Bath's Prologue.*" *TSL,* 11 (1966), 19–33.

2527 DUNCAN, Edgar H. "Chaucer's 'Wife of Bath's Prologue', lines 193–828, and Geoffrey of Vinsauf's *Documentum.*" *MP,* 66 (1969), 199–211.

2528 EISNER, Sigmund. *A Tale of Wonder: A Source Study of* The Wife of Bath's Tale. Wexford, Ireland: John English and Co., 1957.

2529 FOX, Allan B. "The *Traductio* on *Honde* in the *Wife of Bath's Prologue.*" *Notre Dame English Jour.,* 9, i (1973), 3–9.

2530 GARBÁTY, Thomas J. "Chaucer's Weaving Wife." *Jour. of American Folklore,* 81 (1968), 342–346.

2531 GILLAM, D. " 'Cast up the Curtyn'; A Tentative Exploration into the Meaning of *The Wife of Bath's Tale.*" *Australasian Universities Lang. and Lit. Assoc.: Proc . . . Twelfth Congress,* ed. A. P. Treweek (Sydney: AAULA, [1970]), pp. 435–455.

2532 HALLER, Robert S. "The Wife of Bath and the Three Estates." *AnM,* 6 (1965), 47–64.

2533 HAMILTON, Alice. "Helowys and the Burning of Jankyn's Book." *MS,* 34 (1972), 196–207.

2534 HARWOOD, Britton J. "The Wife of Bath and the Dream of Innocence." *MLQ,* 33 (1972), 257–273.

2535 HASKELL, Ann S. "The St. Joce Oath in the Wife of Bath's Prologue." *ChauR,* 1 (1966), 85–87.

2537 HIGDON, David L. "The Wife of Bath and Refreshment Sunday." *PLL,* 8 (1972), 199–201.

2538 HOFFMAN, Richard L. "Ovid and the 'Marital Dilemma' in the *Wife of Bath's Tale.*" *AN&Q,* 3 (1965), 101.

2539 HOFFMAN, Richard L. "Ovid and the Wife of Bath's Tale of Midas." *N&Q,* 211 (1966), 48–50.

2540 HOFFMAN, Richard L. "Ovid's Argus and Chaucer." *N&Q,* 210 (1965), 213–216.

2541 HOFFMAN, Richard L. "The Wife of Bath and the Dunmow Bacon." *N&Q,* 208 (1963), 9–11.

2542 HOLLAND, Norman N. "Meaning as Transformation: The Wife of Bath's Tale." *CE,* 28 (1967), 279–290.

2543 HUPPÉ, Bernard F. "Rape and Woman's Sovereignty in the *Wife of Bath's Tale.*" *MLN,* 63 (1948), 378–381.

2544 JONES, Richard F. "A Conjecture on the Wife of Bath's Prologue." *JEGP,* 24 (1925), 512–547.

2545 KENYON, John S. "Wife of Bath's Tale 1159–62." *MLN,* 54 (1939), 133–137.

2546 KERNAN, Anne. "The Archwife and the Eunuch." *ELH,* 41 (1974), 1–25.

2547 KIESSLING, Nicolas K. "The *Wife of Bath's Tale:* D 878–881." *ChauR,* 7 (1972), 113–117.

2548 KOBAN, Charles. "Hearing Chaucer Out: The Art of Persuasion in the *Wife of Bath's Tale.*" *ChauR,* 5 (1971), 225–239.

2549 LEVY, Bernard S. "Chaucer's Wife of Bath, the Loathly Lady, and Dante's Siren." *Symposium,* 19 (1965), 359–373.

2550 LEVY, Bernard S. "The Wife of Bath's *Queynte Fantasye.*" *ChauR,* 4 (1970), 106–122.

2551 LUMIANSKY, Robert M. "Aspects of the Relationship of Boccaccio's 'Il Filostrato' with Benoit's 'Roman de Troie' and Chaucer's 'Wife of Bath's Tale'." *Italica,* 31 (1954), 1–7.

2552 MAGEE, Patricia A. "The Wife of Bath and the Problem of Mastery." *Massachu-setts Stud. In English,* 3 (1971), 40–45.

2553 MAHONEY, John. "Alice of Bath: Her 'secte' and 'gentil text'." *Criticism,* 6 (1964), 144–155.

2554 MALONE, Kemp. "The Wife of Bath's Tale." *MLR,* 57 (1962), 481–491.

2555 MARGULIES, Cecile S. "The Marriages and the Wealth of the Wife of Bath." *MS,* 24 (1962), 210–216.

2556 MAYNADIER, G. H. *The Wife of Bath's Tale: Its Sources and Analogues.* (Grimm Library, No. 13). London: Nutt, 1901.

2557 MILLER, Robert P. "*The Wife of Bath's Tale* and Mediaeval Exempla." *ELH,* 32 (1965), 442–456.

2558 MOORE, Arthur K. "Alysoun's Other Tonne." *MLN,* 59 (1944), 481–483.

2559 MOORE, Arthur K. "Chaucer and Matheolus." *N&Q,* 190 (1946), 245–248.

2560 MOORE, Arthur K. "The Pardoner's Interruption of the *Wife of Bath's Prologue.*" *MLQ,* 10 (1949), 49–57.

2561 MROCZKOWSKI, P. "Incubi and Friars." *Kwartalnik Neofilologiczny,* 8 (1961), 191–192.

2562 MUSCATINE, Charles. "The Wife of Bath and Gautier's *La Veuve.*" *Romance Stud. in Memory of Edward Billings Ham,* ed. Urban T. Holmes, *Calif. State Coll. Pubns.,* 2, pp. 109–114. Hayward, Calif.: California State Coll., 1967.

2563 PARKER, David. "Can We Trust the Wife of Bath?" *ChauR,* 4 (1970), 90–98.

2564 PITTOCK, Malcolm. See 2325.

2565 PRATT, Robert A. "Chaucer and Isidore on Why Men Marry." *MLN,* 74 (1959), 293–294.

2566 PRATT, Robert A. "The Development of the Wife of Bath." 48, 45–79.

2567 PRATT, Robert A. "Jankyn's Book of Wikked Wyves: Medieval Anti-matrimonial Propaganda in the Universities." *AnM,* 3 (1962), 5–27.

2568 PRATT, Robert A. "A Note on Chaucer and the *Policraticus* of John of Salisbury." *MLN,* 65 (1950), 243–246.

2569 PRATT, Robert A. "Saint Jerome in Jankyn's Book of Wikked Wyves." *Criticism,* 5 (1963), 316–322.

2570 REID, David S. "Crocodilian Humor: A Discussion of Chaucer's Wife of Bath." *ChauR,* 4 (1970), 73–89.

2571 ROPPOLO, Joseph P. "The Converted Knight in Chaucer's *Wife of Bath's Tale.*" *CE,* 12 (1951), 263–269. Cf. *ibid.,* p. 459 (W. P. Albrecht).

2572 ROWLAND, Beryl. "Chaucer's *The Wife of Bath's Prologue,* D. 389." *Explicator,* 24 (1965), item 14.

2573 ROWLAND, Beryl. "The Wife of Bath's 'Unlawfull Philtrum'." *Neophil,* 56 (1972), 201–206.

2574 ROWLAND, Beryl. "Chaucer's Dame Alys: *Critics in Blunderland.*" 52, pp. 381–395.

2575 ROWLAND, Beryl. "On the Timely Death of the Wife of Bath's Fourth Husband." *Archiv,* 209 (1973), 273–282.

2576 RUTTER, George M. "The Wife of Bath." *Western Reserve Univ. Bull.,* n.s. 34, No. 13 (1931), 60–64.

2577 SALTER, F. M. "The Tragic Figure of the Wyf of Bath." *PTRSC,* 3rd Ser., 48, Section 2 (1954), 1–13.

2578 SANDERS, Barry. "Further Puns from the *Prologue* and *Tale* of the Wife of Bath." *PLL,* 4 (1968), 192–195.

2579 SCHLAUGH, Margaret. "The Marital Dilemma in the *Wife of Bath's Tale.*" *PMLA,* 61 (1946), 416–430.

2580 SCHMIDT, A. V. C. "The Wife of Bath's Marital State." *N&Q,* 212 (1967), 230–231.

2581 SHAPIRO, Gloria K. "Dame Alice as Deceptive Narrator." *ChauR,* 6 (1971), 130–141.

2582 SHUMAKER, Wayne. "Alisoun in Wander-Land: A Study in Chaucer's Mind and Literary Method." *ELH,* 18 (1951), 77–89. Reprinted in 1548.

2583 SILVERSTEIN, Theodore. "Wife of Bath and the Rhetoric of Enchantment; or How to Make a Hero See in the Dark." *MP,* 58 (1960–61), 153–173.

2584 SILVIA, Daniel S., Jr. "Glosses to the *Canterbury Tales* from St. Jerome's *Epistola adversus Jovinianum.*" *SP,* 62 (1965), 28–39.

2585 SILVIA, D. S. "The Wife of Bath's Marital State." *N&Q,* 212 (1967), 8–10.

2586 SILVIA, D. S. "Chaucer's *Canterbury Tales,* D. 44a-f." *Explicator,* 28 (1970), item 44.

2587 SLADE, Tony. "Irony in the Wife of Bath's Tale" *MLR,* 64 (1969), 241–247.

2588 SLAUGHTER, Eugene E. " 'Allas! Allas! That Ever Love Was Sinne!' " *MLN,* 49 (1934), 83–86.

2589 SLAUGHTER, Eugene E. "Clerk Jankyn's Motive." *MLN,* 65 (1950), 530–534.

2590 STEADMAN, John M. "The Book-burning Episode in the Wife of Bath's Prologue: Some Additional Analogues." *PMLA,* 74 (1959), 521–525.

2591 STEINBERG, Aaron. "The Wife of Bath's Tale and Her Fantasy of Fulfillment." *CE,* 26 (1964), 187–191.

2592 TOWNSEND, Francis G. "Chaucer's Nameless Knight." *MLR,* 49 (1954), 1–4.

2593 TRAIN, Lilla. "Chaucer's *Ladys Foure and Twenty.*" *MLN,* 50 (1935), 85–87. [D 992]

2594 TUPPER, Frederick. "Saint Venus and the Canterbury Pilgrims." *Nation,* 97 (1913), 354–356.

2595 UTLEY, Francis L. "Chaucer's Way with a Proverb: 'Allas! Allas! That Evere Love was Synne'." *North Carolina Folklore,* 21 (1973), 98–104.

2596 VERBILLION, June. "Chaucer's *The Wife of Bath's Prologue,* 175." *Explicator,* 24 (1966), item 58.

2597 VOGT, George M. "Gleanings for the History of a Sentiment: Generositas Virtus, Non Sanguis." *JEGP,* 24 (1925), 102–124.

2598 WOOD, Chauncey. "Chaucer's The Wife of Bath's Prologue, D. 576 and 583." *Explicator,* 23 (1965), item 73.

2599 WOOLLCOMBE, W. W. "The Sources of the Wife of Bath's Prologue: Chaucer Not a Borrower from John of Salisbury." *Essays on Chaucer,* Part III, pp. 293–306 (Chaucer Soc., 2nd Ser. No. 16).

2600 ZIMBARDO, Rose A. "Unity and Duality in *The Wife of Bath's Prologue and Tale.*" *TSL,* 11 (1966), 11–33.

The Friar's Prologue and Tale

2601 AIKEN, Pauline. "Vincent of Beauvais and the Green Yeoman's Lecture on Demonology." *SP,* 35 (1938), 1–9.

2602 BAIRD, Joseph L. "The Devil in Green." *NM,* 69 (1968), 575–578.

2603 BAIRD, Joseph L. "The Devil's *Privetee.*" *NM,* 70 (1969), 104–106.

2604 BAKER, Donald C. "Exemplary Figures as Characterizing Devices in the *Friar's Tale* and the *Summoner's Tale.*" *UMSE,* 3 (1962), 35–41.

2605 BAKER, Donald C. See 2638.

2606 BEICHNER, Paul E. "Baiting the Summoner." *MLQ,* 22 (1961), 367–376.

2607 BIRNEY, Earle. " 'After His Ymage'—The Central Ironies of the *Friar's Tale.*" *MS,* 21 (1959), 17–35.

2608 BONJOUR, Adrien. "Aspects of Chaucer's Irony in *The Frair's Tale.*" *EIC,* 11 (1961), 121–127.

2609 CARRUTHERS, Mary. "Letter and Gloss in the Friar's and Summoner's Tales." *Jour. of Narrative Technique,* 2 (1972), 208–214.

2610 CAWLEY, A. C. "Chaucer's Summoner, The Friar's Summoner and the *Friar's Tale.*" *Proc. Leeds Philos. and Literary Soc.,* 8, (1957), 173–180.

2611 CLINE, Ruth H. "St. Anne." *ELN,* 2 (1964), 87–89.

2612 CORREALE, Robert M. "St. Jerome and the Conclusion of the *Friar's Tale.*" *ELN,* 2 (1965), 171–174.

2613 ECKHARDT, Caroline D. " 'Canterbury Tales' D 1554: 'Caples Thre'." *N&Q,* 20 (1973), 283–284.

2614 HARRISON, Thomas P. "Chaucer's 'wariangles'." *N&Q,* 199 (1954), 189.

2615 HATTON, Tom. "Chaucer's Friar's 'Old Rebekke'." *JEGP,* 67 (1968), 266–271.

2616 HENNEDY, Hugh L. "The Friar's Summoner's Dilemma." *ChauR,* 5 (1971), 213–217.

2617 HIEATT, Constance. "Oaths in the *Friar's Tale.*" *N&Q,* 205 (1960), 5–6.

2618 IMMACULATE, Sister Mary. "Fiends as 'servant unto man' in the *Friar's Tale.*" *PQ,* 21 (1942), 240–244. [D 1501-3]

2619 KELLOGG, Alfred L. "Chaucer's 'Friar's Tale': line 1314." *N&Q,* 204 (1959), 190–192. Reprinted in 456.

2620 LENAGHAN, R. T. "The Irony of the *Friar's Tale.*" *ChauR,* 7 (1973), 281–294.

2621 MALONE, Kemp. "The Freres Contree." *MLR,* 26 (1931), 75–77.

2622 MROCZKOWSKI, P. "Chaucer's Green 'Yeoman' and 'Le Roman de Renart'." *N&Q,* 207 (1962), 325–326.

2623 MROCZKOWSKI, P. "*The Friar's Tale* and Its Pulpit Background." *English Stud. Today* (Berne), 2nd Ser. (1961), 107–120.

2624 MURTAUGH, Daniel M. "Riming Justice in *The Friar's Tale.*" *NM,* 74 (1973), 107–112.

2625 NATHAN, Norman. "Pronouns of Address in the *Friar's Tale.*" *MLQ,* 17 (1956), 39–42.

2626 PASSON, Richard H. " 'Entente' in Chaucer's *Friar's Tale.*" *ChauR,* 2 (1968), 166–171.

2627 RICHARDSON, Janette. "An Ambiguous Reference in Chaucer's *Friar's Tale.*" *Archiv,* 198 (1962), 388–390.

2628 RICHARDSON, Janette. "Hunter and Prey: Functional Imagery in Chaucer's *Friar's Tale.*" *EM,* 12 (1961), 9–20. Reprinted in 264.

2629 ROBERTSON, D. W., Jr. "Why the Devil Wears Green." *MLN,* 69 (1954), 470–472.

2630 ROWLAND, Beryl. " 'Wood . . . as an Hare' (*The Friar's Tale,* 1327)." *N&Q,* 208 (1963), 168–169.

2631 SOUTHWORTH, James G. "Chaucer's *The Canterbury Tales,* D. 1746–1753." *Explicator,* 11 (1953), item 29.

2632 STROUD, T. A. "Chaucer's Friar As Narrator." *ChauR,* 8 (1973), 65–69.

2633 SUTHERLAND, Raymond C., Jr. "A Note on Lines D 1645–1662 of Chaucer's *Friar's Tale.*" *PQ,* 31 (1952), 436–439.

2634 TAYLOR, Archer. "The Devil and the Advocate." *PMLA,* 36 (1921), 35–59.

2635 TAYLOR, Archer. "Der Richter und der Teufel." *Studies in Honor of Hermann Collitz,* pp. 248–251. Baltimore: Johns Hopkins Press, 1930.

2636 TUPPER, Frederick. See 1721.

The Summoner's Prologue and Tale

√ 2637 ADAMS, John F. "The Structure of Irony in *The Summoner's Tale.*" *EIC,* 12 ✕ (1962), 126–132.

2638 BAKER, Donald C. "Witchcraft in the dispute between Chaucer's Friar and Summoner." *South-Central Bull.,* 21, No. 4 (1961), 33–36.

2639 BAKER, Donald C. See 2604.

2640 BEICHNER, Paul E. "*Non Alleluia Ructare.*" *MS,* 18 (1956), 135–144.

2641 BIRNEY, Earle. "Structural Irony within the *Summoner's Tale.*" *Anglia,* 78 (1960), 204–218.

2642 CURRY, Walter C. "The Bottom of Hell." *MLN,* 38 (1923), 253.

2643 FLEMING, John V. "The Antifraternalism of the *Summoner's Tale.*" *JEGP,* 45 (1966), 688–700.

2644 FLEMING, John V. "Chaucer's 'Syngeth Placebo' and the *Roman de Fauvel.*" *N&Q,* 210 (1965), 17–18.

2645 FLEMING, John V. "The Summoner's Prologue: An Iconographic Adjustment." *ChauR,* 2 (1967), 95–107.

2646 HAMILTON, Marie P. "The Summoner's 'Psalm of Davit'." *MLN,* 57 (1942), 655–657.

2647 HARTUNG, Albert E. "Two Notes in the Summoner's Tale: Hosts and Swans." *ELN,* 4 (1967), 175–180.

2648 HASKELL, Ann S. "St. Simon in the *Summoner's Tale.*" *ChauR,* 5 (1971), 218–224.

2649 KASKE, R. E. "Horn and Ivory in the *Summoner's Tale.*" 52, pp. 122–126.

2650 KELLOGG, Alfred L. "The Fraternal Kiss in Chaucer's *Summoner's Tale.*" *Scriptorium,* 7 (1953), 115. Reprinted in 456.

2651 KOCH, Robert A. "Elijah the Prophet, Founder of the Carmelite Order." *Speculum,* 34 (1959), 547–560.

2652 LEVITAN, Alan. "The Parody of Pentecost in Chaucer's *Summoner's Tale.*" *UTQ,* 40 (1971), 236–246.

2653 LEVY, Bernard S. "Biblical Parody in the *Summoner's Tale.*" *TSL,* 11 (1966), 45–60.

2654 MERRILL, Thomas F. "Wrath and Rhetoric in *The Summoner's Tale.*" *TSLL,* 4 (1962), 341–350.

2655 PEARCY, Roy J. "Chaucer's 'An Impossible' (*Summoner's Tale,* III. 2231)." *N&Q,* 212 (1967), 322–325.

2656 ROOT, Robert K. See 2281.

2657 SEVERS, J. Burke. "Chaucer's *The Summoner's Tale,* D 2184–2188." *Explicator,* 23 (1964), item 20.

2658 SILVIA, Daniel S., Jr. "Chaucer's Friars: Swans or Swains? *Summoner's Tale* D 1930." *ELN,* 1 (1964), 248–250.

2659 STANFORD, Mabel A. "The Sumner's Tale and Saint Patrick's Purgatory." *JEGP,* 19 (1920), 377–381.

2660 SZITTYA, Penn R. "The Friar as False Apostle: Antifraternal Exegesis and the *Summoner's Tale.*" *SP,* 71 (1974), 19–46.

2661 TUPPER, Frederick. "Anent Jerome and the Summoner's Friar." *MLN,* 30 (1915), 63–64.

2662 TUPPER, Frederick. See 1722.

2663 WENZEL, Siegfried. See 2176.

2664 ZIETLOW, Paul N. "In Defense of the Summoner." *ChauR,* 1 (1966), 4–19.

The Clerk's Prologue and Tale

2665 BAIRD, Joseph L. "The 'secte' of the Wife of Bath." *ChauR,* 2 (1968), 188–190.

2666 BAIRD, Joseph. "*Secte* and *Suit* Again: Chaucer and Langland." *ChauR,* 5 (1971), 117–119.

2667 BAKER, Donald C. "Chaucer's Clerk and the Wife of Bath on the Subject of *Gentilesse.*" *SP,* 59 (1962), 631–640.

2668 BETTRIDGE, William E., and Francis L. UTLEY. "New Light on the Origin of the Griselda Story." *TSLL,* 13 (1971), 153–208.

2669 BOWEN, Robert O. "Chaucer, The Clerk's Prologue." *MLN,* 71 (1956), 165.

2670 CATE, Wirt A. "The Problem of the Origin of the Griselda Story." *SP,* 29 (1932), 389–405.

2671 CHERNISS, Michael D. "The *Clerk's Tale* and *Envoy,* the Wife of Bath's Purgatory, and the *Merchant's Tale.*" *ChauR,* 6 (1972), 235–254.

2672 COOK, Albert S. "Chauceriana." *RR,* 8 (1917), 210–226, 353–382.

2673 Cook, Albert S. "Chaucer's Griselda and Homer's Arete." *AJP,* 39 (1918), 75–78.

2674 Cook, James W. "Augustinian Neurosis and the Therapy of Orthodoxy." *Universitas* (Wayne State Univ.), 2 (1964), 51–62.

2675 Cordié, Carlo. "Geoffrey Chaucer e Giovanni da Legnano." *Letterature Moderne,* 2 (1951), 82–85.

2676 Covella, Sister Francis Dolores. "The Speaker of the Wife of Bath Stanza and Envoy." *ChauR,* 4 (1970), 267–283.

2677 Cunningham, J. V. "Ideal Fiction: *The Clerk's Tale.*" *Shenandoah,* 19, ii (1968), 38–41.

2678 Dempster, Germaine. "Chaucer's Manuscript of Petrarch's Version of the Griselda Story." *MP,* 41 (1943), 6–16.

2679 Farnham, Willard E. "Chaucer's *Clerk's Tale.*" *MLN,* 33 (1918), 193–203.

2680 Fichte, Joerg O. "*The Clerk's Tale:* An Obituary to *Gentilesse.*" 282, pp. 9–16.

2681 Frese, Dolores W. "Chaucer's *Clerk's Tale:* The Monsters and the Critics Reconsidered." *ChauR,* 8 (1973), 132–146.

2682 Grennan, Joseph E. "Science and Sensibility in Chaucer's Clerk." *ChauR,* 6 (1971), 81–93.

2683 Griffith, Dudley D. *The Origin of the Griselda Story. (Univ. of Washington Pub. in Lang. and Lit.,* VIII). Seattle, 1931.

2684 Hamilton, George L. "Chauceriana I: The Date of *The Clerk's Tale* [and Chaucer's 'Petrak']." *MLN,* 23 (1908), 169–172.

2685 Hartung, Albert E. "The Clerk's Endlink in the *d* Manuscripts." *PMLA,* 67 (1952), 1173–1177. Cf. *ibid.,* 1177–1181 (Dempster), 1181 (Hartung).

2686 Hendrickson, G. L. "Chaucer and Petrarch: Two Notes on the *Clerkes Tale.*" *MP,* 4 (1906–07), 179–192.

2687 Heninger, S. K., Jr. "The Concept of Order in Chaucer's *Clerk's Tale.*" *JEGP,* 56 (1957), 382–395.

2688 Hornstein, Lillian H. "The Wyf of Bathe and the Merchant: From Sex to 'Secte'. " *ChauR,* 3 (1968),65–67.

2689 Jeffrey, Lloyd N. "Chaucer's Walter: A Study in Emotional Immaturity." *Jour. of Humanistic Psych.,* 3 (1963), 112–119.

2690 Kellogg, Alfred L. "The Evolution of the 'Clerk's Tale': A Study in Connotation." 456, pp. 276–329. Reprinted in 456.

2691 Kökeritz, Helge. "The Wyf of Bathe and 'al hire secte'. " *PQ,* 26 (1947), 147–151.

2692 Lanham, Richard A. "Chaucer's *Clerk's Tale:* The Poem Not the Myth." *L&P,* 16 (1966), 157–165.

2693 Laserstein, Käte. *Der Griseldisstoff in der Weltliteratur: Eine Untersuchung zur Stoff- und Stilgeschichte.* Weimar, 1926 (*Forschungen zur neueren Literaturgeschichte,* No. 58).

2694 Lavers, Norman. "Freud, The Clerk's Tale, and Literary Criticism." *CE,* 26 (1964), 180–187.

2695 Loganbill, Dean. "*The Clerk's Tale* and the *Man of Law's Tale:* Chaucer and Godot Waiting for Beckett." 282, p. 29–34.

2696 LONGSWORTH, Robert. "Chaucer's Clerk as Teacher." 57, pp. 61–66.

2697 MALONE, Kemp. "Patient Griseldus." *RR,* 20 (1929), 340–345.

2698 McCALL, John P. "Chaucer and John of Legnano." *Speculum,* 40 (1965), 484–489.

2699 McCALL, John P. "The *Clerk's Tale* and the Theme of Obedience." *MLQ,* 27 (1966), 260–269.

2700 McNAMARA, John. "Chaucer's Use of the Epistle of St. James in the *Clerk's Tale.*" *ChauR,* 7 (1973), 184–193.

2701 MORROW, Patrick. "The Ambivalence of Truth: Chaucer's 'Clerkes Tale'. " *Bucknell Rev.,* 16, iii (1968), 74–90.

2702 MORSE, J. Mitchell. "The Philosophy of the Clerk of Oxenford." *MLQ,* 19 (1958), 3–20.

2703 PEARSALL, Robert B. "Chaucer's 'Panik' (*Clerk's Tale,* 590)." *MLN,* 67 (1952), 529–531.

2704 PRINS, A. A. "As Fer as last Ytaille." *ES,* 37 (1956), 111–116.

2705 REIMAN, Donald H. "The Real *Clerk's Tale;* or, Patient Griselda Explained." *TSLL,* 5 (1963), 356–373.

2706 ROTHMAN, Irving N. "Humility and Obedience in the *Clerk's Tale,* with the Envoy Considered as an Ironic Affirmation." *PLL,* 9 (1973), 115–127.

2707 SALTER, Elizabeth. See 2084.

2708 SEVERS, Jonathan B. "Chaucer's Source MSS. for the *Clerkes Tale.*" *PMLA,* 47 (1932), 431–452.

2709 SEVERS, J. Burke. "Did Chaucer Rearrange the Clerk's Envoy?" *MLN,* 69 (1954), 472–478.

2710 SEVERS, J. Burke. "Did Chaucer Revise the *Clerk's Tale?*" *Speculum,* 21 (1946), 295–302.

2711 SEVERS, J. Burke. "The Job Passage in the *Clerkes Tale.*" *MLN,* 49 (1934), 461–462.

2712 SEVERS, J. Burke. *The Literary Relationships of Chaucer's Clerkes Tale. (Yale Stud. in English,* No. 96). New Haven, 1942. Reprinted Hamden, Conn.: Archon, 1972.

2713 SLEDD, James. "The *Clerk's Tale:* The Monsters and the Critics." *MP,* 51 (1953–54), 73–92. Reprinted in 628 and 1700.

2714 SPEARING, A. C. "Chaucer's *Clerk's Tale* as a Medieval Poem." 231, pp. 76–106.

2715 UTLEY, Francis L. "Five Genres in the *Clerk's Tale.*" *ChauR,* 6 (1972), 198–228.

The Merchant's Prologue and Tale

2716 BAIRD, Joseph L. " 'Of marriage, which we have on honde.' " *AN&Q,* 11 (1973), 100–102.

2717 BASSAN, Maurice. "Chaucer's 'Cursed Monk', Constantinus Africanus." *MS,* 24 (1962), 127–140.

2718 BAUGH, Albert C. "The Original Teller of the Merchant's Tale." *MP,* 35 (1937–38), 15–26, Cf. *ibid.,* 36 (1938–39), 1–8 (Dempster).

2719 BEIDLER, Peter G. "The Climax in the *Merchant's Tale.*" *ChauR,* 6 (1971), 38–43.

2720 BEIDLER, Peter G. "January, Knight of Lombardy." *NM*, 72 (1971), 735–738.

2721 BEIDLER, Peter G. "Chaucer's Merchant and the Tale of January." *Costerus*, 5 (1972), 1–25.

2722 BEIDLER, Peter G. "Chaucer's *Merchant's Tale* and the *Decameron.*" *Italica*, 50 (1973), 266–283.

2723 BLANCH, Robert J. "Irony in Chaucer's *Merchant's Tale.*" *Lock Haven Rev.*, No. 8 (1966), 8–15.

2724 BLEETH, Kenneth A. "The Image of Paradise in the *Merchant's Tale.*" 57, pp. 45–60.

2725 BOOTHMAN, Janet. See 2119.

2726 BRONSON, B. H. "Afterthoughts on *The Merchant's Tale.*" *SP*, 58 (1961), 583–596.

2727 BROWN, Emerson, Jr. "*The Merchant's Tale:* Why Is May Called 'Mayus'?" *ChauR*, 2 (1968), 273–277.

2728 BROWN, Emerson, Jr. "*Hortus Inconclusus:* The Significance of Priapus and Pyramus and Thisbe in the *Merchant's Tale.*" *ChauR*, 4 (1970), 31–40.

2729 BROWN, Emerson, Jr. "*The Merchant's Tale:* Why Was Januarie Born 'of Pavye'?" *NM*, 71 (1970), 654–658.

2730 BROWN, Emerson, Jr. "*The Merchant's Tale:* Januarie's 'Unlikely Elde'." *NM*, 74 (1973), 92–106.

2731 BURROW, J. A. "Irony in *The Merchant's Tale.*" *Anglia*, 75 (1957), 199–208.

2732 CASSIDY, Frederic G. "Chaucer's 'broken harm'." *MLN*, 58 (1943), 23–27.

2733 CHERNISS, Michael D. See 2671.

2734 DELANY, Paul. "Constantinus Africanus and Chaucer's *Merchant's Tale.*" *PQ*, 46 (1967), 560–566.

2735 DEMPSTER, Germaine, "On the Source of the Deception Story in the *Merchant's Tale.*" *MP*, 34 (1936–37), 133–154.

2736 DONALDSON, E. Talbot. "The Effect of the Merchant's Tale." 272, pp. 30–45.

2737 DONOVAN, Mortimer J. "The Image of Pluto and Proserpine in the *Merchant's Tale.*" *PQ*, 36 (1957), 49–60.

2738 DONOVAN, Mortimer J. "Three Notes on Chaucer's Marine Life." *PQ*, 31 (1952), 439–441.

2739 ECONOMOU, George D. "Januarie's Sin against Nature: The *Merchant's Tale* and the *Roman de la Rose.*" *CL*, 17 (1965), 251–257.

2740 ELLIOTT, John R., Jr. "The Two Tellers of *The Merchant's Tale.*" *TSL*, 9 (1964), 11–17.

2741 FERRIS, Sumner J. " 'Wades Boot': *Canterbury Tales* E. 1424 and 1684." *AN&Q*, 9 (1971), 71–72.

2742 FIELD, P. J. C. "Chaucer's Merchant and the Sin against Nature." *N&Q*, 215 (1970), 84–86.

2743 GARBÁTY, Thomas J. "The Monk and the *Merchant's Tale:* An Aspect of Chaucer's Building Process in the Canterbury Tales." *MP*, 67 (1969), 18–24.

2744 GRENNEN, Joseph E. "Another French Source for *The Merchant's Tale.*" *Romance Notes*, 8 (1966), 109–112.

2745 GRIFFITH, Philip M. "Chaucer's *Merchant's Tale.*" *Explicator,* 16 (1957), item 13.

2746 HARRINGTON, David V. "Chaucer's *Merchant's Tale,* 1427–28." *N&Q,* 209 (1964), 166–167.

2747 HARRINGTON, Norman T. "Chaucer's Merchant's Tale: Another Swing of the Pendulum." *PMLA,* 86 (1971), 25–31.

2748 HARTUNG, Albert E. "The Non-Comic *Merchant's Tale,* Maximianus, and the Sources." *MS,* 29 (1967), 1–25.

2749 HOFFMAN, Richard L. "Ovid's Priapus in the Merchant's Tale." *ELN,* 3 (1966), 169–172.

2750 HOLMAN, C. Hugh. "Courtly Love in the Merchant's and the Franklin's Tales." *ELH,* 18 (1951), 241–252. Reprinted in 628.

2751 HOLTHAUSEN, F. "Die Quelle von Chaucers *Merchant's Tale.*" *ESt,* 43 (1910–11), 168–176.

2752 HUSEBOE, Arthur R. "Chaucerian Puns on 'Brotel'. " *NDQ,* 31 (1963), 35–37.

2753 JORDAN, Robert M. "The Non-dramatic Disunity of the *Merchant's Tale.*" *PMLA,* 78 (1963), 293–299.

2754 KASKE, Robert E. "January's 'aube'. " *MLN,* 75 (1960), 1–4.

2755 KEE, Kenneth. See 453.

2756 KELLOGG, Alfred L. "Susannah and the *Merchant's Tale.*" *Speculum,* 35 (1960), 275–279. Reprinted in 456.

2757 KIRBY, Thomas A. "A Note on the Irony of the *Merchant's Tale.*" *PQ,* 21 (1942), 433–435.

2758 KREISLER, Nicolai von. "An Aesopic Allusion in the *Merchant's Tale.*" *ChauR,* 6 (1971), 30–37.

2759 MAGOUN, Francis P., Jr. " 'Muchel *broken* harm', *C.T.,* E. 1425." *Anglia,* 52 (1929), 223–224.

2760 MAIN, William W. "Chaucer's *The Merchant's Tale,* 2257–2261." *Explicator,* 14 (1955), item 13.

2761 MATTHEWS, William. "Eustache Deschamps and Chaucer's *Merchant's Tale.*" *MLR,* 51 (1956) 217–220.

2762 McGALLIARD, John C. "Chaucerian Comedy: The *Merchant's Tale,* Jonson, and Molière." *PQ,* 25 (1946), 343–370.

2763 McGALLIARD, John C. "Chaucer's *Merchant's Tale* and Deschamps' *Miroir de Mariage.*" *PQ,* 25 (1946), 193–220.

2764 MILLER, Milton. "The Heir in the *Merchant's Tale.*" *PQ,* 29 (1950), 437–440.

2765 MUKHERJEE, Meenakshi. "*The Merchant's Tale:* A Study in Multiple Meaning." *IJES,* 7 (1966), 17–23.

2766 OLSON, Paul A. "Chaucer's Merchant and January's 'hevene in erthe heere'. " *ELH,* 28 (1961), 203–214.

2767 OLSON, Paul A. "The Merchant's Lombard Knight." *TSLL,* 3 (1961), 259–263.

2768 OTTEN, Charlotte F. "Proserpine: *Liberatrix Suae Gentis.*" *ChauR,* 5 (1971), 277–287.

2769 PACE, George B. "The Scorpion of Chaucer's *Merchant's Tale.*" *MLQ,* 26 (1965), 369–374.

2770 Pittock, Malcolm. "The Merchant's Tale." *EIC* 17 (1967), 26-40.

2772 Robbins, Rossell H. "January's Caress." *Lock Haven Rev.,* 10 (1968), 3-6.

2773 Rosenberg, Bruce A. "The 'Cherry-Tree Carol' and the *Merchant's Tale.*" *ChauR,* 5 (1971), 264-276.

2774 Schaar, Claes. "The Merchant's Tale, Amadas et Ydoine, and Guillaume au Faucon." *K. Humanistika vetenskapssamfundet i Lund: Årsberättelse, 1952-53,* pp. 87-95.

2775 Schlauch, Margaret. "Chaucer's *Merchant's Tale* and Courtly Love." *ELH,* 4 (1937), 201-212.

2776 Schroeder, Mary C. "Fantasy in the 'Merchant's Tale'." *Criticism,* 12 (1970), 167-179.

2777 Sedgewick, G. G. "The Structure of *The Merchant's Tale.*" *UTQ,* 17 (1948), 337-345.

2778 Shores, David L. "*The Merchant's Tale:* Some Lay Observations." *NM,* 49 (1970), 119-133.

2779 Stevens, Martin. "'And Venus laugheth': An Interpretation of the *Merchant's Tale.*" *ChauR,* 7 (1972), 118-131.

2780 Tatlock, John S. P. "Chaucer's *Merchant's Tale.*" *MP,* 33 (1935-36), 367-381. Reprinted in 1700.

2781 Tatlock, John S. P. "The Marriage Service in Chaucer's *Merchant's Tale.*" *MLN,* 32 (1917), 373-374.

2782 Taylor, Willene P. "Chaucer's Technique in Handling Anti-Feminist Material in 'The Merchant's Tale': An Ironic Portrayal of the Senex-Amans and Jealous Husband." *CLAJ,* 13 (1969), 153-162.

2783 Turner, W. Arthur. "Biblical Women in *The Merchant's Tale* and *The Tale of Melibee.*" *ELN,* 3 (1965), 92-95.

2784 Utley, Francis L. "Mannysch Wood—*Merchant's Tale* (IV) 1530-1536." *MLN,* 53 (1938), 359-362.

2785 Wentersdorf, Karl P. "Chaucer's Merchant's Tale and Its Irish Analogues." *SP,* 63 (1966), 604-629.

2786 Wentersdorf, Karl P. "Theme and Structure in the Merchant's Tale: The Function of the Pluto Episode." *PMLA,* 80 (1965), 522-527.

2787 Wentersdorf, Karl P. "A Spanish Analogue of the Pear-Tree Episode in the *Merchant's Tale.*" *MP,* 64 (1967), 320-321.

2788 White, Gertrude M. "'Hoolynesse or Dotage': The Merchant's January." *PQ,* 44 (1965), 397-404.

2789 Wichert, Robert A. "Chaucer's The Merchant's Tale, 1662." *Explicator,* 25 (1966), item 32.

The Squire's Prologue and Tale

2790 Bennett, Josephine W. "Chaucer and *Mandeville's Travels.*" *MLN,* 68 (1953), 531-534.

2791 Braddy, Haldeen. "Cambyuskan's Flying Horse and Charles VI's 'Cerf Volant'." *MLR,* 33 (1938), 41-44. Reprinted in 258.

THE SQUIRE'S TALE

2792 BRADDY, Haldeen. "The Genre of Chaucer's *Squire's Tale.*" *JEGP,* 41 (1942), 279–290. Reprinted in 258.

2793 BRADDY, Haldeen. "The Oriental Origin of Chaucer's Canacee-Falcon Episode." *MLR,* 31 (1936), 11–19. Reprinted in 258.

2794 BRANDL, Alois. "Über einige historische Anspielungen in den Chaucer-Dichtungen." *ESt,* 12 (1889), 161–186. Cf. 2809.

2795 BROWN, Calvin S., Jr., and Robert H. WEST. "'As by the Whelp Chastised Is the Leon.'" *MLN,* 55 (1940), 209–210. Cf. *ibid.,* 481 (Grace Frank).

2796 CLOUSTON, W. A. *On the Magical Elements in Chaucer's Squire's Tale, with Analogues.* (Chaucer Soc., 2nd Ser., No. 26.) London, 1890.

2797 DUNCAN, Charles F., Jr. "'Straw for youre gentilesse': The Gentle Franklin's Interruption of the Squire." *ChauR,* 5 (1970), 161–164.

2798 EMERSON, Francis W. "Cambalus in the Squire's Tale." *N&Q,* 203 (1958), 461.

2799 FINKELSTEIN, Dorothee. *The Celestial Origin of* Elpheta *and* Algarsyf *in Chaucer's Squire's Tale. (Euroasiatica,* No. 4.) Naples: Instituto Universitario Orientale, 1970.

2800 FRIEND, Albert C. "The Tale of the Captive Bird and the Traveler: Nequam, Berechiah, and Chaucer's *Squire's Tale.*" *M&H,* n.s. 1 (1970), 57–65.

2801 GÖLLER, Karl H. "Chaucer's 'Squire's Tale': 'The knotte of the tale'." 54, pp. 163–188.

2802 GREENE, Richard L. "'Foules of ravyne' and 'foules smale' in Chaucer's *Squire's Tale.*" *N&Q,* 210 (1965), 446–448.

2803 HALLER, Robert S. "Chaucer's *Squire's Tale* and the Uses of Rhetoric." *MP,* 62 (1964–65), 285–295.

2804 HAWKINS, Laurence F. *The Place of Group F in the Canterbury Chronology.* [New York Univ. diss.], 1937.

2805 HINCKLEY, Henry B. "Chaucer and the *Cléomedès.*" *MLN,* 24 (1909), 95. Cf. *ibid.,* 158 (H.S.V. Jones).

2806 JONES, H. S. V. "The Cléomadès and Related Folk-Tales." *PMLA,* 23 (1908), 557–598.

2807 JONES, H. S. V. "Some Observations upon the Squire's Tale." *PMLA,* 20 (1905), 346–359.

2808 KAHRL, Stanley J. "Chaucer's *Squire's Tale* and the Decline of Chivalry." *ChauR,* 7 (1973), 194–209.

2809 KITTREDGE, George L. "Supposed Historical Allusions in the Squire's Tale." *ESt,* 13 (1889), 1–25.

2810 LOOMIS, Roger S. "Gawain in the *Squire's Tale.*" *MLN,* 52 (1937), 413–416.

2811 LOWES, John L. "'As by the whelp chasted is the leoun'." *Archiv,* 124 (1910), 132.

2812 LOWES, John L. "The Squire's Tale and the Land of Prester John." *Washington Univ. Stud.,* 1, Part ii, No. 1 (1913), 3–18.

2813 MAGOUN, F. P., Jr. "Chaucer and the Roman de la Rose, vv. 16096–105." *RR,* 17 (1926), 69–70.

2814 MAGOUN, F. P., Jr. "Chaucer's Sir Gawain and the OFr. *Roman de la Rose.*" *MLN,* 67 (1952), 183–185.

2815 MANLY, John M. "Marco Polo and the Squire's Tale." *PMLA*, 11 (1896), 349–362.

2816 McCALL, John P. "The Squire in Wonderland." *ChauR*, 1 (1966), 103–109.

2817 NEVILLE, Marie. "The Function of the *Squire's Tale* in the Canterbury Scheme." *JEGP*, 50 (1951), 167–179.

2818 OSGERBY, J. R. "Chaucer's Squire's Tale." *Use of English*, 11 (1959), 102–107.

2819 PEARSALL, D. A. "The Squire as Story-teller." *UTQ*, 34 (1964), 82–92.

2820 PETERSON, Joyce E. "The Finished Fragment: A Reassessment of the Squire's Tale." *ChauR*, 5 (1970), 62–74.

2821 TATLOCK, John S. P. "Chaucer's Whelp and Lion." *MLN*, 38 (1923), 506–507.

2822 TOLLENAERE, F. de. " 'To maken of fern-asshen glas' . . . (*Squire's Tale* 246)." *ES*, 31 (1950), 97–99.

2823 WHITING, B. J. "Gawain: His Reputation, His Courtesy and His Appearance in Chaucer's *Squire's Tale.*" *MS*, 9 (1947), 189–234.

The Franklin's Prologue and Tale

2824 AMAN, Anselm. *Die Filiation der Frankeleynes Tale in Chaucers Canterbury Tales.* Erlangen, 1912 (Munich diss.).

2825 ARCHER, Jerome W. "On Chaucer's Source for 'Arveragus' in the *Franklin's Tale.* " *PMLA*, 65 (1950), 318–322.

2826 BAKER, Donald C. "A Crux in Chaucer's *Franklin's Tale:* Doringen's Complaint." *JEGP*, 60 (1961), 56–64.

2827 BEIDLER, Peter G. "The Pairing of the *Franklin's Tale* and the *Physician's Tale.* " *ChauR*, 3 (1969), 275–279.

2828 BENJAMIN, Edwin B. "The Concept of Order in the *Franklin's Tale.* " *PQ*, 38 (1959), 119–124.

2829 BLENNER-HASSETT, Roland. "Autobiographical Aspects of Chaucer's Franklin." *Speculum*, 28 (1953), 791–800.

2830 BØGHOLM, N. "A Rash Promise." *SN*, 15 (1942), 41–42.

2831 BURLIN, Robert B. "The Art of Chaucer's Franklin." *Neophil*, 51 (1967), 55–73.

2832 BURNLEY, J. D. "Chaucer's Art of Verbal Allusion: Two Notes." *Neophil*, 56 (1972), 93–99. [*FranklT*, 899; *BD* 874]

2833 CLARK, John W. "*Does* the Franklin Interrupt the Squire?" *ChauR*, 7 (1972), 160–161.

2834 COLMER, Dorothy. "The Franklin's Tale: A Palimpsest Reading." *EIC*, 20 (1970), 375–380. (A reply to 2855.)

2835 DAVID, Alfred. "Sentimental Comedy in *The Franklin's Tale.* " *AnM*, 6 (1965), 19–27.

2836 DEMPSTER, Germaine. "Chaucer at Work on the Complaint in *The Franklin's Tale.* " *MLN*, 52 (1937), 16–23.

2837 DEMPSTER, Germaine. "A Further Note on Dorigen's *Exempla.* " *MLN*, 54 (1939), 137–138.

2838 DONOVAN, Mortimer J. "The *Anticlaudian* and Three Passages in the *Franklin's Tale.* " *JEGP*, 56 (1957), 52–59.

2839 FRENCH, W. H. "*The Franklin's Tale,* line 942." *MLN,* 60 (1945), 477–480.

2840 GAYLORD, Alan T. "The Promises in *The Franklin's Tale.*" *ELH,* 31 (1964), 331–365.

2841 GERHARD, Joseph. "The *Franklin's Tale:* Chaucer's Theodicy." *ChauR,* 1 (1966), 20–32.

2842 GOLDING, M. R. "The Importance of Keeping 'Trouthe' in *The Franklin's Tale.*" *MÆ,* 39 (1970), 306–312.

2843 GRAY, Paul E. "Synthesis and the Double Standard in the *Franklin's Tale.*" *TSLL,* 7 (1965), 213–224.

2844 HARRISON, Benjamin S. "The Rhetorical Inconsistency of Chaucer's Franklin." *SP,* 32 (1935), 55–61.

2845 HART, Walter M. "The Franklin's Tale." *Haverford Essays* [in honor of] *Francis B. Gummere,* pp. 183–234. Haverford, 1909.

2846 HATTON, Thomas J. "Magic and Honor in *The Franklin's Tale.*" *PLL,* 3 (1967), 179–181.

2847 HERZ, Judith S. "A Syncretic Reading of *The Franklin's Tale.*" *RUO,* 40 (1973), 587–601.

2848 HOLMAN, C. Hugh. See 2750.

2849 HOWARD, Ronnalie R. "Appearance, Reality, and the Ideal in Chaucer's *Franklin's Tale.*" *Ball State Univ. Forum,* 8, iii (1967), 40–44.

2850 HUME, Kathryn. "Why Chaucer Calls the *Franklin's Tale* a Breton Lai." *PQ,* 51 (1972), 365–379.

2851 HUME, Kathryn. "The Pagan Setting of the *Franklin's Tale* and the Sources of Dorigen's Cosmology." *SN,* 44 (1972), 289–294.

2852 HUNTER, William B., Jr. "Canterbury Tales V, 1031ff." *MLN,* 68 (1953), 174.

2853 JOHNSTON, Grahame. "Chaucer and the Breton Lays." *Proc. and Papers of the Fourteenth Congress of the Australasian Universities Lang. and Lit. Assoc.,* ed. K. I. D. Maslen, pp. 230–241. Dunedin: AULLA, 1972.

2854 JOSEPH, Gerhard. "The *Franklin's Tale:* Chaucer's Theodicy." *ChauR,* 1 (1966), 20–32.

2855 KEARNEY, A[nthony] M. "Truth and Illusion in *The Franklin's Tale.*" *EIC,* 19 (1969), 245–253.

2856 KEARNEY, Anthony [M.] "The *Franklin's Tale.*" *EIC,* 21 (1971), 109–111. (Reply to 2834)

2857 KEE, Kenneth. See 453.

2858 KELLY, Francis J. "The Franklin's Tale, F. 942." *Explicator,* 24 (1966), item 81.

2859 KNIGHT, Stephen. "Rhetoric and Poetry in the *Franklin's Tale.*" *ChauR,* 4 (1970), 14–30.

2860 LOOMIS, Laura H. "Chaucer and the Breton Lays of the Auchinleck MS." *SP,* 38 (1941), 14–33. Reprinted in 194.

2861 LOOMIS, Roger S. "A Parallel to the Franklin's Discussion of Marriage." *Philologica: The Malone Anniversary Studies,* pp. 191–194. Baltimore: Johns Hopkins Press, 1949.

2862 Lowes, John L. "The *Franklin's Tale*, the *Teseide*, and the *Filocolo*," *MP*, 15 (1918), 689–728.

2863 Lumiansky, Robert M. "The Character and Performance of Chaucer's Franklin." *UTQ*, 20 (1951), 344–356.

2864 Magoun, F. P., Jr. "*Canterbury Tales*, F 1541–44." *MLN*, 70 (1955), 173.

2865 Mallikarjunan, S. "On Three Interpretations of Chaucer's *The Franklin's Tale*." *IJES*, 3 (1962), 1–11.

2866 Mann, Lindsay A. " 'Gentilesse' and the Franklin's Tale." *SP*, 63 (1966), 10–29.

2867 Milosh, Joseph. "Chaucer's Too-Well Told *Franklin's Tale:* A Problem of Characterization." *Wisconsin Stud. in Lit.*, No. 5 (1968), 1–11.

2868 Mukerji, N. "Chaucer's Franklin's [Tale] and the Tale of Madanasena of Vetalapachisi." *Folklore* (Calcutta), 9 (1968), 75–85.

2869 Pearcy, Roy J. "Chaucer's Franklin and the Literary Vavasour." *ChauR*, 8 (1973), 33–59.

2870 Peck, Russell A. "Sovereignty and the Two Worlds of the *Franklin's Tale*." *ChauR*, 1 (1967), 253–271.

2871 Prins, A. A. "Notes on the Canterbury Tales (3)." *ES*, 35 (1954), 159–162. [F 1141, 1143]

2872 Rajna, Pio. "Le origini della novella narrata del 'Frankeleyn' nei *Canterbury Tales* del Chaucer." *Romania*, 32 (1903), 204–267.

2873 Schofield, W. H. "Chaucer's Franklin's Tale." *PMLA*, 16 (1901), 405–449.

2874 Severs, J. Burke. "Appropriateness of Character to Plot in the *Franklin's Tale*." 55, pp. 385–395.

2875 Sledd, James. "Dorigen's Complaint." *MP*, 45 (1947), 36–45.

2876 Tatlock, John S. P. "Astrology and Magic in Chaucer's *Franklin's Tale*." 51, pp. 339–350.

2877 Tatlock, John S. P. *The Scene of the Franklin's Tale Visited.* (Chaucer Soc., 2nd Ser., No. 51.) London 1914.

2878 Tripp, Raymond P., Jr. "The Franklin's Solution to the 'Marriage Debate'. " 282, pp. 35–41.

2879 White, Gertrude M. "The Franklin's Tale: Chaucer or the Critics." *PMLA*, 89 (1974), 454–462.

2880 Witke, Charles. "*Franklin's Tale*, F 1139–1151." *ChauR*, 1 (1966), 33–36.

2881 Wood, Chauncey. "Of Time and Tide in the *Franklin's Tale*." *PQ*, 45 (1966), 688–711.

2882 Wright, Constance S. "On the Franklin's Prologue, 716–721, Persius, and the Continuity of the Mannerist Style." *PQ*, 52 (1973), 739–746.

The Physician's Tale

2883 Amoils, E. R. "Fruitfulness and Sterility in the 'Physician's' and 'Pardoner's Tales'." *ESA*, 17 (1974), 17–34.

2884 Beidler, Peter G. See 2827.

2885 Hanson, Thomas B. "Chaucer's Physician as Storyteller and Moralizer." *ChauR*, 7 (1972), 132–139.

2886 HOFFMAN, Richard L. "Pygmalion in the *Physician's Tale.*" *AN&Q,* 5 (1967), 83–84.

2887 HOFFMAN, Richard L. "Jephthah's Daughter and Chaucer's Virginia." *ChauR,* 2 (1967), 20–31.

2889 LONGSWORTH, Robert. "The Doctor's Dilemma: A Comic View of the 'Physician's Tale'." *Criticism,* 13 (1971), 223–233.

2890 MIDDLETON, Anne. "The *Physician's Tale* and Love's Martyrs: 'Ensamples mo than ten' as a Method in the *Canterbury Tales.*" *ChauR,* 8 (1973), 9–32.

2891 OWEN, Charles A., Jr. See 3079.

2892 RAMSEY, Lee C. " 'The sentence of it sooth is': Chaucer's *Physician's Tale.*" *ChauR,* 6 (1972), 185–197.

2893 ROWLAND, Beryl. "The Physician's 'Historial Thyng Notable' and the Man of Law." *ELH,* 40 (1973), 165–178.

2894 YOUNG, Karl. "The Maidenly Virtues of Chaucer's Virginia." *Speculum,* 16 (1941), 340–349.

The Pardoner's Prologue and Tale

(including the *Physician-Pardoner Link*)

2895 ADELMAN, Janet. " 'That We May Leere Som Wit'." 2894, pp. 96–106.

2896 AMOILS, E. R. See 2883.

2897 ANDERSON, George K. *The Legend of the Wandering Jew.* Providence: Brown Univ. Press, 1965.

2898 ANDERSON, George K. "*Die Silberlinge des Judas* and the Accursed Treasure." *SP,* 48 (1951), 77–86.

2899 BARAKAT, Robert A. "Odin: Old Man of *The Pardoner's Tale.*" *SFQ,* 28 (1964), 210–215.

2900 BARNEY, Stephen A. "An Evaluation of *The Pardoner's Tale.*" 2920, pp. 83–95.

2901 BARRER, John W. "Influencia de la literatura española en la literatura inglesa." *Universidad: Revista de Cultura y Vida Universitaria* (Saragossa), 23 (1946), 593–610.

2902 BEICHNER, Paul E. "Chaucer's Pardoner as Entertainer." *MS,* 25 (1963), 160–172.

2903 BISHOP, Ian. "The Narrative Art of *The Pardoner's Tale.*" *MÆ,* 36 (1967), 15–24.

2904 BUSHNELL, Nelson S. "The Wandering Jew and the *Pardoner's Tale.*" *SP,* 28 (1931), 450–460.

2905 CALDERWOOD, James L. "Parody in *The Pardoner's Tale.*" *ES,* 45 (1964), 302–309.

2906 CANBY, Henry S. "Some Comments on the Sources of Chaucer's *Pardoner's Tale.*" *MP,* 2 (1904–05), 477–487.

2907 CANDELARIA, Frederick H. "Chaucer's 'Fowle Ok' and *The Pardoner's Tale.*" *MLN,* 71 (1956), 321–322.

2908 CHAPMAN, Coolidge O. "Chaucer on Preachers and Preaching." *PMLA,* 44 (1929), 178–185.

2909 CHAPMAN, Coolidge O. "*The Pardoner's Tale:* A Medieval Sermon." *MLN,* 41 (1926), 506–509.

2910 CONDREN, Edward I. "The Pardoner's Bid for Existence." *Viator,* 4 (1973), 177–205.

2911 CURRY, Walter C. "The Secret of Chaucer's Pardoner." *JEGP,* 18 (1919), 593–606. Reprinted in 170.

2912 CURTIS, Penelope. "The Pardoner's 'Jape'." *CR,* 11 (1968), 15–31.

2913 DAVID, Alfred. "Criticism and the Old Man in Chaucer's *Pardoner's Tale.*" *CE,* 27 (1965), 39–44.

2914 DEAN, Christopher. "Salvation, Damnation and the Role of the Old Man in the *Pardoner's Tale.*" *ChauR,* 3 (1968), 44–49.

2915 DENEEF, A. Leigh. "Chaucer's *Pardoner's Tale* and the Irony of Misinterpretation." *Jour. of Narrative Technique,* 3 (1973), 85–96.

2916 DUINO, Russell. "The Tortured Pardoner." *EJ,* 46 (1957), 320–325.

2917 ELLIOTT, Charles, and R. George THOMAS. "Two Points of View: *The Pardoner's Prologue* and *Tale.*" *AWR,* 14, No. 33 (1964), 9–17.

2918 ELLIOTT, R. W. V. "Our Host's 'triacle': some Observations on Chaucer's *Pardoner's Tale.*" *REL,* 7, ii (1966), 61–73.

2919 ETHEL, Garland. "Chaucer's Worste Shrew: The Pardoner." *MLQ,* 20 (1959), 211–227.

2920 FAULKNER, Dewey R., ed. *Twentieth-Century Interpretations of the Pardoner's Tale: A Collection of Critical Essays.* Englewood Cliffs: Prentice-Hall, 1973.

2921 FRIEND, Albert C. "Analogues in Cheriton to the Pardoner and His Sermon." *JEGP,* 53 (1954), 383–388.

2922 FRIEND, Albert C. "The Dangerous Theme of the Pardoner." *MLQ,* 18 (1957), 305–308.

2923 GROSS, Seymour L. "Conscious Verbal Repetition in the Pardoner's *Prologue.*" *N&Q,* 198 (1953), 413–414.

2924 HALVERSON, John. "Chaucer's Pardoner and the Progress of Criticism." *ChauR,* 4 (1970), 184–202.

2925 HAMILTON, Marie P. "The Credentials of Chaucer's Pardoner." *JEGP,* 40 (1941), 48–72.

2926 HAMILTON, Marie P. "Death and Old Age in *The Pardoner's Tale.*" *SP,* 36 (1939), 571–576.

2927 HARRINGTON, David V. "Narrative Speed in the *Pardoner's Tale.*" *ChauR,* 3 (1968), 50–59. Reprinted in 2920.

2928 HARRIS, Richard L. "Odin's Old Age: A Study of the Old Man in *The Pardoner's Tale.*" *SFQ,* 33 (1969), 24–38.

2929 HART, Walter M. "*The Pardoner's Tale* and *Der Dot im Stock.*" *MP,* 9 (1911–12), 17–22.

2930 HEMINGWAY, Samuel B. "The Two St. Pauls." *MLN,* 32 (1917), 57–58.

2931 HENCH, Atcheson L. "On the Subtly Creeping Wine of Chaucer's Pardoner." *MLN,* 52 (1937), 27–28.

2932 HENKIN, Leo J. "Jacob and the Hooly Jew." *MLN,* 55 (1940), 254–259.

2933 HENKIN, Leo J. "The Pardoner's Sheep-bone and Lapidary Lore." *Bull. Hist. of Medicine,* 10 (1941), 504–512.

2934 KANTOR, Betty. *The Sin of Pride in 'The Pardoner's Tale.'* (*Stanford Honors Essays in Humanities,* No. V.) Stanford, Calif., 1962.

2935 KELLOGG, Alfred L. "An Augustinian Interpretation of Chaucer's Pardoner." *Speculum,* 26 (1951), 465–481. Reprinted in 456.

2936 KHINOY, Stephen A. "Inside Chaucer's Pardoner?" *ChauR,* 6 (1972), 255–267.

2937 KITTREDGE, George L. "Chaucer and Maximianus." *AJP,* 9 (1888), 84–85.

2938 KITTREDGE, George L. "Chaucer's Pardoner." *Atlantic Mo.,* No. 72 (1893), pp. 829–833. Reprinted in 628.

2939 KRISHNAMURTI, S. "A Note on *The Pardoner's Tale,* lines 237–239." *MLR,* 39 (1944), 398.

2940 LUMIANSKY, Robert M. "A Conjecture Concerning Chaucer's Pardoner." *TSE,* 1 (1949), 1–29.

2941 MANNING, Stephen. "Chaucer's Pardoner: Sex and Non-Sex." *So. Atlantic Bull.,* 39 (1974), 17–26.

2942 McNAMARA, Leo F. "The Astonishing Performance of Chaucer's Pardoner." *PMASAL,* 46 (1961), 597–604.

2943 MILLER, Clarence H., and Roberta B. Bosse. "Chaucer's Pardoner and the Mass." *ChauR,* 6 (1972), 171–184.

2944 MILLER, Robert P. "Chaucer's Pardoner, the Scriptural Eunuch, and the Pardoner's Tale." *Speculum,* 30 (1955), 180–199. Reprinted in 1700, 2920.

2945 MITCHELL, Charles. "The Moral Superiority of Chaucer's Pardoner." *CE,* 27 (1966), 437–444.

2946 NICHOLS, Robert E., Jr. "The Pardoner's Ale and Cake." *PMLA,* 82 (1967), 498–504.

2947 NORRIS, Dorothy M. "Chaucer's *Pardoner's Tale* and Flanders." *PMLA,* 48 (1933), 636–641.

2948 O'NEAL, Cothburn M. "The Syndrome of Masochism in Chaucer's Pardoner: Synopsis of the Pardoner." *Proc. Conference of College Teachers of English,* 32 (Lubbock: Texas Tech. Coll., 1967), pp. 18–23.

2949 OSSELTON, N. E. "Chaucer's 'clumsy transition' in the Pardoner's Tale." *ES,* 49 (1968), 36–38.

2950 OWEN, Nancy H. "The Pardoner's Introduction, Prologue, and Tale: Sermon and Fabliau." *JEGP,* 66 (1967), 541–549.

2951 OWEN, W. J. B. "The Old Man in *The Pardoner's Tale.*" *RES,* n.s. 2 (1951), 49–55. Reprinted in 628.

2952 PITTOCK, Malcolm. "*The Pardoner's Tale* and the Quest for Death." *EIC,* 24 (1974), 107–123.

2953 PRATT, Robert A. "Chaucer's *Pardoner's Prologue,* 444–447." *Explicator,* 21 (1962), item 14.

2954 REISS, Edmund. "The Final Irony of the *Pardoner's Tale.*" *CE,* 25 (1964), 260–266.

2955 ROACHE, Joel. "Treasure Trove in the *Pardoner's Tale.*" *JEGP,* 64 (1965), 1–6.

2956 ROSS, Alan S. C. "To Go A-blackberrying." *N&Q,* 218 (1973), 284–285.

2957 RUTTER, G. M. "An Holy Jewes Shepe." *MLN,* 43 (1928), 536.

2958 SCHMIDT, Philip. "Reexamination of Chaucer's Old Man of the Pardoner's Tale." *SFQ,* 30 (1966), 249–255.

2959 SEDGEWICK, G. G. "The Progress of Chaucer's Pardoner, 1880–1940." *MLQ,* 1 (1940), 431–458. Reprinted in 628 and 1700.

2960 SEDGEWICK, W. B. "Chaucer's *'Pardoner's Prologue'.*" *MLR,* 19 (1924), 336–337.

2961 SLEDD, James. "*Canterbury Tales,* C 310, 320: 'By Seint Ronyan.'" *MS,* 13 (1951), 226–233. Cf. Eric P. Hamp, "St. Ninian/Ronyan Again." *Celtica,* 3 (1956), 290–294.

2962 STEADMAN, John M. "Chaucer's Pardoner and the *thesaurus meritorium.*" *ELN,* 3 (1965), 4–7.

2963 STEADMAN, John M. "'My Modres Gate' and 'El Palo del Viejo'." *N&Q,* 203 (1958), 323.

2964 STEADMAN, John M. "Old Age and *Contemptus Mundi* in *The Pardoner's Tale.*" *MÆ,* 33 (1964), 121–130. Reprinted in 2920.

2965 STEWART, Donald C. "Chaucer's Perplexing Pardoner." *CEA Critic,* 29, (1966), 4–6.

2966 STOCKTON, Eric W. "The Deadliest Sin in *The Pardoner's Tale.*" *TSL,* 6 (1961), 47–59.

2967 STRANG, Barbara M. H. "Who Is the Old Man in *The Pardoner's Tale?*" *N&Q,* 205 (1960), 207–208.

2968 SWART, J. "Chaucer's Pardoner." *Neophil,* 36 (1952), 45–50.

2969 TAITT, P. S. "Harry Bailly and the Pardoner's Relics." *SN,* 41 (1969), 112–114.

2970 TODD, Robert E. "The Magna Mater Archetype in *The Pardoner's Tale.*" *L&P,* 15 (1965), 32–40.

2971 TOOLE, William B. "Chaucer's Christian Irony: The Relationship of Character and Action in the *Pardoner's Tale.*" *ChauR,* 3 (1968), 37–43.

2972 TUPPER, Frederick. "The Pardoner's Tavern." *JEGP,* 13 (1914), 553–565.

2973 WEATHERLY, Edward H. "A Note on Chaucer's *Pardoner's Tale.*" *MLN,* 50 (1935), 310–311.

2974 WHITING, B. J. "More on Chaucer's Pardoner's Prologue (VI [C], 377–390)." *MLN,* 51 (1936), 322–327.

The Second Nun's Prologue and Tale

2975 BEICHNER, Paul E. "Confrontation, Contempt of Court, and Chaucer's Cecilia." *ChauR,* 8 (1974), 198–204.

2976 BROWN, Carleton. "Chaucer and the Hours of the Blessed Virgin." *MLN,* 30 (1915), 231–232.

2977 BROWN, Carleton. "The Prologue of Chaucer's *Lyf of Seint Cecile.*" *MP,* 9 (1911–12), 1–16.

2978 CAMPBELL, J. M. See 357.

2979 CLOGAN, Paul M. "The Figural Style and Meaning of *The Second Nun's Prologue and Tale.*" *M&H,* n.s. 3 (1972), 213–240.

2980 CORNELIUS, Roberta D. "Corones Two." *PMLA,* 42 (1927), 1055–1057.

2981 ELIASON, Norman E. "Chaucer's Second Nun?" *MLQ,* 3 (1942), 9–16.

2982 EMERSON, O. F. "Saint Ambrose and Chaucer's *Life of St. Cecilia.*" *PMLA,* 41 (1926), 252–261. Reprinted in 395.

2983 GARDNER, William B. "Chaucer's 'Unworthy Sone of Eve'." *Stud. in English* (Univ. of Texas), 1947, pp. 77–83.

2984 GEROULD, G. H. "A Note on St. Caecelia." *MLN,* 68 (1953), 173.

2985 GIFFIN, Mary. " 'Hir Hous the Chirche of Scinte Cecilie Highte'." 413, pp. 29–48.

2986 GRENNEN, Joseph E. "Saint Cecilia's 'chemical wedding': The Unity of the Canterbury Tales, Fragment VIII." *JEGP,* 65 (1966), 466–481.

2987 HENSHAW, Millett. "The Preface of St. Ambrose and Chaucer's *Second Nun's Tale.*" *MP,* 26 (1928–29), 15–16.

2988 HOLTHAUSEN, F. "Zu Chaucers Cecilien-Legende." *Archiv,* 87 (1891), 265–273.

2989 JONES, Claude. "The 'Second Nun's Tale', a Medieval Sermon." *MLR,* 32 (1937), 283.

2990 LOWES, John L. "The Corones Two of the Second Nun's Tale." *PMLA,* 26 (1911), 315–323; "A Supplementary Note," *ibid.,* 29 (1914), 129–133.

2991 LOWES, John L. "The Second Nun's Prologue, Alanus, and Macrobius." *MP,* 15 (1917–18), 193–202.

2992 MACCRACKEN, Henry N. "A Further Parallel to the 'Corones two' of the Second Nun's Tale." *MLN,* 27 (1912), 63.

2993 PARKER, Roscoe E. "A Note on 'Corones Two'." *MLN,* 41 (1926), 317–318.

2994 PECK, Russell A. "The Ideas of 'Entente' and Translation in Chaucer's *Second Nun's Tale.*" *AnM,* 8 (1967), 17–37.

2995 REILLY, Cyril A. "Chaucer's Second Nun's Tale: Tiburce's Visit to Pope Urban." *MLN,* 69 (1954), 37–39.

2996 ROSENBERG, Bruce A. "The Contrary Tales of the Second Nun and the Canon's Yeoman." *ChauR,* 2 (1968), 278–291.

2997 ROSENFELD, Mary-Virginia. See 2259.

2998 TATLOCK, John S. P. "St. Cecilia's Garlands and Their Roman Origin." *PMLA,* 45 (1930), 169–179.

The Canon's Yeoman's Prologue and Tale

2999 ADAMS, George R. "The Canon's Yeoman: Alchemist, Confidence Man, Artist." *English Notes* (Oshkosh, Wis.), 3, No. 2 (1969), 3–14.

3000 AIKEN, Pauline. "Vincent of Beauvais and Chaucer's Knowledge of Alchemy." *SP,* 41 (1944), 371–389.

3001 BALDWIN, R. G. "The Yeoman's Canons: A Conjecture." *JEGP,* 61 (1962), 232–243.

3002 BAUM, Paull F. "*The Canon's Yeoman's Tale.*" *MLN,* 40 (1925), 152–154.

3003 COFFMAN, George R. "Canon's Yeoman's Prologue, G. II. 563–566: Horse or Man." *MLN,* 59 (1944), 269–271.

3004 DAMON, S. Foster. "Chaucer and Alchemy." *PMLA,* 39 (1924), 782–788.

3005 DUNCAN, Edgar H. "Chaucer and 'Arnold of the Newe Toun'." *MLN,* 57 (1942), 31–33.

3006 DUNCAN, Edgar H. "The Yeoman's Canon's 'Silver Citrinacioun'." *MP*, 37 (1939–40), 241–262.

3007 DUNCAN, Edgar H. "The Literature of Alchemy and Chaucer's Canon's Yeoman's Tale: Framework, Theme, and Characters." *Speculum*, 43 (1968), 633–656.

3008 DUNLEAVY, Gareth W. "The Chaucer Ascription in Trinity College Dublin Ms. D.2.8." *Ambix*, 13 (1965), 1–21.

3009 FINKELSTEIN, Dorothee. "The Code of Chaucer's 'Secree of Secrees': Arabic Alchemical Terminology in *The Canon's Yeoman's Tale.*" *Archiv*, 207 (1970), 260–276.

3010 FOLCH-PI, Willa B. "Ramón Lull's *Felix* and Chaucer's *Canon's Yeoman's Tale.*" *N&Q,* 212 (1967), 10–11.

3011 GARDNER, John. "*The Canon's Yeoman's Prologue and Tale:* An Interpretation." *PQ,* 46 (1967), 1–17.

3012 GRENBERG, Bruce L. "The *Canon's Yeoman's Tale:* Boethian Wisdom and the Alchemists." *ChauR*, 1 (1966), 37–54.

3013 GRENNEN, Joseph E. "The Canon's Yeoman and the Cosmic Furnace: Language and Meaning in the *Canon's Yeoman's Tale.*" *Criticism*, 4 (1962), 225–240.

3014 GRENNEN, Joseph E. "The Canon's Yeoman's Alchemical 'Mass'." *SP*, 62 (1965), 546–560.

3015 GRENNEN, Joseph E. "Chaucer's Characterization of the Canon and His Yeoman." *JHI*, 25 (1964), 279–284.

3016 GRENNEN, Joseph E. "Chaucer's 'Secree of Secrees': An Alchemical 'Topic'." *PQ,* 42 (1963), 562–566.

3017 GRENNEN, Joseph E. "Chaucer and the Commonplaces of Alchemy." *C&M*, 26 (1965), 306–333.

3018 HAMILTON, Marie P. "The Clerical Status of Chaucer's Alchemist." *Speculum*, 16 (1941), 103–108.

3019 HARRINGTON, David V. "Dramatic Irony in the Canon's Yeoman's Tale." *NM*, 66 (1965), 160–167.

3020 HARRINGTON, David V. "The Narrator of the *Canon's Yeoman's Tale.*" *AnM*, 9 (1968), 85–97.

3021 HARTUNG, Albert E. "Inappropriate Pointing in the Canon's Yeoman's Tale, G 1236–1239." *PMLA*, 77 (1962), 508–509.

3022 HASKELL, Ann S. "The St. Giles Oath in the *Canon's Yeoman's Tale.*" *ChauR*, 7 (1973), 221–226.

3023 HERZ, Judith S. "*The Canon's Yeoman's Prologue* and *Tale.*" *MP*, 58 (1960–61), 231–237.

3024 KITTREDGE, George L. "The Canon's Yeoman's Prologue and Tale." *Trans. Royal Soc. Lit.*, 2nd Ser., 30 (1910), 87–95.

3025 LOWES, John L. "The Dragon and His Brother." *MLN*, 28 (1913), 229.

3026 McCRACKEN, Samuel. "Confessional Prologue and the Topography of the Canon's Yeoman." *MP*, 68 (1971), 289–291.

3027 OLMERT, K. Michael. "*The Canon's Yeoman's Tale:* An Interpretation." *AnM*, 8 (1967), 70–94.

3028 O'REILLY, William M., Jr. "Irony in the *Canon's Yeoman's Tale.*" *Greyfriar: Siena Stud. in Lit.,* 10 (1968), 25–39.

3029 REIDY, John. "Chaucer's Canon and the Unity of *The Canon's Yeoman's Tale.*" *PMLA,* 80 (1965), 31–37.

3030 ROSENBERG, Bruce A. "Swindling Alchemist, Antichrist." *CRAS,* 6 (1962), 566–580.

3031 ROSENBERG, Bruce A. See 2996.

3032 RUSKA, Julius. "Chaucer und das Buch Senior." *Anglia,* 61 (1937), 136–137.

3033 RYAN, Lawrence V. "The Canon's Yeoman's Desperate Confession." *ChauR,* 8 (1974), 297–310.

3034 SANDERS, Barry. " 'Point': *Canon's Yeoman's Tale* 927." *N&Q,* 212 (1967), 325.

3035 WHITTOCK, T. G. "Chaucer's *Canon's Yeoman's Tale.*" *Theoria,* 24 (1965), 13–26.

3036 WILSON, W. J. "An Alchemical Manuscript by Arnoldus de Bruxella." *Osiris,* 2 (1936), 220–405.

3037 YOUNG, Karl. "The 'secree of secrees' of Chaucer's Canon's Yeoman." *MLN,* 58 (1943), 98–105.

The Manciple's Prologue and Tale

3038 BIRNEY, Earle. "Chaucer's 'Gentil' Manciple and his 'Gentil' Tale." *NM,* 61 (1960), 257–267.

3039 BRODIE, Alexander H. "Hodge of Ware and Geber's Cook: Wordplay in the 'Manciple's Prologue'." *NM,* 72 (1971), 62–68.

3040 CADBURY, William. "Manipulation of Sources and the Meaning of the *Manciple's Tale.*" *PQ,* 43 (1964), 538–548.

3041 CAMPBELL, Jackson J. "Polonius among the Pilgrims." *ChauR,* 7 (1972), 140–146.

3042 DONNER, Morton. "The Unity of Chaucer's Manciple Fragment." *MLN,* 70 (1955), 245–249.

3043 ELLIOTT, J. D. "The Moral of the Manciple's Tale." *N&Q,* 199 (1954), 511–512.

3044 GRUBER, Loren C. "The *Manciple's Tale:* One Key to Chaucer's Language." 282, pp. 43–50.

3045 HARWOOD, Britton J. "Language and the Real: Chaucer's Manciple." *ChauR,* 6 (1972), 268–279; 7 (1972), 84.

3046 HAZELTON, Richard. "The *Manciple's Tale:* Parody and Critique." *JEGP,* 62 (1963), 1–31.

3047 MUSTANOJA, Tauno F. "Chaucer's *Manciple's Tale,* lines 311–13." *Franciplegius: Medieval and Linguistic Studies in Honor of Francis Peabody Magoun, Jr.,* pp. 250–254. New York: New York Univ. Press, 1965.

3048 PEARCY, Roy J. "Does the Manciple's Prologue Contain a Reference to Hell's Mouth?" *ELN,* 11 (1974), 167–175.

3049 PLESSOW, Gustav, ed. *Des Haushälters Erzählung aus den Canterbury Geschichten Gottfried Chaucers.* (Trübners Philol. Bibliothek, 12.) Berlin: de Gruyter, 1929.

3050 REID, T. B. W. "The She-Wolf's Mate." *MÆ,* 24 (1955), 16–19. [H 183–6]

3051 ROOT, Robert K. "The Manciple's Prologue." *MLN,* 44 (1929), 493–496.

3052 SCATTERGOOD, V. J. "The Manciple's Manner of Speaking." *EIC,* 24 (1974), 124–146.

3053 SEVERS, J. Burke. "Is the *Manciple's Tale* a Success?" *JEGP,* 51 (1952), 1–16.

3054 SHUMAKER, Wayne. "Chaucer's *Manciple's Tale* as Part of a Canterbury Group." *UTQ,* 22 (1953), 147–156.

3055 SPECTOR, Robert D. "Chaucer's *The Manciple's Tale.*" *N&Q,* 202 (1957), 26.

3056 STILLWELL, Gardiner. "Analogues to Chaucer's *Manciple's Tale* in the *Ovide Moralisé* and Machaut's *Voir-dit.*" *PQ,* 19 (1940), 133–138.

3057 WORK, James A. "The Manciple's Prologue." *SP,* 29 (1932), 11–14.

The Parson's Prologue and Tale

3058 ALLEN, Judson B. "The old way and the Parson's way: an ironic reading of the Parson's Tale." *JMRS,* 3 (1973), 255–271.

3059 BIGGINS, D. "*Canterbury Tales* X (I) 424: 'The hyndre part of a she-apè in the fulle of the moone'." *MÆ,* 33 (1964), 200–203.

3060 BIGGINS, D. "Chaucer: *CT X* (I) 42–46." *PQ,* 42 (1963), 558–562.

3061 CHAPMAN, Coolidge O. "*The Parson's Tale:* A Medieval Sermon." *MLN,* 43 (1928), 229–234.

3062 DICKSON, Arthur. "*Canterbury Tales,* I. 355 ff." *MLN,* 62 (1947), 562.

3063 EILERS, Wilhelm. "Dissertation on *The Parson's Tale* and the *Somme de Vices et de Vertus* of Frère Lorens." *Essays on Chaucer,* Part V, pp. 501–610 (Chaucer Soc., 2nd Ser., No. 19).

3064 FINLAYSON, John. "The Satiric Mode and the *Parson's Tale.*" *ChauR,* 6 (1971), 94–116.

3065 FOX, Robert C. "Chaucer and Aristotle." *N&Q,* 203 (1958), 523–524.

3066 FOX, Robert C. "The Philosophre of Chaucer's Parson." *MLN,* 75 (1960), 101–102.

3067 FRIEND, Albert C. "Sampson, David, and Solomon in the Parson's Tale." *MP,* 46 (1948–49), 117–121.

3068 GUINAGH, Kevin. "Source of the Quotation from Augustine in *The Parson's Tale,* 985." *MLN,* 55 (1940), 211–212.

3069 HAZELTON, Richard. "Chaucer's Parson's Tale and the 'Moralium Dogma Philosophorum'." *Traditio,* 16 (1960), 255–274.

3070 HOMANS, George C. "Free Bull." *RES,* 14 (1938), 447–449.

3071 IVES, Doris V. " 'A Man of Religion'." *MLR,* 27 (1932), 144–148.

3072 JOHNSON, Dudley R. " 'Homicide' in the *Parson's Tale.*" *PMLA,* 57 (1942), 51–56.

3073 KELLOGG, Alfred L. "St. Augustine and the Parson's Tale," *Traditio,* 8 (1952), 424–430. Reprinted in 456.

3074 KELLOGG, Alfred L. " 'Seith Moyses by the Devil': A Problem in Chaucer's Parson's Tale." *Revue Belge de Philologie et d'Histoire,* 31 (1953), 61–64. Reprinted in 456.

3075 LIDDELL, Mark H. "A New Source of *The Parson's Tale.*" 50, pp. 255–277.

3076 MARIELLA, Sister. "The Head, the Foot, and the Rib of Adam." *N&Q,* 171 (1936), 119.

3077 MARIELLA, Sister. "The Parson's Tale and the Marriage Group." *MLN,* 53 (1938), 251–256.

3078 MYERS, D. E. "Justesse rationnelle: le 'Myrie Tale in Prose' de Chaucer." *Moyen Age,* 78 (1972), 267–286.

3079 OWEN, Charles A., Jr. "Relationship between the *Physician's Tale* and the *Parson's Tale." MLN,* 71 (1956), 84–87.

3080 PECK, Russell A. "Number Symbolism in the Prologue to Chaucer's *Parson's Tale." ES,* 48 (1967), 205–215.

3081 PETERSON, Kate O. *The Sources of the Parson's Tale. (Radcliffe College Monographs,* No. 12.) Boston: Ginn, 1901.

3082 PFANDER, H. G. "Some Medieval Manuals of Religious Instruction in England and Observations on Chaucer's Parson's Tale." *JEGP,* 35 (1936), 243–258.

3083 REGAN, Charles L. "Chaucer's *Parson's Tale* 1025: A Probable Source." *N&Q,* 209 (1964), 210.

3084 ROWLAND, Beryl. "Chaucer's She-Ape (*The Parson's Tale,* 424)." *ChauR,* 2 (1968), 159–165.

3085 SANDERLIN, George. "Quotations from St. Bernard in 'The Parson's Tale'." *MLN,* 54 (1939), 447–448.

3086 SCHMIDT, A. V. C. "Chaucer's 'Philosophre': A Note on *The Parson's Tale,* 534–7." *N&Q,* 213 (1968), 327–328.

3087 SIMON, H. "Chaucer a Wicliffite: An Essay on Chaucer's Parson and *Parson's Tale." Essays on Chaucer,* Part III, pp. 227–292 (Chaucer Soc., 2nd Ser., No. 16).

3088 SPIES, H. "Chaucers religiöse Grundstimmung und die Echtheit der Parson's Tale." *Festschrift für Lorenz Morsbach,* pp. 626–721. (*Studien zur engl. Phil.,* L.) Halle, 1913.

3089 WENZEL, Siegfried. "The Source for the 'Remedia' of the Parson's Tale." *Traditio,* 28 (1971), 433–453.

Chaucer's Retraction

3090 CAMPBELL, A. P. "Chaucer's 'Retraction': Who Retracted What?" *RUO,* 35 (1965), 35–53. Reprinted in *HAB,* 16, i (1965), 75–87.

3091 CLARK, John W. See 2382.

3092 GORDON, James D. "Chaucer's Retraction: A Review of Opinion." 48, pp. 81–96.

3093 JAMES, Stanley B. "The 'Repentance' of Chaucer." *Month,* 163 (1934), 41–46.

3094 LUMIANSKY, Robert M. "Chaucer's Retraction and the Degree of Completeness of the *Canterbury Tales." TSE,* 6 (1956), 5–13.

3095 MADDEN, William A. "Chaucer's Retraction and Mediaeval Canons of Seemliness." *MS,* 17 (1955), 173–184.

3096 SAYCE, Olive. "Chaucer's 'Retractions': The Conclusion of the *Canterbury Tales* and Its Place in Literary Tradition." *MÆ,* (1971), 230–248.

3097 SPIES, Heinrich. "Chaucer's 'Retractatio'." *Festschrift Adolf Tobler* (Braunschweig, 1905), pp. 383–394 (*Berliner Gesellschaft für das Studium der neueren Sprachen*).

3098 TATLOCK, John S. P. "Chaucer's *Retractions.*" *PMLA,* 28 (1913), 521–529.

3099 WORK, James A. "Chaucer's Sermon and Retractations." *MLN,* 47 (1932), 257–260.

The Astrolabe

3100 ELMQUIST, Karl E. "An Observation on Chaucer's *Astrolabe.*" *MLN,* 56 (1941), 530–534.

3101 GUNTHER, R. T. *Chaucer and Messahalla on the Astrolabe.* Now printed in full for the first time . . . Oxford, 1929.

3102 HARVEY, S. W. "Chaucer's Debt to Sacrobosco." *JEGP,* 34 (1935), 34–38.

3103 MOORE, Samuel. "On the Date of Chaucer's *Astrolabe.*" *MP,* 10 (1912–13), 203–205.

3104 NAGUCKA, Ruta. *The Syntactic Component of Chaucer's* Astrolabe. (*Zeszyty Naukowe Uniwersytetu Jagiellonskiego,* 199.) Cracow, 1968.

3105 Pintelon, P. *Chaucer's Treatise on the Astrolabe: MS. 4862–4869 of the Royal Library in Brussels. (Rijksuniversiteit te Gent: Werken Uitgegeven door de Faculteit . . . , Afl. 89.)* Antwerp: De Sikkel, 1940.

3106 VEAZIE, Walter B. "Chaucer's Text-book of Astronomy: Johannes de Sacrobosco." *Univ. of Colorado Stud., Ser. B: Stud. in the Humanities,* I (1940), 169–182.

3107 WILSON, Winifred G. "Chaucer's Astrolabe." *Life and Letters Today,* 37 (1943), 75–81.

Short Poems
Criticism: Collective

3108 CARTER, Thomas H. "The Shorter Poems of Geoffrey Chaucer." *Shenandoah,* 11, iii (1960), 48–60.

3109 DOYLE, A. I., and George B. PACE. "A New Chaucer Manuscript." *PMLA,* 83 (1968), 22–34.

3110 GREEN, A. Wigfall. "Chaucer's Complaints: Stanzaic Arrangement, Meter and Rhyme." *UMSE,* 3 (1962), 19–34.

3111 GREEN, A. Wigfall. "Structure of Three Minor Poems by Chaucer." *UMSE,* 4 (1963), 79–82. [*Truth, Gentilesse, Lak of Sted.*]

3112 NICHOLS, Robert E., Jr. "Chaucer's *Fortune, Truth,* and *Gentilesse:* The 'Last' Unpublished Manuscript Transcriptions." *Speculum,* 44 (1969), 46–50.

3113 REISS, Edmund. "Dusting Off the Cobwebs: A Look at Chaucer's Lyrics." *ChauR,* 1 (1966), 55–65.

3114 ROBBINS, Rossell H. "The Lyrics." 296, pp. 313–331.

Criticism: Individual Poems

An A B C

3115 D[OYLE], A. I. "Unrecorded Chaucer Manuscript." *Durham Philobiblon*, 1 (1953), 54–55.

3116 KLINEFELTER, Ralph A. "Chaucer's *An A B C*, 25 –32." *Explicator*, 24 (1965), item 5.

3117 LANGHANS, Viktor. "A.B.C." In 284, pp. 302–304.

3118 SEVERS, J. Burke. "Two Irregular Chaucerian Stanzas." *MLN*, 64 (1949), 306–309.

The Complaint of Chaucer to his Purse

3119 FERRIS, Sumner. "The Date of Chaucer's Final Annuity and of the 'Complaint to his Empty Purse'." *MP*, 65 (1967), 45–52.

3120 FINNEL, Andrew J. "The Poet as Sunday Man: 'The Complaint of Chaucer to His Purse'." *ChauR*, 8 (1973), 147–158.

3121 GIFFIN, Mary. " 'O Conquerour of Brutes Albyon'." 413, pp. 89–105.

3122 LEGGE, M. Dominica. " 'The Gracious Conqueror'." *MLN*, 68 (1953), 18–21.

3123 PACE, George B. "The Text of Chaucer's *Purse*." *PBSUV*, 1 (1948), 103–121.

3124 PACE, George B. See 3181.

3125 SCOTT, Florence R. "A New Look at *The Complaint of Chaucer to His Empty Purse*." *ELN*, 2 (1964), 81–87.

3126 SMITH, Roland M. See 601.

The Complaint of Mars

3127 BRADDY, Haldeen. See 764.

3128 BREWER, D. S. "Chaucer's *Complaint of Mars*." *N&Q*, 199 (1954), 462–463.

3129 COWLING, G. H. "Chaucer's *Complaintes of Mars and of Venus*." *RES*, 2 (1926), 405–410.

3130 EMERSON, O. F. See 396.

3131 HULTIN, Neil C. "Anti-Courtly Elements in Chaucer's *Complaint of Mars*." *AnM*, 19 (1968), 58–75.

3132 LAIRD, Edgar S. "Chaucer's *Complaint of Mars*, line 145: 'Venus valaunse'." *PQ*, 51 (1972), 486–489.

3133 LAIRD, Edgar S. "Astrology and Irony in Chaucer's *Complaint of Mars*." *ChauR*, 6 (1972), 229–231.

3134 LANGHANS, Viktor. "Die Klage des Mars." In 284, pp. 229–252.

3135 STILLWELL, Gardiner. "Convention and Individuality in Chaucer's *Complaint of Mars*." *PQ*, 35 (1956), 69–89.

3136 WILLIAMS, George G. "What is the Meaning of Chaucer's *Complaint of Mars?*" *JEGP*, 57 (1958), 167–176.

The Complaint of Venus

3137 BRADDY, Haldeen. See 764.

3138 LANGHANS, Viktor. ["Klage der Venus."] In 284, pp. 246–252.

A Complaint to his Lady

3139 TIMMER, B. J. "La Belle Dame sans Merci," *ES,* 11 (1929), 20–22.

The Complaint unto Pity

3140 LOWES, John L. See 795.

3141 PITTOCK, Malcolm. "Chaucer: The Complaint unto Pity." *Criticism,* 1 (1959), 160–168.

3142 TEN BRINK, Bernard. "Specimen of a Critical Edition of Chaucer's *Compleynte to Pite.*" *Essays on Chaucer,* Part I, pp. 165–177 (Chaucer Soc., 2nd Ser., No. 2).

The Former Age

3143 NORTON-SMITH, J. "Chaucer's 'Etas Prima'." *MÆ,* 32 (1963), 117–124.

3144 PACE, George B. "The True Text of *The Former Age.*" *MS,* 23 (1961), 363–367.

3145 PRESTON, Raymond. "Poyson, Manslauhtre, and Mordre in Sondry Wise." *N&Q,* 195 (1950), 95.

3146 SEVERS, J. Burke. See 3119.

Fortune

3147 GALWAY, Margaret. "Chaucer among Thieves." *TLS,* April 20, 1945, p. 187.

3148 HAMMERLE, Karl. "Das Fortunamotiv von Chaucer bis Bacon." *Anglia,* 65 (1941), 87–100.

3149 LANGHANS, Viktor. See 284, pp. 247–252.

3150 PATCH, Howard R. See 217.

3151 RIDEOUT, Edna. "Chaucer's 'Beste Frend'." *TLS,* Feb. 8, 1947, p. 79.

Gentilesse

3152 BRITTAIN, Robert E. "A Textual Note on Chaucer: *Gentilesse,* 20." *MLN,* 51 (1936), 433–435.

3153 DAVIS, Norman. "Chaucer's *Gentilesse:* A Forgotten Manuscript, with Some Proverbs." *RES,* 20 (1969), 43–50.

3154 VOGT, George M. See 2597.

Lak of Stedfastnesse

3155 BRADDY, Haldeen. "The Date of Chaucer's *Lak of Steadfastnesse.*" *JEGP,* 36 (1937), 481–490. Reprinted in 258.

3156 CROSS, J. E. "The Old Swedish *Trohetsvisan* and Chaucer's *Lak of Stedfastnesse* —A Study in Mediaeval Genre." *Saga-Book,* 16 (1965), 283–314.

3157 HOLT, Lucius H. "Chaucer's *Lac of Stedfastnesse.*" *JEGP,* 6 (1907), 419–431.

3158 PACE, George B. "Chaucer's *Lak of Stedfastnesse.*" *SB*, 4 (1951–52), 105–122.

3159 PACE, George B. See 3182.

Lenvoy de Chaucer a Bukton

3160 BRADDY, Haldeen. "Sir Peter and the *Envoy to Bukton.*" *PQ*, 14 (1935), 368–370.

3161 HÉRAUCOURT, W. "What is troughe or soothfastnesse." *Englische Kultur in sprachwissenschaftlicher Deutung: Max Deutschbein zum 60. Geburtstage*, pp. 75–84. Leipzig: Quelle & Meyer, 1936.

3162 KITTREDGE, George L. "Chaucer's *Envoy to Bukton.*" *MLN*, 24 (1909), 14–15.

3163 KUHL, E. P. "Chaucer's 'My Maistre Bukton'." *PMLA*, 38 (1923), 115–132. Reprinted in 475.

3164 LOWES, John L. "The Date of the *Envoy to Bukton.*" *MLN*, 27 (1912), 45–48.

3165 TATLOCK, John S. P. See 616.

Lenvoy de Chaucer a Scogan

3166 DAVID, Alfred. "Chaucer's Good Counsel to Scogan." *ChauR*, 3 (1969), 265–274.

3167 FRENCH, Walter H. "The Meaning of Chaucer's *Envoy to Scogan.*" *PMLA*, 48 (1933), 289–292.

3168 GOFFIN, R. C. " 'Lenvoy de Chaucer a Scogan'." *MLR*, 20 (1925), 318–321.

3169 KITTREDGE, George L. "Henry Scogan." [Harvard] *Stud. and Notes in Phil. and Lit.*, 1 (1892), 109–117.

3170 PHIPPS, Thomas M. "Chaucer's Tullius." *MLN*, 58 (1943), 108–109.

Merciles Beaute

3171 FRANÇON, Marcel. "Note on Chaucer's Roundels and His French Models." *Annali Istituto Orientale di Napoli (Sezione Germanica)*, 9 (1966), 195–197.

3172 LOWES, John L. "The Chaucerian 'Merciles Beaute' and Three Poems of Deschamps." *MLR*, 5 (1910), 33–39.

3173 RENWICK, W. L. "Chaucer's Triple Roundel, 'Merciles Beaute'." *MLR*, 16 (1921), 322–323.

3174 SKEAT, W. W. "The Chaucerian 'Merciles Beaute'." *MLR*, 5 (1910), 194.

Proverbs

3175 PACE, George B. "The Chaucerian *Proverbs.*" *SB*, 18 (1965), 41–48.

To Rosemounde

3176 KÖKERITZ, Helge. "Chaucer's *Rosemunde.*" *MLN*, 63 (1948), 310–318.

3177 REISS, Edmund. See 3113.

3178 ROBBINS, Rossell H. "Chaucer's 'To Rosemounde'." *Stud. in the Literary Imagination* (Georgia State Coll.), 4, ii (1971), 73–81.

Truth

3179 LAMPE, David E. "The Truth of A 'Vache': The Homely Homily of Chaucer's 'Truth'." *PLL*, 9 (1973), 311–314.

3180 MANLY, John M. "A Note on the Envoy of *Truth.*" *MP*, 11 (1913–14), 226.

3181 PACE, George B. "Four Unpublished Chaucer Manuscripts." *MLN*, 63 (1948), 457–462.

3182 PEAVLER, James M. "Analysis of Corpora of Variations." *Computers and the Humanities*, 8 (1974), 153–159.

3183 RAGAN, James F. "The 'hevenlich mede' in Chaucer's *Truth.*" *MLN*, 68 (1953), 534–535.

3184 RICKERT, Edith. "Thou Vache." *MP*, 11 (1913–14), 209–225.

Words unto Adam

3185 BRESSIE, Ramona. "Chaucer's Scrivener." *TLS*, May 9, 1929, p. 383. Cf. *ibid.*, May 16, p. 403 (Manly), June 13, p. 474 (B. M. Wagner).

3186 KUHL, Ernest P. "A Note on Chaucer's Adam." *MLN*, 29 (1914), 263–264. Reprinted in 475.

3187 MANLY, John M. "Chaucer's Scrivener." *TLS*, May 16, 1929, p. 403.

Lost and Apocryphal Works

Criticism: General

3188 BONNER, Francis W. "The Genesis of the Chaucer Apocrypha." *SP*, 48 (1951), 461–481.

3189 MOORE, Arthur K. "Chaucer's Lost Songs." *JEGP*, 48 (1949), 196–208.

3190 SEATON, Ethel. *Sir Richard Roos, c. 1410–1482, Lancastrian Poet.* London: R. Hart-Davis. 1961.

Criticism: Individual Poems

The Book of the Lion

3191 DEAR, F. M. "Chaucer's *Book of the Lion.*" *MÆ*, 7 (1938), 105–112.

3192 LANGHANS, Viktor. "Chaucers Book of the Leoun." *Anglia*, 52 (1928), 113–122.

Envoy to Alison

3193 CHEWNING, Harris. "The Text of the 'Envoy to Alison'." *SB*, 5 (1952), 33–42.

The Equatorie of the Planetis

3194 HERDAN, G. "Chaucer's Authorship of *The Equatorie of the Planetis:* The Use of Romance Vocabulary as Evidence." *Language*, 32 (1956), 254–259.

3195 KENNEDY, E. S. "A Horoscope of Messahalla in the Chaucer Equatorium Manuscript." *Speculum,* 34 (1959), 629–630.

3196 PRICE, Derek J., ed. *The Equatorie of the Planetis.* With a Linguistic Analysis by R. M. Wilson. Cambridge: Cambridge Univ. Press, 1955.

3197 PRICE, Derek J. "The Equatorie of the Planetis." *Jour. of the SW Essex Tech. Coll.,* 3 (1952), 154–168. See also *TLS,* Feb. 29, 1952, p. 164; March 7, p. 180. Cf. *ibid.,* p. 173 (C. T. Onions).

Gamelyn

3198 HIBBARD, Laura. "Gamelyn." *Medieval Romance in England,* pp. 156–163. New York: Oxford Univ. Press, 1924.

3199 MENKIN, Edward Z. "Comic Irony in the Sense of Two Audiences in the *Tale of Gamelyn.*" *Thoth,* 10 (1969), 41–53.

3200 ROGERS, Franklin R. See 1691.

3201 SHANNON, Edgar F., Jr. "Medieval Law in *The Tale of Gamelyn.*" *Speculum,* 26 (1951), 458–464.

A Love Epistle

3202 ROBBINS, Rossell H. "A Love Epistle by 'Chaucer'." *MLR,* 49 (1954), 289–292.

The Plowman's Tale

3203 IRVINE, Annie S. "A Manuscript Copy of *The Plowman's Tale.*" *Stud. in English* (Univ. of Texas), No. 12 (1932), pp. 27–56.

3204 WAWN, Andrew N. "Chaucer, *The Plowman's Tale* and Reformation Propaganda: The Testimonies of Thomas Godfray and *I Playne Piers.*" *BJRL,* 56 (1973), 174–192.

3205 WAWN, Andrew W. "Chaucer, Wyclif and the Court of Apollo." *ELN,* 10 (1972), 15–20.

The Tale of Beryn

3206 BASHE, E. J. "The Prologue of *The Tale of Beryn.*" *PQ,* 12 (1933), 1–16.

The Wreched Engendrynge of Mankind

3207 BROWN, Beatrice D. "Chaucer's *Wreched Engendrynge.*" *MP,* 35 (1937–38), 325–333.

3208 BROWN, Carlton. "Chaucer's *Wreched Engendring.*" *PMLA,* 50 (1935), 997–1011.

3209 BROWN, Carleton. "*An Holy Medytacion*—by Lydgate?" *MLN,* 40 (1925), 282–285.

3210 DEMPSTER, Germaine. "Chaucer's *Wretched Engendering* and *An Holy Medytacion.*" *MP,* 35 (1937–38), 27–29.

3211 DEMPSTER, Germaine. "Did Chaucer Write *An Holy Medytacion?*" *MLN,* 51 (1936), 284–295. Cf. "An Affirmative Reply," *ibid.,* 296–300 (Brown).

3212 LANGHANS, Viktor. "Chaucers Angebliche Übersetzung des Trakates *De Contemptu Mundi* von Innocenz III," *Anglia,* 52 (1928), 325–349.

3213   Lewis, Robert E. "What Did Chaucer Mean by *Of the Wreched Engendrynge of Mankynde?*" *ChauR,* 2 (1968), 139–158.

3214   Tatlock, John S. P. "Has Chaucer's *Wretched Engendering* Been Found?" *MLN,* 51 (1936), 275–284. Cf. "An Affirmative Reply," *ibid.,* 296–300 (Brown).

3215   Webster, Mildred. "The Vocabulary of *An Holy Medytacion.*" *PQ,* 17 (1938), 359–364.

Index

INDEX

INDEX

INDEX

INDEX

INDEX

INDEX

INDEX

INDEX

INDEX

INDEX

Notes